Youth in the information society

Council of Europe Publishing

French edition:

Les jeunes dans une société d'information

ISBN 92-871-3513-4

Council of Europe Publishing
F-67075 Strasbourg Cedex

ISBN 92-871-3514-2

Contents

Foreword

The "information society" has become the symbol of a new hope for the future of humanity as the value of the information technology resides in its capacity to facilitate human communication with no limit of time and distance and to provide instantaneous access to knowledge that took millennia to build up. Experts in social science and social work commonly consider that an international political strategy is essential for a successful transition to the information society on a global scale and that apart from matters concerning the technical and legal infrastructure, such a strategy should include a vision of the kind of civilisation we wish to evolve towards.

However, many observers warn that the development of the social applications of information technology along market lines alone would lead to stronger social divisions and less individual responsibility and participation in public decision-making, as the means of communication and the definition of the content of communication would be in the hands of the elite. Although we can obviously not subscribe to all of the opinions expressed in the papers presented in this book, we strongly agree with the belief shared by all participants in the symposium: that the global information society should be a synonym for a civilisation of human rights and social justice. Furthermore, the practical implications of the concept of social justice should be a subject of permanent debate involving citizens as much as possible. We are confident that massive participation in political debate is a guarantee that the collective wisdom of humanity can control the destructive potential of technological progress.

We also believe that education is the domain where societies should invest a larger part of their human and material resources. New technologies require individuals trained to use them adequately and creatively in professional and leisure contexts. Skills for finding, sorting and sharing information and turning it into knowledge, for finding solutions to non-standard problems, will be more than ever necessary to maximise benefits and control risks at individual and societal level. Coherent value frameworks and a critical attitude will be indispensable for making informed choices in the extraordinary range of products designed for leisure and professional consumption.

Our educational and training systems, methods and even objectives will have to be radically adapted to a rapidly changing world which is more demanding than ever on each individual's learning abilities.

New socialisation environments, more sensitive to each individual's needs, capacities and rhythms, should be created in order to facilitate personality development and social integration.

The political construction of the information society should not be an exercise in social engineering but the instigation of a community-based framework for the support and empowering of individuals. Its primary objective ought to be to ensure for each citizen access to the global information infrastructure but, equally importantly, it should envisage means for promoting diversity of content, culture and language of information transactions. A serious effort must be made to guarantee that the information technology remains a device that people master and not one that masters them. In this respect, the protection of young people from any attempt of intrusion on their privacy and integrity by means of information technology is a duty that governments must not neglect.

The book you are about to discover contains a selection of the papers presented at a symposium organised by the Youth Directorate of the Council of Europe in November 1996. The subject of the symposium – youth in the information society – was an obvious choice for us who, working with young people, are constantly incited to look into the future. This subject provided endless possibilities for discussion, in an international setting, of a variety of issues from a multitude of angles, types of expertise and disciplines. The young people who took part in the symposium were considered as experts. Young people and the information society seem to be naturally linked: this will be their society and therefore it is essential to take into account their perspectives, visions and expectations while taking decisions which will shape the world of tomorrow.

Franco Marziale
Youth Director

Virtually there?
Young Europeans and the information society

A synthesis report of the 2nd Council of Europe youth research symposium

Opening

The symposium was opened with a welcome and presentation by Peter Lauritzen, Executive Director of the European Youth Centre, Budapest. Before Peter Lauritzen spoke, the chair of the session, Francine Meyer emphasised the importance of the meeting. Not only was the substantive topic of youth in the information society an important one, but the symposium was a convention of different parties – researchers, governmental representatives, and representatives of youth work and NGOs – who, here, had an opportunity to identify and define new routes for youth policy and youth research. It was an opportunity that should be embraced by all those participating, all of whom had an equal contribution to make.

Peter Lauritzen then spoke briefly about the European Youth Centre in Budapest, its continuing lack of adequate computing resources (!), and the programmes being run at the Centre. Significantly, he drew attention to the last youth research symposium – held in Strasbourg in 1986 – which had shaped the pattern of youth research within and beyond the Council of Europe over the past decade. It had, therefore, been an important convention but subsequent events had still not resolved persisting tensions concerning relationships between youth research, youth policy and practice. Moreover, there continued to be disciplinary conflicts and dissent between different forms of (academic and evaluative) youth research.

There was, therefore, a general responsibility to develop more effective communication systems and improved shared understandings: to this end, the symposium could promote dialogue and make relevant recommendations. It could, and should, be demanding of the secretariat, the Advisory Committee[1], the CDEJ, and the Governing Board[2], in mapping the framework and pathway for youth policy for the forthcoming years, especially with

---

1 A statutory body with a consultative status at the Youth Directorate composed of representatives of international non-governmental youth organisations.
2 A statutory body of the Council of Europe's Youth Directorate taking decisions on the programme of the European Youth Centre and on the grants given by the European Youth Foundation.

regard to young people's relationship with the emerging technological age and the information society.

The subject matter of the symposium was of immense importance, but there were still many more questions than answers. What kind of knowledge was important? What was the meaning of "conversation" within virtual communities? Language, terminology and information conferred very different meanings in the technological age and often bore little relation to traditional cultural understandings. There seemed to be four core questions which needed to be addressed concerning:

– resource allocation,

– participation,

– access,

– opportunities.

Peter Lauritzen concluded by outlining his aspirations for the symposium. He hoped that it would find time to reflect on the ideals of the European Youth Centre and offer an honest appraisal of the reality (not virtual reality!) of its contribution to intercultural learning by young people throughout Europe. The symposium might also indicate how the work of the European youth centres might have to change in response to the information age: what was the role of educators in an information society? And, clearly, it was very likely that there would be budgetary implications which would have to be given careful consideration.

The symposium might therefore make a valuable contribution to the re-orientation of the Centre's work. Why should the Centre not be at the leading edge of technological change?

An introduction to the substantive theme of the symposium was then provided by a "double act" of Ola Stafseng (who reported on the academic and youth research antecedents to the information society) and Lasse Siurala (who reported on some more practical historical and contemporary questions concerning the information society).

The presentation of their paper, entitled "Opening windows for youth in the information society", skipped back and forth between profound theoretical and grounded empirical questions and observations.

The postindustrial society, or postmodern society has altered basic relationships. Whereas industrial production was characterised by relationships between human beings and objects, the information society is characterised by relationships between individuals and other human beings. New forms of relationships and communication, notably computer-mediated communication (CMC) are especially attractive to young people and therefore should be considered as a central mechanism for developing effective youth work. Digital media needs to be promoted as a pedagogical instrument. The contexts of transition and maturation have altered and the means of navigating them successfully have also altered. Old forms of institutional intervention (through, for example, schools, family and youth organisations) to promote various forms of moral and political citizenship are being replaced by new goals such as membership of cultural communities which can be achieved only through different kinds of intervention and experience: non-formal educational intervention, peer group learning, direct participation, virtual democracy.

That is the provocative contention which needs careful consideration by the symposium. How much has the world moved in the direction of the cyber-punks living in a virtual world? Has the medium become more important that the message? Can one really find authentic communities and relation-ships inside the Internet? What, anyway, is "authentic"? Are electronic com-munication and communities pedagogically useful, or socially empty and ethically dubious? Do they stifle and deflect from reality, or do they provide choice and enrichment? There is limited knowledge of new technologies: how are they used?, what is their impact?, what is their meaning?, and what is their potential?

There have always been connections between new technological develop-ments, young people and wider questions of socialisation and social out-comes. Youth and youth culture make use of such resources in unexpected and often hard-to-understand ways. But, invariably, it all contributes to the development of their "communicative competence". Style, language, cloth-ing, music all transmit "codes of meaning" on an analogue dimension, a dimension which is very different from the digital dimension of formal, sing-ular mechanisms such as teachers, parents, books or newspapers. Yet they are connected, through different levels of interaction. One is not necessarily a threat to the other and indeed, more "analogisation" arguably leads to more "digitalisation": "teenagers making video films write more text than ever, being good in music means to write notes for your own compositions", and so on.

So if computer technology promotes skills and qualifications in many differ-ent ways, then questions of access become important. Clearly, access oppor-tunities are very differentially distributed. In Helsinki, computers are located in schools, libraries and youth clubs, and over 25 per cent of young people have recently made use of computer-mediated communication. But how can the Internet be used as an instrument of youth work? Beyond promoting access, there are questions of training, guidance and the provision of infor-mation, as well as communication between youth projects. Moreover, CMC can be used to facilitate international co-operation.

But is there a "problem" of overload and chaos. This may be no bad thing. In contrast to the effects of globalisation, there may be the possibility for local flexibilisation (note: close to what Phil Cohen once described as the "narcissism of minor differences"): it is now quite possible for a young per-son to be against rock music and in favour of Mozart.

Of course, new technological development can be subjected to criticism. Is it little more than a marketing device and a commercial trick? Does it herald great potential for human progress or is it little more than the means to "amuse ourselves to death". What kinds of ethical considerations does it enshrine? Can it be harnessed to new social and political agendas? Should it be?

We can tell ourselves that attitude is the problem (the English Luddites smashed up new spinning machinery because they saw "progress" threatening jobs and working conditions; there are now many technological luddites). But it is crucial that we explore, as dispassionately as possible, both the threats and potentialities of the information society. And, specifically, it is crucial to debate the extent to which new technologies can provide new tools for the delivery of effective youth work and the implementation of constructive youth policy.

Papers and discussions

John Bynner (youth research) presented the first plenary lecture, focusing on key questions for youth research in the information society. There is now clearly a common understanding across Europe about what "new technology" is and what are its information technology components.

The new technological revolution has, albeit differentially across time and space, been a significant mediator in the new life course paths which young people throughout Europe are having to navigate and negotiate. Adolescent development has, of course, become increasingly problematised and problematic – in both sociological analysis and social policy debate. There is emerging evidence of new forms of social exclusion on the "technological periphery", for while there is migration towards technological centres, other young people are experiencing a "revolving door syndrome", within which they become subjected to ever more marginalising processes of exclusion and self-exclusion. The life course for young people is now characterised in terms of individualisation, risk and uncertainty. The relationship between (changes in) the workplace, (changes in) youth culture, (changes in) the family, and (changes in) individual and group experience is in a state of constant flux. Youth cultural forms, in particular, are evolving in ways in which technological media are central. Questions arise about the relation between the "social citizen" (the individual firmly embedded within the social web) and the "consumer citizen" (individuals shaping their own futures with the resources available and accessible to them), and the capacity of different individuals and groups to take control of their own destinies. Within the framework of technological change, young people are both subjected to negative forces and agents of change through processes of self-actualisation. The "power" of youth culture across Europe, as evidenced by the opening of the Berlin Wall, has been assisted by the development of communication technologies but, while there is considerable evidence of young people not "signing up" to old ways, there is countervailing evidence that those young people who remain most distant from technology continue to display a strong adherence to traditional values and conventional aspirations.

Both within and without the framework of new technologies, the agenda for youth research must be developed in terms of the concept of "life management" and an analysis of the factors which obstruct and support transitions to adult life and "citizenship", that is full participation in civil society. There are clearly fundamental questions about the distribution of resources and access to those resources, but a research agenda might be usefully constructed around four core themes:

1. the shaping of transitions and biographies;
2. vulnerable groups;
3. the social construction of identity;
4. political and social participation and citizenship.

New technologies may (or may not) have a central place within these critical research questions about the changing conditions of young people's lives throughout Europe. It is often argued that the emerging world is framed not by an information society but by an information economy – driven by the "narrow" grid of investment, profit and loss, and contributing increasingly to social inequality. Others argue that the information age is promoted self-centredness and moral denegeracy, which are themselves contributing to social decay and collapse. The challenge is to discover whether or not the information economy can be converted into an information society, harnessed to secure wider societal objectives of social inclusion and renewed opportunities. The information age must not be "colonised" by the old and established and must be connected to young people in ways which enable broader goals of youth policy to be realised. Such goals – and the contribution of the information society to them – may be scrutinised and "tested" by reference to this new agenda for youth research in Europe. The agenda has been re-shaped in view of the disappearance of the old "trajectories" of the life cycle and the emergence of the new (and uncertain) navigations within the life course but, in some senses, it is still addressing "old" issues in youth research: transition, vulnerability, identity and citizenship. The terminology may have changed and the issues may now be circumscribed by new technological clothing, but the questions will – as always – require collective and political will if they are to be addressed effectively.

Many of these points were revisited and addressed in more detail by Andre Vitalis (youth research) in his sub-plenary presentation on "European information society and citizenship". He challenged the unequivocal positive evaluations of new technological development, arguing instead for the risks such development produced: increasingly inequalities, the "stupidisation" of the masses, dangers to private life, the disintegration of society, threats to democracy, and the undermining of public services. This was a plank for devil's advocacy. There was no "ready made" information society, which was inherently beneficial. A constructive information society would have to be shaped and regulated. Key questions needed to be asked about the locus of control over information, the relevance of information, and the ways in which available information was used. There were questions about privacy and anonymity. There needed to be far greater transparency and understanding of the rules governing networks and databases. There needed to be guarantees, otherwise individuals risked becoming little more than the puppets of market forces. Of course, information technology offered great potential as a tool for communication and the development of active citizens but, for this to be realised, the debate had to move beyond the technical to a consideration of the social and political implications of its usage.

A number of important conceptual distinctions were made: between information itself and the medium of information (the content and the vessel); between the signs and the meanings (what lies behind the symbols/who deciphers the signals?); between virtual neighbours and real neighbours (can technological contact substitute for physical human contact?); between hard and soft information (once more, who provides the interpretation of "soft" communication?). It is essential to emphasise that images do not reproduce reality and, for those images to forge appropriate connections with reality, there needs to be people trained and equipped to provide appropriate interpretation and analysis. The quality of information will always be variable; measures need to be developed to enable young people to be critical of what they receive or access. At a broader level, the state and civil society must be equipped and prepared to resist the threats posed within the information society by untrammeled economic forces. Educational practice must be reshaped and renewed to facilitate self-directed learning and to ensure responsible and empowering use of available information, and to develop the competencies to resist the disempowering and negative practices which will inevitably come to occupy some of the vast space now being made available through new communication technologies. In short, there are both considerable threats and enormous opportunities. It is necessary to be aware of the former and to develop the capacity to promote the latter.

Tanja Rener (youth research), in her sub-plenary on "Time out for youth in the 1990s" described the findings from a survey of the student population of Slovenia. Students had been chosen since they were at the vanguard of social change in Slovenia and because they provided the most clear indicator of the elements of "postmodern" lifestyles. Despite this, a significant minority (some 30-40 per cent) of students aged between 25 and 30 years still lived with their parents, although this was characterised as "living apart together". Fundamentally, although there was change (arising from political transformation and the availability of new technologies), many young people in Slovenia were still sustained by traditions, especially traditions around family life. Indeed, there was strong integration between the generations.

Although young people expressed ideals around peace, environmental issues and solidarity, these were rarely converted into concerted public and social action. Young people mapped their individual life course, usually in the context of and with the support of their families. Many families possessed personal computers and use of the Internet was widespread. But even with this access to new technology, the family still played a central role in the socialisation of young people. Moreover, "old" media (booklets, radio and television) still exerted a strong hold on the interests and "education" of the young.

Sven Mørch (youth research) presented a sub-plenary paper entitled "Information society and normative action", arguing initially that the information society has become a new, if still ill-defined, metaphor for actual society. In many respects, people have lost their authentic relation to the world and much significant learning about life derives from the media. Indeed, they often know more about the "global" world than they do about their "local world".

However, it is important to recognise that the information society is part of the broader contextual change which has transformed "youth life" – the life led by young people during a period of increasingly extended "adolescence". The greater openness of societies and of the world has led, certainly, to greater "individualisation" – both of possibility and opportunity, and of risk. "Youth life" is not only increasingly complicated and demanding but it is increasingly central to individual development. And while societal conditions present both possibilities and constraints on individual action, it is also more possible for individuals to use previous experiences and personal capacities as tools for their own "self-actualisation". But the scope for that self-actualisation is contigent upon the individual's understanding of social and individual conditions. The development of this self-understanding takes place within social relationships and social contexts.

Clearly, modern life for young people has become bewildering, undirected and often contradictory. "Youth life" is no longer a space before adult responsibilities set in (as youth cultural analysis suggested in the 1960s and early 1970s) but a time of education and learning and a central landmark in individual development. The way young people deal with it is critical to social mobility. The old certainties and securities (and inequalities) of social class stratification have vanished; "today "youth life" seems to have become an individual fight".

Individuals now have to forge their own life course, carving their own individual track. Modern "youthhood" represents the landscape through which individual young people seek to make their best way in society – and those who do make the "best way" do so by maximising the benefits within the social conditions and contexts affecting them. Hence "youth life" has been transformed from learned norms to negotiated normativity. Young people are the constructors of modern social lives and individual tracks, not the fol-

13

lowers of parental normative expectations and generational recipients of class cultural continuities.

If "youth life" is a road, navigated with different degrees of success by young people, the "old" influences of school, peer group, family (and organised free time) still exert their power, but in different ways from the past. They are now resources through which children develop active self-managing and young people develop qualified self-determination. So while "youth life" may be open to all, it is actualised in different ways by different groups of young people. For some, the perception that no adult life possibilities are open to them may lead them to disengage, or switch off, or engage only with the peer group, sometimes with negative consequences. Others who do not avail themselves of the opportunities and support presented by the school or family, end up in a "container" situation – held, as young adults, in a symbolic "warehouse" as a result of being denied admittance to the adult world.

And while the school and family are still important, youth activities and projects have become more important. Because the "tracks" within "youth life" are created, it is possible to influence and support their positive direction. Youth projects need, therefore, to be planned in order to face the challenge of developing mechanisms for supporting youth development by providing clearer "maps" by which young people may be helped in developing their own tracks to adult life. Such projects must therefore not jump from an analysis of problems to the formulation of plans; a critical intervening consideration must be an understanding of the nature of the problems in order to develop appropriate interventions. The task of all youth projects (author's note: which presumably includes those concerning new information technologies) is to support constructive tracks to adult life by connecting with existing tracks and thereby developing individual young people.

Prior to the plenary session on the second day, Lasse Siurala re-emphasised this core message of the symposium. The first youth research symposium had established an infrastructure for communication and co-management of research within the Council of Europe producing, *inter alia*, the *European Directory of Youth Research*, the post of youth research co-ordinator, national youth research co-ordinators, library co-operation, a research and development unit and, most recently, the decision to conduct national youth policy surveys. This could not have been achieved without the contribution and support of governments and NGOs. The first symposium had, however, been unapologetically concerned with increasing the profile of youth research within the Council of Europe. This second symposium had a broader task: not only to sustain the profile of youth research but also to identify – on account of the opportunities now presented by the information age – new working methods and strategies for the promotion of youth policies and youth work under the umbrella of the Council of Europe. In other words, the goal was to engender an even more dynamic, and more broadly based, agenda through effective co-management by the three "constituencies" present. Researchers clearly did not have privileged access to any absolute truth; there were "regimes of truth", albeit with different levels of credibility and persuasiveness, to which all parties were able to make an equal contribution. This was what was expected and hoped for from the participants at the symposium.

Anke Bahl (youth research) provided a more concrete understanding of young people's involvement with new technologies in her plenary presentation on "Identity switches on Internet on-line activities". Her account projected the voice of the user: students whom she had interviewed who were immersed in the world of the Internet and who had forged different relationships between their "virtual" and "real" worlds and selves. For outward appearances and personalities could be transformed on the Net, although reconciling them in "real life" – as her story of Klaus and Amy (Ovlor and Sita) illustrated – could be both fraught and, ultimately, romantic! Klaus and Amy, through their participation in the MUD (multi-user dungeon) game "Nightfall", were able to experiment with alternative identities and to be what they could not be in real life. For Amy, her MUD friends also offered a therapeutic outlet for her personal problems in her real life. Amy's involvement with CMC (computer-mediated communication) enabled her, eventually, to work through important personal concerns about her identity and relationships.

For Jack, an American student in Germany, the use of IRC (Internet Relay Chat) assisted in enhancing his awareness of questions of nationality, racism and historical identities and, incrementally, in improving his use of the German language and integration into German society. For Reina and Tracey, who allocated a vast amount of their personal time to a special type of MUD game called "World of Darkness" MUSH (multi-user shared hallucination), it offered a basis for "therapeutic learning", allowing them to experiment with different aspects of a theoretical life, in which they were completely in control and had complete freedom as a result of their total anonymity. However, they became so absorbed in the game that their real lives were constructed around participation.

These accounts provide important illustrations of the different boundaries of virtual culture. They provide exemplars of the ways in which young people may develop and make use of their on-line selves, which may be aspects of their real selves or completely different personae, to the point of switching gender (or, indeed, ethnicity). It is possible to be anyone, anywhere, on the Net. Thus on-line environments like MUDs have the potential to be laboratories for the construction of identity: people are able to build a real self by "cycling" through many virtual selves. They offer a possibility for change, but they also offer a site for "unproductive repetition": there are both risks and opportunities. It seems important to improve our understanding of the dynamics of virtual experiences, in order to anticipate the dangers (and find ways of addressing them) and to put these experiences to best use. Amy, on reflection, had "mixed feelings" about her experience – that was about as much as she could say. It encapsulates the current state of much understanding about the ways in which (some) young people are becoming involved with the opportunities made available by new technological communication. Some concerns may be overstated: many MUD users also meet face to face for parties and gatherings in real life. Other concerns may have greater legitimacy, such as the cultural colonisation, through the Net, by the Americans and by the English language. But the essential question is to what extent should the kind of role-playing described be supported, criticised, or simply left alone?

In the following sub-plenary, Mohammed Dhalech (youth work practitioner) also explored questions of identity, more from the point of view of ethnic origin than on-line technology. Concern was expressed about differential access to the information society, especially on the part of Muslim young people. Did the information society compound the exclusion of some groups of young people; could it be used to promote their integration? Young people from ethnic minorities constantly switch identities in real life (is experimentation in virtual life unnecessary?): between home life, school life and their friendship groups. There is increasing cross-over, imitation and cross-fertilisation between young people across ethnic backgrounds in terms of image, culture, food and music (see Les Back, *New Ethnicities and Urban Culture*, London: UCL Press, 1996). However, skin colour cannot be changed, and so Muslim youth continues to be subjected to insidious forms of racism, which must be combated, if their aspirations for involvement, respect and active citizenship are to be supported.

That support can, to some extent be delivered through effective youth work. But effective youth work suffers from lack of access to, and connection with, European and global networks of information. It is critical that young people are both directly and indirectly (through youth work practice) provided with access to the information society. Only through ensuring that this takes place can core youth work principles (of equality, access, empowerment and opportunity) be firmly translated into practice. Youth workers have a specific responsibility to generate access and thereby promote equality of opportunity, particularly for young people from ethnic minorities.

Ensuing discussion confirmed and extended the complexity of this debate, around both access to the information society and questions of identity. The case for broadening access to communication technology, irrespective of how it was used, was argued for, if "only" on the grounds of equalising opportunity. Equality of access was, therefore, to some extent, a symbolic issue, which would not address or solve any wider issues. Those issues raised further questions about the support required and educational methods needed for particular forms of on-line communication. Indeed, was the Internet (potentially or actually) a support system, an experimental system or a learning system? It might, for example, be used by young people from ethnic minorities to contact other young people and promote intercultural learning. It was agreed that a *"laissez faire"* approach to communication technologies might well do nothing for social life and community development, which was the goal for youth organisations and youth workers, not just securing access *per se*. How could the Internet be used for empowering young people to make sense of their lives and assist them in moving towards constructive futures?

In a more theoretical sub-plenary contribution, Ulrike Nagel (youth research) discussed new types of schooling and forms of participation under the title of "Second chances in a risk society". There was a "scissors movement" which, for a number of reasons including globalisation, individualisation and risk, was fomenting the greater polarisation of opportunity in society and producing greater inequality. There was, however, between the possibilities of permanent employment and the risks of unemployment, a "third arena", based on the shadow or informal economy and self-employment networks. Engagement with this third arena requires specific skills and competencies of flexibility, opportunism and enterprise. It demands the exercise of individual choice and the heightened application of individual autonomy. Education and training needs to be restructured to enable young people to avail themselves of opportunities within this third arena: the pedagogical task is to train young people for coping with discontinuous life course patterns and with status inconsistencies and to prepare them for multiple or mixed participation patterns – between formal employment, unemployment and the third arena. Work must not be seen any longer as a central life value; other kinds of activities and roles must be accorded equal value. Second chance schools – as recently advocated by the EU's DG XXII as part of its strategy to combat social exclusion – may contribute to equipped more marginalised young people with the skills needed to participate in the third arena, thus assisting their re-entry into the labour force.

The vision is that such provision can provide a solution to the precarious predicament of socially excluded young people. Theoretically, it is a credible mechanism for encouraging the renewed participation of those who have dropped out of, or are excluded from, the formal labour market, and it provides an alternative to them slipping into prolonged unemployment. In practice, numerous questions remain about the impact and effectiveness of such a strategy. There is a risk of romanticising notions of "lifelong learning", alternative education, and new forms of economic activity, thereby clouding the persistence of central problematics such as real social participation and the distribution of real resources with which young people can equitably participate as full members of civil society.

Workshop presentations included an account by Brigitta Myrman (government) on the establishment of a website on youth issues in Sweden (http://www.youth.se). This includes a database for all young people and for those working with young people. People can meet, communicate and learn about activities by youth organisations. This initiative has three objectives: to energise municipalities in promoting their youth policies and activities; to encourage participation by young people; and to promote and communicate relevant publications. Of the two million young people aged 7 to 25 years in Sweden, some seventy thousand are in youth organisations. However, there has been concern about declining membership of youth organisations. In recognition of the fact that young people have new ways, new cultural pursuits and new interests, the information network was (recently – September 1996) established. The website contains a calendar of events and activities, contact names and addresses, international connections, information for youth workers and, most significantly perhaps, "The Sluice". This is a young people's guide to society, giving them direct access to a host of relevant information. It is acknowledged that, while it is clear that young people are deserting formal systems, there are others who will remain disinterested in, or excluded from, even this initiative; nevertheless, it is viewed as providing a bridge to broader participation and thereby ensuring the maintenance (by new means) of democracy. The site is very new and it is difficult to know how things will work out, but that is the rationale for having established it. It will be funded by the government as a pilot project until 1998.

Many practical questions were raised following this presentation, largely about the resources required for developing this project, the reasons for Swedish youth deserting traditional youth organisations, levels of usage, the spread of access sites, and the competitiveness of this site (compared to more commercial ones) in terms of attracting and retaining the attention of young people. Many of the answers remain to be discovered!

Marcel Kreuger (NGO), Director of an anti-racism information centre in the Netherlands, spoke of the importance of establishing Internet sites for the accessing and dissemination of information. He outlined six key reasons: cheap, particularly with free software and other services, as a result of increasing competition; easy to use; fits in with individualisation; serves the needs of education; enables individuals to deal personally with many issues; and there are no rules and no rulers! The Internet will soon be available for everyone, so we have to learn how to involve ourselves with it and to influence it – or else we leave it to Microsoft.

When ARIC decided, as a social organisation with social goals, to establish a website, some key questions emerged, which are relevant to all similar organisations with similar objectives:

– What is your message?

– How do you intend to present your information?

– How will you encourage people to access your information?

– What balance do you aim to strike between being proactive and reactive?

Clearly different organisations will wish to convey and transmit different messages. But the presentation of information demands careful thought and reflection: what "languages" will you use (national or international)?; in what ways will you make it attractive?; what role do you intend for it?; which services are priorities?; what plans do you have for updating?; how much specialist support are you likely to require?

The ARIC experience suggests that, if organisations move forward in this direction, then a quite radical reorganisation of staffing and labour will be necessary. The key point is that one has to be clear about the market you intend to reach and to plan your services accordingly. There will always remain a problem of not really knowing who your "customers" are and what they do with any information they acquire from your site: all you can count is the number of visits. However, for sensitive work (such as issues around anti-racism), such anonymity is perhaps a strength. But the investment in delivering anti-racist information through new technologies continues to be largely an act of faith and conviction, rather than an act of science; it is impossible to gauge its effectiveness in either quantitative or qualitative terms.

Both of the practical initiatives outlined indicate that a core challenge is to educate youth organisations about how to use new communication technologies as a tool for enhancing their aims, rather than simply engaging with it "because it is there".

In another workshop, three presentations were made by youth researchers, but they provided a platform for practical discussion. Anita Eliasson commented on her research on well-educated teenagers in Finland under the title of "Youth: virtual travellers in and outside the Internet". She described the more technical orientation of young men to new technologies compared with the more social orientation of young women. Nonetheless, in her small sample, both young men and young women switched comfortably between their "real" and their "virtual" activities. There were two important questions which surfaced from this presentation, concerning issues of identity and control. For those who regularly make use of Internet Relay Chat (and perhaps other facilities on the Net), there needs to be more consideration of the potential problems arising from the integration of personality and identity between on-line and off-line selves. Secondly, despite the claims concerning autonomy and independence on the Net, users do not control the Net. It is controlled by commercial interests. For greater control to be exercised by users, users would have to pay for it and this would run counter to the objective of broadening access so that poorer people can make use of it.

Vladimir Dubski (youth research) offered some observations on "Czech Youth and the information society". Since "independence" in 1989, the Czech Republic has been relatively slow in introducing the use and ownership of computers. The youngest age group in the study, those aged between 19 and 25 years, were in fact those least likely to own or make use of computers. This was probably due to the fact that they had other priorities for their resources, since this was the age of marriage and starting a family. However, use of new technologies in the Czech Republic was slowly on the increase, with some 7 per cent now having access to the Internet.

The study was concerned with the values of Czech youth. There were some important differences in values between those who used computers and those who did not, with the former placing greater emphasis on values such as "social prestige" and "enterprise". But there were few differences in value orientations towards, for example, family and friends. Czech youth generally attached limited importance to collective values, perhaps because this resonated too closely with the communist old guard, but nevertheless they valued "solidarity". They also attached considerable importance to "ecology".

Debi Roker (youth research) talked about the "Information and advice needs of rural youth". The importance of young people themselves articulating their needs was stressed. Rural youth tends to be neglected in youth studies, possibly as a result of (misguided) perceptions that country life is idyllic and unproblematic. In fact, the situation of young people living in rural areas is often limiting, impoverished and isolated. Young people are cut off from opportunity and advice. To develop appropriate support measures to meet the needs of rural youth, there need to be mobile advice units, some with telephones and Internet terminals and other opportunities for contact and communication, such as the "youth clubs in the radio" initiative run by rural youth. New technologies are an important dimension in provision for rural youth, but they should not be seen as a substitute for more personal human contact and support.

In another workshop, Tuuli Toomere (youth research) considered the historical vertical hierarchy in the transmission and consumption of information and suggested that this is transformed by the Internet, since there is free movement of information. The same was true of feedback routes. The information society might be defined as the society formed in the Internet by the users.

The research reported concerned the findings of a questionnaire placed on a chat channel, which had elicited 274 responses. Young men accounted for 80 per cent of the participants. Highest levels of participation were amongst those aged 16 to 23 years peaking at 18 to 19 years. Boys had tended to have more computer-related studies in high school. Users not only saw the Internet as a tool, but also as a friend. Within the Net, they found a sense of freedom, democracy and anonymity. One of the reasons young people reduced or ceased participating was perhaps because the virtual world was becoming too much like the real world and losing its democratic and egalitarian aspects. However, questions were raised about the potential for democratic development if users could detach themselves from all ascribed qualities and play any role they wished.

Meral Alguidas (youth work), in her presentation on "Youth and Internet relations in Turkey", discussed the "politics" of Internet use and development. The development of use of the Internet in Turkey has largely been pioneered by university students, though within a questionable legal framework: the Internet is under the control of the Turkish Government and other use is therefore arguably illegal. Indeed, Microsoft has declined to establish a Microsoft network in Turkey due to legal problems. Yet, despite legal, technical and financial difficulties, Turkish youth has become part of the Net. Long before the creation of more "established" Internet outlets, students had started their own bulletin board services and communicating through e-mail. They facilitated chat, exchanged programmes and assisted in the formation of interest groups. Despite the slow growth of "official" accounts, students have found ways – for example, through sharing accounts – of extending access to the Net. Internet use has grown at an unbelievable pace, although formal development of systems has been slow, and the basis for considerable protest. Informal development has, however, been facilitated and accelerated by the knowledge of students returning from studying (and making use of information technologies) abroad. And what often started as friendly chat has turned into serious debates on different issues.

José Cabrita Nascimento (NGO) talked about the question of "Multicultural training of youth volunteers: participation and citizenship in the creation of a new European identity". This is a project designed to promote an authentic sense of European citizenship, something which may prove difficult given the problems of social exclusion and unemployment. Nonetheless, if we really want to develop an "ideal" Europe of democracy, cultural and ethnic tolerance, solidarity and co-operation, then it is an urgent task to find effective and active means to promote the participation of young people throughout Europe, but particularly those living in disadvantaged social, economic and cultural environments.

The project described concerns the training of volunteer social workers to carry out work designed to combat racism and exclusion. Young people from distinct cultural groups lived together and learned from each other, thus ensuring that they have an important and active role in contributing to the training process. The methods used included video, journalism, compact disk production and photography.

One idea which emerged from this multicultural training was to set up a European network (YouthNet Communication) between associations and organisations having broadly the same aims. The network is planned and intends to make use of Internet and e-mail and to provide a website for the exchange of information. A major aim of the network will be the preparation of European events, such as exchanges, seminars and training courses. Geographical distance will be overcome through the exploitation of new information technologies. Real action and youth work has led to the development of new ideas and hopes for activities and projects, all of which emphasise that individual countries do not stand alone and that all of Europe has a common destiny. New information technologies represent an important tool for contributing to that destiny.

Muhamed Sestanovic (youth research), departing from the focus on new technologies, wished instead to reflect on the "Problems of youth in Bosnia and Herzegovina – a state in transition". The country has suffered, as a result of the war in former Yugoslavia, the greatest social problems of all European countries experiencing profound social and economic transition at the end of the twentieth century. Immediately before the war, the socio-political life of young people totally faded away. There were no longer any youth organisations where young people could display their creativity. Young people have since had little option but to gather in war trenches, bomb shelters and cafe shops. Young people have suffered dreadful physical hardship as a result of the war: displacement from their homes, appalling injury and disability, fractured or non-existent education and training, and emotional and mental trauma. It is the latter – the mental integrity of young people following the war – which has been the subject of research.

Beyond the deaths of over sixteen thousand children and young people, over thirty-five thousand have been wounded and nearly twenty thousand have lost one or both parents. On average, every young person has witnessed nine traumatic events, considerably more than young people in Kuwait, Iraq or Lebanon. Yet despite the mental disorder which has arisen, this research also shows that the experience of the war has not significantly changed the value orientations of young people to anything like the same extent as it has changed their mental health. Young people still subscribe to multicultural and multiethnic values and still place a very high priority on values such as honesty, tolerance and patience – the historical values and attributes of the Bosniaks and Herzegovinians.

The plenary lecture for the third day of the symposium was presented by Phil Brown (youth research) on the subject of "Globalisation, youth and employment in the information age". (Phil had persisting problems dealing with the amplification technology from an earlier time!)

Issues concerning the information age – encompassing new forms of knowledge, information, technology and computers – need to be placed firmly in a wider social, political and economic context. There is clearly evidence to support contentions of both economic and cultural globalisation, but it is the political debate about globalisation which will affect what governments will do. That debate is taking place largely within the "new rules of economic organisation": eligibility, engagement and wealth creation. Everyone can now join in the competition: the truly global character of multinational organisations is used as evidence by, for example, the British Government for its stance on competitiveness and failure to endorse the social chapter. There is now a "global auction", for jobs, workers and technologies, and one can no longer afford expensive infrastructure. The new rules of engagement demand that, to remain competitive, nations endeavour to develop high skill, high technology niches in the global market, producing high quality goods and services. To achieve this, there is a consensus that a successful future for national societies will depend upon investment in human resources, quality education and training and a commitment to lifelong learning. New technologies will, inevitably, be at the very centre of these processes.

Such arguments do not, however, deal adequately with the social and political issues (conflicts?) which are accentuated through such global competition in global markets. The economic prognosis produces deep concerns about social and economic division and inequality. The invocation of new information technologies as the salvation for this growing divide tends to cloud the real issues – which need to focus on positional, distribution and relational issues. Put simply: who is in and who is out as processes of inclusion and exclusion exert their hold. The proclaimed need for "lifelong learning" is held to be intrinsically a "good thing", without it being subjected to deeper interrogation and potential counter-argument. There are fundamental questions, even if it is a "good thing", to do with resourcing it, structuring it and accessing it. The Internet – as a central resource for the promotion of lifelong learning – cannot compensate for society.

Furthermore, there is no cross-national consensus on how economic development can make the difference in promoting citizenship and combating exclusion. On the one hand, there is the ideology of the "enterprise economy", as epitomised by the United Kingdom, which argues for the centrality of reduced public intervention in order to promote wealth creation and liberate individual choice. On the other hand, there is the stakeholder model, which incorporates a social vision and detects a role for social welfare in underpinning effective economic development.

For young people, these models reflect two competing versions of inclusion and exclusion, success and failure. For there have always been patterns and processes of inclusion and exclusion; they are now just perhaps more visible and more acute. Within the enterprise model, the market rules: the exercise of individual choice and the commitment of personal resources, as well as an astute reading of the market, will effect outcomes. Within the stakeholder model, more meritocratic principles persist, within which greater equality of opportunity is sustained through public sector intervention. However, all societies throughout Europe are steadily moving away from stakeholding social models towards (if not embracing fully) the concepts prevailing in enterprise economies, such as the marketisation of education.

There is a reluctance on the part of governments to acknowledge the scale of marginalisation of significant proportions of young people. The political rhetoric has not been adequately subjected to a social audit of grounded realities. The rhetoric is, nevertheless, influencing strongly the directions being taken by governments in economic and social policy. Learning for all, and the proliferation of new technologies as a tool for learning and for economic innovation, must be more carefully analysed. The consignment of many of the difficulties experienced by young people to the arena of "private troubles" must be challenged, for many of these need to be retrieved and repositioned in the arena of "public issues". Only then will the social hardware be effectively related to the information software and the more insidious effects of globalisation. Social questions cannot be dislocated from economic change and new information technologies need to be firmly connected not only to economic development but also to wider social agendas concerned with participation, equal opportunities, learning, communication, respecting diversity and social justice. Talk about the task of promoting social cohesion must be followed by action which harnesses new information technologies to that objective.

In a stark recognition of the still widespread exclusion of many young people, the sub-plenary presentation by Jacques Ogier and Peggy Simmons (NGO youth work campaigners) on the work of the Fourth World Youth Movement considered the information needs, hopes and demands for change amongst the poorest groups of young people and those committed to working with them. There was a dire risk that such groups would be abandoned as the first casualties of global economic competition, and it was imperative that work was done alongside such young people to re-energise them and sustain the possibilities for their inclusion in their societies. It would not be sufficient simply to set up public Internet sites which they could access; such young people required support and encouragement if they were to make productive use of such opportunities.

As for many people, the first technological contact experienced by the poorest is through television and perhaps subsequently through electronic games. But this is technology to be consumed: users cannot be creators or producers. More creative and productive technology is seldom available or accessible to the poorest sections of society: it is perceived to belong to the world of wealthy people.

A computer network for the fourth world (the very poorest), YODEM, is being established by the Fourth World Youth Movement. It will be part of follow-up work, after more physical, personal and human encounters designed to instil confidence and provide support. The objective of setting up the network is quite explicitly about assisting the most disadvantaged young people in developing real relationships in the real world, not providing access to virtual relationships in a virtual world.

It is important that the information society does not exclude anyone, particularly on the grounds of cost. Even if every household and every public library was provided with a computer, it would still not reach everyone. The poor will not find a place within the information society without support. New information technologies present a new opportunity precisely because of their interactivity. Those who have access to them have, simultaneously, the possibility of sharing in the making of the information society. Those who

24

do not, do not. Therefore the Fourth World Youth Movement has established dialogue on issues such as human rights, social justice and equality through Internet Relay Chat (IRC) and through the UNICEF Voice of youth page.

But for young people to participate effectively they need skill, belief and motivation – something which can be developed through relating involvement in new technologies to their interests: science, art, other countries, music or sport. The Fourth World Youth Movement therefore runs workshops which involve young people and enable them to learn and communicate through tapping their natural curiosity and creativity. Young people feel that they are part of something bigger, not individualised and isolated. The issue is about communicating, with and without technology. To this end, the project cultivates different ways of communicating with each other: through a multilingual journal, personal visits, international meetings and electronic media. Through the YODEM, young people can send personal messages, discuss themes and issues and get involved in campaigns.

There needs to be a re-thinking of human activity, so that training and learning is not simply focused on access to jobs, but also celebrates personal creativity, self-education and growth, and providing support for others. The latter is becoming especially important – and new technologies have a central role to play here – as the social world becomes increasingly isolating and atomised. New opportunities for participation and communication are imperative in order to foment and cement social integration.

(Note: There were very few researchers in attendance at this very practical sub-plenary, a point which was noted with some concern by those participating.)

The sub-plenary presentation by Maurice Devlin (youth research) raised the question "Young people today: virtually adult?". It traced some of the historical influences on defining youth and conferring status on young people, including the influence of socio-economic change. The prevailing low status and lack of independence of youth is indicative of a "crisis" in traditional understandings of how youth relates to adulthood, for "youth" is no longer a time of relative lack of commitment in preparation for the relative commitment of adulthood, precisely because the adulthood available is changing – many young people are now faced with a "virtual" adulthood. In other words, they are almost adults but they remain without the most basic material security to allow other aspects of adulthood to fall into place. The adulthood on offer has become dematerialised; identity exploration may be about the only thing available.

New information and communication technologies (NICTs) look as if they will become another unequally distributed resource. And even if the more optimistic projections are accurate and all young people will eventually gain acess, there must still be questions about the capacity of NICTs to enhance democracy. NICTs may, however, come to exert a significant influence on relations between the generations: indeed, when combined with demographic change, they could lead to the erosion of "youth" as a separate stage in the life course.

So what should youth work do in relation to NICTs? First, NICTs need to become accessible to youth workers and youth workers need to be familiar with their possibilities. For it is youth work which may make use of NICTs in order to promote young people's development, rather than allowing engagement with new information technology to remain largely a leisure activity and a potentially negative force in young people's lives.

Specifically, youth work can use NICTs to develop young people's emotional and intellectual resources. It can help to counteract the "stupidisation" possibilities: even if the Net becomes stupidised, young people's use of it need not be. It can place the "escapist" dimensions of the Net in context for, while some element of escapism is vital for all of us, there needs to be a sense of balance with other human dimensions of our lives. It can support young people becoming consuming citizens, rather than simply consumers. And it can provide the social and political education to enable young people to make discerning use of the NICTs.

Policy-makers therefore need to provide incentives for youth workers to acquaint themselves with NICTs, ensure that they have access, and provide the resources to enable youth work to resist the increasing encroachment of commercial NICT-based provision on young people's lives. Youth work therefore needs to develop new attitudes, a new image, and new forms of engagement with young people, in order to become a leading component in what the Australian academic and politician Barry Jones (*Sleepers Wake*) has called the "convivial sector" – a sector which will be complementary to, but not dependent upon, the new information and communication technologies.

Elke Stolzenburg (youth research) made a sub-plenary presentation on "Out-of-school work and information superhighways". Even in Germany there are still many technical limitations to applying and accessing new information technologies. Cable networks are not available for youth clubs; reliance on telephone lines and modem connections limits the use of Internet to e-mails, IRCs, websurfing and CD-roms. There is no possibility to transfer, for example, moving pictures and advanced versions of multimedia.

If Internet is to provide a service for youth then clearly it needs to be accessible and it must be available to all partners in youth policy, particularly to youth organisations. However, it has considerable potential for involving young people and those who work with them in computer-mediated communication. One example was of the production of CD-roms by young people themselves (on the sensitive topic of rape and sexual assault). Another was concerned with a joint project between those centrally responsible for political education in Germany and youth workers in order to provide, via the

Internet, a service for young people and parents about "educative" games. This databank was itself a product of the viewpoints and evaluations of educators, young "game fans", and interviews conducted by educators with young game fans, which had themselves been collected via the Internet. The broader message was to highlight the potential of making use of the Internet to deal with topical subjects and to demonstrate the versatility of new information technologies in accumulating the knowledge of both young people and youth workers to achieve this objective. But to do this, computer-mediated communication must be consciously applied as an instrument of youth work.

Workshop presentations included an account by Ivan Marinov (NGO) of training courses being developed in Bulgaria to familiarise young people with new technologies. Local networks have been established through the Council for Youth and Children. In times of rapid social and economic change, the information society provides a means of overcoming time and place, and offers a social forum for new forms of expression. Increasingly, familiarity with new technologies is also an essential prerequisite for being considered for any prestigious job. Young people need to internalise the message that there are other, new, ways of organising themselves; the training course essentially equips young people with the "research methods" needed to access and make use of information effectively, particularly the youth database which has been established on the Internet.

Matti Viirimaki (NGO) discussed the question of the delivery of information by the Youth Council of Finland to its one hundred member organisations. It still used traditional methods (a magazine, leaflets and library resources) but had recently invested in information technology to develop new methodologies. It had a server on the web to provide information for youth organisations and youth workers, and it used Internet Relay Chat for meetings. Its main service, however, is PROYOUTH, an interactive resource for youth organisations. Access is secured by a user ID, and therefore users have to register. The problem which is emerging is overcrowding and the difficulties of finding information. Furthermore, there is a key issue around updating, and the resources required to do so. Nonetheless, the site has some one thousand visits a month. Most users are active, if their e-mail communication is a guide. But there are still problems about the unwillingness (or inability?) of youth workers to make use of these facilities, and there is currently training for youth workers on technical issues. (Discussion raised questions about whether youth workers also needed to be trained in more ethnical and substantive issues.) It was possible to do some virtual training on the Net. And money was no problem! The Finnish government had enthusiastically supported these developments.

Juri Saarniit (youth research) and Ilse Trapenciere (youth research) presented some very different observations from their experiences in Estonia and Latvia. (Apparently, there are only sailors, nor surfers, on the Net in Estonia!)

It was noted that throughout much of the symposium there had been only very general and common "visions" about the relationship between young people and new technologies. Certainly everybody understood that the technological revolution was an inevitable process, which could not be resisted. But, within such structural determinism, there were psychological and pedagogical aspects of the debate which had rarely surfaced. In Estonia, the commitment by the government to equip all schools with computers had been accompanied by a "new curriculum" for the information society. In essence, the aim of computer science in schools was to teach the purposeful use of information – enabling children and young people to make educated use of new technologies and developing their competence to do so. The achievement of such aims was, however, highly constrained by resources. It had been stated many times at the symposium but it was critical to re-state the differential resource capacity of different nations to realise their visions of the potential educational use of new technologies.

Ilse Trapenciere considered the many "roadblocks" facing young people in Latvia on the path to accessing and making use of new technology. Indeed, few even associate computers with the "information society", referring more frequently to books, newspapers, libraries, conversation and school. Those who mentioned computers tended to be the most successful young people (namely, those who had overcome the roadblocks). Many young people do not even have a basic education, others live in poorly-resourced rural areas, and others have not had a secondary education. Even many of those with a secondary education have not had access to computer classes and, of those who have, few have access to computers (only 2-3 per cent of households have computers). So the Internet road map leading to the information highway has many diversions and obstructions, meaning that only about 10 per cent of young people gain access to new technologies and have the competence to use them – in after-school centres, universities and in the NGO centres. A significant majority are young men who do use information technology for their education, but more for games and interaction in virtual communities. Young women appear less concerned with entertainment and more interested in information.

Conny Reuter (NGO), who had throughout the symposium emphasised that the information society was more than the Internet, presented a practical case study of "A multimedia education network". Supported under the Telematics Programme of DG XIII of the European Union, the network currently covers five countries but was developed as part of the French youth organisation La Ligue's responsibility to educate young people as citizens – and the view was that new technologies might help! Yet in France there still remain problems around the technical aspects of linking into new technological networks, in both households and schools. Nevertheless, the DG XIII Telematics Programme presented an opportunity, although also problems in terms of finding institutional educational partners, securing industrial involvement, having to work in the English language and having to produce bi-monthly reports!

As always, the starting point was not new technology but the needs of young people. An increasingly observed need is that for social integration. The potential role of multimedia in contribution to meeting that need then had to be understood and a suitable pedagogy (the "information and communication architecture") developed. To make anything happen, stakeholders such as young people (low achievers), teachers, associations, and software providers had to be brought on board. Institutional, financial and personal commitment had to be secured. The network has been designed so that access is gained through the use of a smart card, which guides young people to accessible and relevant sites. (It also focuses and limits costs and does permit a very detailed understanding of levels and types of usage.) Further information is available from http.//www.la ligue.cie.fr.

Sites have now been installed and a process is underway for the selection and training of the trainees. The pedagogical dimensions relate to a series of step-wise interventions, from basic skills, through social skills to professional skills. Informal education is directed at the most excluded young people. Non-formal education is aimed at those with no qualifications. Pre-vocational education is targeted at unemployed young people who do possess some level of qualification.

Time will tell about the impact of this adventurous initiative, but it is a reminder not only of the social/societal agenda which informs the interest of youth organisations in new technologies, but also of the traditional sequence of questions which youth workers have always asked prior to making interventions: who are the users or the target group?; what are their needs?; what resources do I have available, or can I make available (including information technology and multimedia) in order to meet those needs? These are very practical questions which may have, at least partially, technological answers.

Paul Kloosterman (NGO) made a sub-plenary presentation on the work of "Spectrum", a provincial organisation in the Netherlands. Three central questions informed a subsequent discussion: what skills do young people need to deal with the overflow (or overload) of information; how can youth work use the "new media" as a tool for its aims and objectives?; what skills and training do youth workers need in this area if they are to work effectively? The questions rest on the assumption that the new media are important and that therefore youth work needs to engage with it, but there are few ideas about the pedagogy or methodology for doing it.

Since technologies are changing so rapidly, and since some young people at least are already competent and committed to their use (while others remain mystified, along with their youth workers!), one methodology is to engage in "learning by doing" – to work alongside young people to demystify technology and to discover its potential. This approach in itself serves wider objectives of promoting citizenship and participation. It will, of course, be necessary to reflect on the type of knowledge which is accessed (are young people able to find what they are looking for?), levels of understanding (can and do young people use this knowledge in their daily life?), and judgements about the importance of this process (how does this new knowledge assist young people in being "critical citizens"?).

The process of intervention is critical and is an emphatic reminder that engagement by youth work with new information technologies is an educative, social, political and cultural project. This provides an answer to the question "why" should youth work get involved: new information technologies provide a new way to democratisation. Of course, it can also be suggested that increasing the competences of those who are often already competent serves to exacerbate the polarisation of young people and to reinforce the exclusion of some. But, more positively, new technologies may be seen as offering a possible space for the development of a critical citizenship – new space, when old space in social and formal educational life has steadily been declining. New technological space may allow the co-production of knowledge and provide collective intelligent space, in which young people are equal producers of knowledge, ideas and information, which can be shared with others. Youth workers do not need to know everything about these technologies before they feel, or are deemed competence to practice in this arena. They can embark on a process of discovery alongside the young people with whom they work. Both can learn from their mistakes and through asking inquisitive questions. The important thing is not to miss the train!

The final plenary paper was presented by Claude Baltz (researcher) who argued, like others before him, that recent times have witnessed the emergence of a whole series of knowledge and new visions of the world. This knowledge has to be acquired in order to play a part and therefore it should be part of everybody's experience.

The "information society" may be the new buzzword, but what does it mean? It has many layers and dimensions, and is accorded different levels of priority within some cultures than others. Opportunities to access new technologies are very differentially distributed. Different regions are subject to a different pace of development. However, even within the most traditional and isolated regions, there is still space and possibility to make use of new technologies. But how?

In a mountainous region of France, an ambitious project is taking place to address local problems through computerised networks. Schools are being linked through computers and software to permit the exchange of information, curriculum issues, newsletters, and advertisements. There is a high degree of flexibility in how the system is used, since it has been established to fulfil a range of purposes. But, fundamentally, it is the application of new technologies in the context of old communities and traditions. For those to survive, investment in new technologies is essential. It is too early to evaluate the impact of these developments, but the view is that they have been a positive initiative, capable of addressing key local issues around education, training and employment. The objectives are social objectives: counteracting isolation and broadening horizons. It is a cultural agenda, designed to preserve human resources by stalling the outflow of young people from the region.

This illustration raises a host of questions about the information society and its role and place within economic and cultural life. Many questions remain unresolved, because it is still too early to say. Despite the strong image projected by the media of the information society, we have to learn much more about the relationship of people to information. We must move beyond technological stocktaking to securing a grasp of information cultures. Prior to the information age, communication was direct and often spontaneous. Now it is shaped in different ways and may have different consequences. We have to retain an open mind about its possibilities and problematics.

We need to think in terms of a new map of the world and to develop a form of "cultural adjustment" which will permit us to read the map correctly. The Internet is a new way of touching space, of reaching out into the world, indeed of being in the world. We need to develop new ways of observing the world if we are really to see what is emerging in terms of the relationship between computer science and the organisation of the social world.

Summary report

Introduction

Some of the paradoxical experiences of the symposium were noted: the fact that at a symposium on young people and the information society, not only were there few young people but there had also been recurrent problems with microphones and amplification, as well as some difficulties with photocopiers and overhead projectors – old technological breakdown was the context of debate about technological innovation and communication.

The symposium had provided a great deal of food for thought, generating more questions than answers. And while it was recognised that there had been concerns about the over-representation of theory and research, there had also been a strong injection of practice accounts with important implications for the shaping of future youth policy. The symposium, the first Council of Europe youth research symposium for ten years, had – as Lasse Siurala had hoped – reinvigorated a partnership between youth researchers, youth organisations and youth policy. Participants had displayed a strong commitment to the symposium, especially in the workshops, as active creators rather than as passive consumers. Workshops had generated lively and constructive dialogue.

Divisions, of course, remained. Even amongst the academics, there were sociologists, psychologists, economists, computer scientists, students of cultural studies and historians. Amongst the practitioners, there was even a cheese specialist! As a result, a vast array of perspectives and arguments had been presented. Some of the gaps between theoretical contention and the experience of policy and practice were quite transparent and, indeed, predictable: the problem is always that theoretical analysis does not always command empirical credibility just as experiential assertions may not have academic validity.

Further, the nature of the papers presented suggested that while the "information society" is – for some – a central theoretical and practical concern, it remains – for others – a long way from their central academic and practice agendas, which are focused more around questions of social division, unemployment and even the consequences of war. And, as Phil Brown said, the Internet cannot compensate for society. We must relate the social hardware to the information software. Much of the social hardware has been about the social exclusion of significant groups of young people (and others) and increasingly differentiated societies. Jacques Ogier and Peggy Simmons argued forcefully that introducing more disadvantaged young people to new technologies must follow physical, personal encounters and framed within the provision of motivation and support. Their network (YODEM) is to assist young people in developing real, not virtual, relationships.

So the symposium has had a twin-track agenda. And the information society is not the dominant agenda, although it clearly remains a central policy issue for our societies. The dominant agenda lies around the capacity of youth researchers, respresentatives of youth organisations and representatives of government youth policy, to produce a persuasive and meaningful framework for youth policy within the Council of Europe member states. Within this framework, clearly the relationship of young people to new information and communication technologies is likely to be paramount.

Questions have remained about the pervasiveness of the so-called information society. Is it a modern myth, perpetrated by Bill Gates and others who stand to profit from it? Or is it an essential connection point for participation and progress in modern society? It is clear from the debate at this symposium that, whichever is the answer, the information society is firmly embedded in the social and political dimensions of "real life". Some young people are clearly still trapped behind the "information Berlin Wall", but a prevalent view expressed here has been that in only a few years information technologies will be accessible to everyone.

Predictions have, indeed, been rife at this symposium. Whatever the forward pace of change, there are always possibilities of unexpected and unanticipated sideways and even backwards moves, as a result of further technological progression (or regression), often mediated by changing cultural priorities. Mid-nineteenth century England was fearful that the growth in the popularity of horse-drawn carriages would lead to the land being covered in manure within fifty years, but it did not anticipate the invention of the motor car. Commercial business proclaimed that all children would soon want for Christmas was a new or improved computer; last year, they wanted "pogs" (as simple a recreational toy as you could think of). A few years ago, the view in the music world was that performing artists would cease to be the pivotal individuals in pop music production, because the technicians would have taken over; instead, we have seen a return to traditional instruments and "unplugged" performance. So we have to tread carefully!

Even at this symposium, there are many initiatives planned relating to connecting young people to the information age, but very little has been operational for sufficient time to judge whether or not it is having a desired effect. There is some sense of treading in the dark.

And, of course, there have been the usual problems regarding language – arising not simply from the many people who are having to consider complex issues without being able to present their thinking in their native tongue, but also from the different understandings of concepts and ideas. Indeed, there have been a number of "languages" in circulation at the symposium: conceptual language, our own native languages, second and third languages, research terminology, the language of the Net and, last if not least, the language of the Council of Europe! Meanings and interpretations are different; common ground and shared understanding cannot be presumed. Where we are all at one, however, is that – in all our societies, albeit in different ways – there has been a massive fracturing and restructuring of the life course, creating new possibilities but also dire consequences in the personal, social, economic and political worlds of young people.

It might be argued that the goal of any, and all, youth policy is citizenship. Citizenship is clearly a contested and controversial concept but in simply terms it conveys something about full participation in society. And if that is its simple definition, then – whatever the wider ramifications for young people of the technological age – our concern must be with the role that information technology might plan in the fomentation and development of citizenship.

Tensions and contradictions

Whether or not this is a postmodern world, it is riddled with contradictions. The world of high technology runs parallel with other worlds in which old traditions are sustained. The enterprising computer-literate unemployed have to contemplate their (unsuccessful) efforts in the context of the unqualified but compliant young people working for McDonalds. I take young people to a cottage with no electricity – with a mobile phone in my pocket.

The symposium has generated a vast array of contradictory messages, competing ideas and inherent tensions in our dialogue about youth in the information society. Lasse Siurala pointed to the space between the technophiles and the "luddites". We have been reminded frequently of tensions between tradition and change. John Bynner said that young people are not signing up to "old ways", yet much research also points to young people's entrenched conformity and conventionality. Much probably depends on which young people we are talking about, and where they live. Tanja Rener emphasised the persisting socialising influence of the family in Slovenia.

There have also been contrasting observations between discipline and freedom, order and chaos, reminding me of Julius Nyrere's famous saying that "Freedom without discipline is anarchy, discipline without freedom is tyranny". A path must be struck between the two. I was also reminded of the gulf between the worlds of young people displaying a disciplined commitment to the use of the Internet, in contrast with those who have little choice but to continue ducking and diving in the "rough economy of the streets". It has been argued that new technologies offer a promise of liberation, yet we have also been told of the insidious cultural colonisation and oppression which comes with the domination of American software and the need to communicate in the English language. We have been told of the enormous potential of new technologies for education in the essential skills for life in the modern age and the shaping of identity; there have also been allusions to technological immersion as little more than a new, sophisticated toy for experimentation with pet ideas. Similarly, while different information technologies are promoted as sites for personal growth and development and social integration, they are also spaces for escapism, addiction. Anke Bahl described two young women who had concluded that virtual life was better than real life. André Vitalis referred to the "stupidisation" accruing from participation on the Internet, and Vladimir Dubsky expressed concern about evidence of young people's dependency on new technologies. Far from cultivating enterprise and empowering young people in "self-actualisation", there are countervailing suggestions that new technologies present a new form for controlling and suppressing the flair and initiative of young people. A related question is the extent to which the generation of new forms of human contact via the Internet may be jeopardising existing social relations in living communities.

But perhaps the most significant question concerns the countervailing forces of globalisation and localism, and the implications which flow from this in terms of risk and stability. Arguments about the consequences of globalisation have to be tempered by what Dubravka Vrgoc described as a retreat into private life. Nevertheless, globalisation and other forces have patently led to great disparities in resource allocation, including new technological resources, within countries, between countries and amongst young people. The technological "haves" have been contrasted with the technological "have-nots" throughout this symposium, and no-one has really challenged expectations that such division is likely to increase in the future. John Bynner

crystalised the issue when he asked whether we were discussing an information society or an information economy.

Throughout the symposium, then, emphasis has repeatedly been placed
upon the polarising circumstances and opportunities for young people –
something clearly replicated in their relation to technology. We have heard
Maurice Devlin's account of young people as "virtual adults", which is not
dissimilar to their characterisation of having "citizenship by proxy" (Gill Jones
and Claire Wallace, *Youth, Family and Citizenship*, Open University Press,
1992) and could be related to my contention, from 1985, that some young
people at least were becoming "trapped as teenagers". It may be a postmodern world of permeable boundaries, life management, self actualisation
and manufactured risk but, for many young people, it also remains a world
circumscribed by local culture and traditional aspirations. Surfin' – if it means
anything (and it would mean nothing in Estonia, where the term in relation
to exploring the Net is "sailing") – would bring thoughts of old Volkswagen
camper vans rather than the Internet. On the other hand, as Vesa Puuronen
maintained, the Internet offers a possibility to develop a new form of democracy, which is based on the accessibility of information, the transparency of
decision-making and direct involvement of citizens in politics. This remains a
possibility; part of the youth policy project is, perhaps, making it a reality.

Substantive themes and issues

Beyond the tensions and contradictions lie some important substantive
themes concerning youth in the information society. Claude Baltz noted the
strong image of the information society which is persistently presented in the
media. Juri Saarniit described the technological revolution as an inevitable
process which nobody can resist. There is clearly an evolving process of globalisation, information revolution and technological change which suggests –
without argument? – that young people need to be connected. But should it
be "taken for granted" (as Vesa Puuronen suggests) that we have already
approached the information society? And, if we have, is lack of contact with
it a private trouble or a public issue?

Curiously, few participants offered a definition of the "information society".
Conny Reuter repeatedly stressed that it was more than the Internet. Tuuli
Toomere hazarded that it was the "society formed on the Internet by the
users". Others presumably made general assumptions about the constituent
components of the information society. What is more, presentations and
commentary implicitly defined the information society by reference to those
who were excluded from it. Indeed, a persistent thread of the symposium
was the striking inequalities in the distribution of opportunities and access to
new information technologies.

Jacques Ogier and Peggy Simmons noted crisply that the Internet belongs to
the world of wealthy people. This observation concealed some strange
anomalies in access to and usage of the Net. While 25 per cent of young

people in Helsinki have used the Internet, only ten million of three hundred million people in the USA will be "wired up" by the turn of the century. In Italy only ten to fifteen thousand are on the Net. There are two hundred thousand in France, but there remain technical limits to expansion. Yet around one fifth of young people in Croatia are users of the Internet and it is "widespread" in Slovenia. In Romania, individuals may be familiar with the theory of its use, but have limited opportunities for practical involvement.

The use of new information technologies, even in those countries and regions where usage is relatively commonplace, would appear to still be mainly the prerogative of students, accessing them through their universities. Beyond easy access, use within universities is usually cheap and users have acquired the competence to participate, both for learning and for "fun".

A key message emerging from the symposium was the need to promote and extend access. Such a blanket aspiration was rarely subjected to critical inter-rogation, beyond how this might be done. Few asked why or what for? Yet these are vital questions. Certainly a range of possible objectives were raised, both implicitly and explicitly. Extending access was seen to be "useful" for broadening leisure activity and self-realisation, for educative and training purposes and providing skills for employment, and for promoting citizenship and political participation. But there was limited debate on the support mechanisms and methodologies which might be applied in order to achieve such objectives. Some practice accounts talked generally of shaping a new pedagogy for social ends: Brigitta Myrman described the development of a new network for youth organisations in Sweden as providing a bridge to broader participation. Likewise, Marcel Kreuger's anti-racist website offered a channel for communication. But the detail of how such a voice might be encouraged and how it was likely to was listened to was left largely undevel-oped.

There are inevitably significant costs attached to public (government) or vol-untary sector commitment to linking young people with new technologies. Therefore there needs to be clarity about the rationale for doing so. Yuri Saarniit encapsulated the issue when he asked whether the Internet was an institution for public intervention or simply a mechanism and arena for inter-personal interaction. If it was the latter, then presumably it was not of inter-est or the business of public institutions. If it was the former, however, the first issue was to establish a socially-oriented agenda around certain core principles, such as expression, authentic participation, learning, communica-tion, respecting diversity, social justice and equal opportunities. Such themes have certainly not been the driving force behind the development and allo-cation of new technologies, so it is a corner which will have to be fought for.

The second issue would be to develop clear aims and objectives. In Estonian schools, the overriding aim of the new curriculum for the information society is to ensure that computer science educates for the "purposeful use" of information. "Purposeful" might relate, presumably, to specific objectives around leisure and creativity, education and employment, or citizenship and political participation.

And the third issue is then to establish the pedagogical methods which would be consistent with the principles and effective in achieving the goals. Many young people will need to be equipped with skills, belief and motivation before they can even start to make use of information technologies in ways in which a public project believes to be of value to them. Some (such as the 25 per cent of young people in Latvia who have had no basic education, or the poorest young people with whom the Fourth World Movement works) may need to acquire basic literacy skills before they are able to participate at even a rudimentary level.

Active pedagogical tools to promote such competencies were subjected to only limited debate during the symposium. There were, of course, exceptions. Peggy Simmons and Jacques Ogier described how young people's engagement was secured by connecting technological learning to their broader social interests. Vesa Puuronen offered an account of simulated voting through the Internet. Conny Reuter explained how his multimedia project sought to develop "stepwise" interventions based on the differential needs of different groups of young people. Paul Kloosterman emphasised the importance of "learning by doing" in order to develop vocational skills and to promote citizenship.

All this begs some important questions. It is clear that the rationale for extending access to information technology through public initiatives stems significantly from the fact that young people are departing from organised social sites and youth organisations. New avenues for participation therefore need to be created by broadening access to technological sites. Young people are certainly often at the vanguard of progress in the use of the Internet (as Meral Alguidas, for example, noted in the context of Turkey), and the Net offers the possibility of equality or, as Tuuli Toomere put it, freedom, democracy and anonymity. But there is, as ever, another side to the argument. Is there a need for stronger legislative and ethic frameworks to govern the use of new technologies? How should they be framed and how can they be enforced? What about the quality and reliability of information? Participants at the symposium referred to the time-consuming nature of maintaining databases and sustaining the "sexiness" and attractiveness of their sites. There are risks of information overload and databases just lying there and gathering digital dust. There was some suggestion that new technologies are male-dominated: how can greater participation by young women be secured? Indeed, how can participation by those young people about whom the symposium was most concerned be secured? As Ivan Marinov pointed out, young people need to be trained in the "research methods" necessary to access the information which is of importance to them. Privacy and anonymity are all very well, but there are questions of public accountability. Simply telling funders the scale of visits to a website may not be enough, but the use of smart cards or passwords in order to monitor usage in more detail has potentially sinister overtones. Yet the use of smart cards, as Conny Reuter noted, helps to keep control on costs and does permit detailed scrutiny of how the network is being used. On the other hand, the simulated voting described by Vesa Puuronen, if operationalised for a real election, might pose a threat to democracy rather than enhancing democratic participation, for passwords might become commodities to be bought and sold. What kinds of balances need to be struck between the "personal" and the "political" in terms of, for example, young people making use of Internet Relay Chat for "private" use when their participation has been encouraged for other reasons?

There are endless permutations to such substantive problematics. One might ask "does it really matter?" But answers to many of these questions will matter to those who provide resources for initiatives to extend access, particularly if they do so in order to achieve specific social objectives. It might be argued, cynically, that extending access to more marginal groups of young people might serve as a kind of technological warehousing operation, holding such young people in a kind of limbo – out of the circulation of real life. That, in itself, might represent a saving to the public purse, when placed against other costs incurred. But constructive youth policy initiatives around young people and the information society clearly revolve around three core positions: education (learning); training (for employment); and politics (for citizenship). One might, tentatively, add a leisure dimension, not for warehousing, but for experimentation, leisure, and identity formation – but this has rarely been a public priority in pre-technological times.

If these points do represent the key elements of a youth policy agenda, then closer attention needs to be paid to how they might be achieved, by harnessing information technologies to wider social and political priorities.

The main agenda – "political" themes and issues

It has been argued recently that there has been a transformation in knowledge production: transdisciplinarity, the expansion of knowledge sites beyond their historical location in universities (and the communication between these sites: universities, private consultancies, research agencies, think-tanks) has led to a diversified "socially distributed knowledge production system" in which researchers, politicians and those who formulate policy all contribute to the production, consumption and critique of both research and practice (Michael Gibbons et al., *The new production of knowledge: The dynamics of science and research in contemporary societies*, Sage, 1994).

It might be suggested that, at the first youth research symposium in Strasbourg in 1986, a momentum was established by the youth research community across Europe to heighten its profile and exert greater influence on the direction of youth policy. At the time, such an approach was possibly appropriate. In 1996, not only would there be firmer resistance to such an initiative but it would be received with some degree of scepticism. Any agenda for action must emanate from dialogue and consensus between youth research, youth organisations and governmental representatives. This is the new framework within which youth policy has to be shaped. All parties have a central interest in contributing to effective youth policy; all must be aware that unconstructive dialogue will lead to reduced youth policy, less effective youth policy or positively misguided youth policy. The kind of dialogue which was hoped for at this symposium and which (by and large) has taken place must therefore be made to work and to prove influential in shaping the direction of youth policy.

There are no doubt residual concerns (and resentments) about the primacy of academic and research thinking on "youth questions" but it is the responsibility of both youth practitioners and youth policy-makers to contribute to the formulation of a youth research agenda and to assist in the "translation" of its findings in order that it may influence policy and practice. Otherwise, powerful and persuasive youth researchers and youth research will distort our understanding of the significant issues which affect young people's lives. The great strength of this symposium has been the challenges made by practitioners and governmental representatives to some of the main assertions of youth research participants – assertions which derive from particular theoretical traditions or the specific circumstances of particular countries. As Phil Brown observed, some "regimes of truth" (the example he gave was "globalisation") can exert disproportionate influence on policy formulation and development (or the lack of it). They need to be dissected, contested and constantly re-evaluated. Lasse Siurala told us that there are many "regimes of truth"; youth researchers certainly do not have any monopoly over the "truth". And with or without research, policy and practice agendas will be established. What is needed, therefore, in order to secure greater integration (and, thereby, less suspicion and conflict) is for increased social sensibility and sensitivity on the part of politicians and their government representatives, more practical engagement by researchers in the policy arena, and more political awareness on the part of practitioners. Only through such a partnership can a constructive and reflective youth policy agenda be promoted, shaped, defined and implemented.

Trialogue, to make use of the term coined by Catalin Ghenea, is what is required, to ensure cohesion at European level, even if at some national levels insufficient dialogue is taking place. Otherwise, political and policy direction will move in ways often at odds with research analysis and implications. Rumiana Stoilova provided an interesting example of the role of researchers in contributing to policy and in promoting and evaluating a particular form of practice.

It has been reassuring that the diversity of the contextual theoretical papers with very grounded policy and empirical presentations have, albeit in very different ways, broadly conformed to John Bynner's formulation of a European youth research agenda, framed around the nature of transitions, the experiences and circumstances of vulnerable groups, the construction of identity, questions of citizenship and political participation.

However, we should not get carried away with the potential of new technologies in restructuring transitions and their basis for rethinking human activity. The Internet cannot compensate for society, and there remain questions about access to basic income, for real social and political participation can only be made possible with sufficient economic resources. It is a convenient and reassuring position for those in more secure and privileged positions to argue that there are other ways for the insecure and underprivileged to live constructive lives. That is why I had some problems with Ulrike Nagel's idea that second-chance schools might assist marginalised young people with the skills needed to participate in what she calls the third arena – the grey economic area between the formal, established labour market and unemployment. They are spurious arguments. The British criminologist Jock Young once argued that leisure can only be purchased with the credit card of work. And, to consolidate the point, I usually tell the following story. Just after the Berlin Wall came down, three well-heeled west German professors sat in a cafe in former East Berlin extolling the virtue of community enterprise and self-employment to a group of unemployed former middle-ranking employees in the German Democratic Republic. There was no applause when they finished. After an awkward silence, one member of the audience said to the professors, "if it's all so good, we'll have your jobs and you go and do it".

Theoretical formulations and research issues

The most pressing need is to subject the concept of the "information society" to more rigorous theoretical analysis and empirical description.

Secondly, is technology essentially a private or commercial sphere, or is it (can it be) a social sphere for leisure, learning, occupation, participation or escape? How do new information technologies contribute to, or relate to, youth cultural forms, social transformation, alternative lifestyles, identity formation, interpersonal relationships. I do not know.

The youth research agenda set out by John Bynner is an important and powerful one, in which the impact of new technologies is clearly a central component. However, new sociological concepts (or reworked old ones) must not cloud what has emerged quite firmly during this symposium: the persistence of those old chestnuts of social stratification – class, race, gender and region – in the distribution and rationing of resources and opportunity, and mediated through family, education and peer groups. All seem to me to be a significant influence on access to new technologies. The rush to embrace postmodernity or anti-modernity is premature even if old certainties and trajectories no longer apply. Late modern times in postindustrial society clearly enshrines more risk and demands greater individualisation but such change is also mediated by persisting continuities. Part of the research agenda should be to assess the relative impact of continuity and change.

John Bynner recounted the question asked of a child as to where elephants were to be found; her reply was that they were too big and too intelligent to get lost in the first place. People shape their lives through their experience and have particular perspectives on that experience. This cameo reminded me of Eric Midwinter's recollection of a child writing that Jean d'Arc had been "condomed" to death. The message here is that many of us are unable to position ourselves so that we acquire the same perspectives on the world as the next generation. Few of us, I suspect, have made the necessary "cultural adjustment", to which Claude Baltz referred. Many young people will not have done so either. Some have, but we have not had a chance to hear their arguments, views, orientations and perspectives, although Anke Bahl, Tuuli Toomere and Anita Eliasson have provided us with some flavour of these in their presentations.

New technologies are still the domain of the intellectual and cultural elite, and a key question is how long they will continue to monopolise these sites of cultural and economic capital. My view is that there has been an academic polarisation whereby, in a strange reflection of what is going on out there for young people, some researchers are evaluating new technology and the learning society while others are studying the underbelly of social exclusion – where new technologies are rarely in young people's mind sets (or anybody else's). Forging the connections between these two polarised realities is also a task for research, as is the more applied task – suggested by Phil Brown – of conducting a "social audit" to establish the degree to which the aspiration of securing "learning for all" is being realised.

The political project, following obtaining a firmer grasp on key issues around young people and the information society, is to build appropriate bridges including, centrally, the capacity to access and make use of information – for economic and social independence and self-determination. Otherwise, the objectives of citizenship are likely to be doomed. Alternative forms of self-realisation, without access to some level of economic autonomy, remain a concept for the privileged.

Towards policy and practice

Much use of new technology remains largely recreational, unless wider goals are established and supported. It has been argued that there needs to be a "social envelope" to support the use of new information technologies if social and educational goals are to be achieved (J Giaquinta et al., *Beyond Technology's Promise*, Cambridge University Press, 1992).

The policy task is to define the constructive "social" potential of new technologies and to develop a strategic vision based on social priorities and individual needs. Can, for example, improving access to new technologies present a new mechanism for combating social exclusion – either for itself or as a stepping stone for further social integration? Or is there a risk that it would become yet another increasingly discredited warehousing strategy, not significantly altering the life chances or material circumstances of those involved?

Within this strategic vision, which would specify how new technologies might be "harnessed" to the social, political and economic objectives of the "real world", would be some understanding of the legal and ethical framework around it, and of the principles which informed it, such as democratic participation or intercultural learning. Anticipated obstacles would have to be overcome. For example, one great strength of the Internet highlighted by a number of participants during the symposium was the fact that "everyone can say what they like": there are no rules and no rulers. But such unconditionality is hardly conducive to the promotion of objectives such as "citizenship" which demands reciprocity and is firmly premised upon rights and responsibilities. In real life, the whole idea of citizenship is bound up with questions of civil obligation: it is almost the very antithesis of citizenship to think in terms of "being and saying what you like".

Furthermore, a strategic vision for youth policy and the information society should be firmly embedded within the wider strands of youth policy. Consideration of new information technology possibilities should not inhibit consideration of other ways of providing information and support to young people – ways which also offer real human contact and guidance. Debi Roker, Jacques Ogier and Peggy Simmons, all spoke of the importance of this dimension to supporting more disadvantaged and isolated young people.

Throughout youth policy, there are always questions about structures, training, curriculum and programmes. Youth policy relating to the information society will need to address the same questions.

The question of resources will inevitably rear its head. This is, as always, an issue of political and collective will. Although resources are always scarce, it is a question of priorities. As Marcel Kreuger commented bluntly, "It is one jet fighter or ..." The British Government, famed for its non-intervention in the labour market and free market ideology, in fact spends some three billion pounds each year effectively subsidising poor employers in the retail sector, since their increasingly part-time employees earn so little they have also to seek state support. Whether or not, however, the necessary resources should be committed to improving young people's access to new information technologies (despite this symposium's view that this is a critical dimension to contemporary youth policy) will depend on methods of evaluating success in meeting pre-determined objectives. That, in turn, raises further practical and ethical questions about the monitoring and mapping of usage. It is possible. The smart card which accesses Conny Reuter's multimedia network provides both a mechanism for monitoring and accountability plus a routemap to relevant sites. But others may feel some disquiet at such possibilities for "surveillance".

And who should deliver whatever is decided? A number of participants have noted the resistance or reluctance amongst youth workers to engage with new information technologies. There will need to be training for those who work with young people as well as for young people themselves. To date, such training as has taken place has tended to focus on technical issues (as Matti Viirimaki informed us) but should there not also be training around ethical, substantive and more issue-based matters?

Conclusion

No doubt Paul Willis would have drawn out the grounded aesthetics and creative cultural possibilities in the common everyday use of technologies by the young – the MUD and MUSH games plus Internet Relay Chat (Paul Willis et al., *Common Culture*, Open University Press, 1990).

From the evidence presented at this symposium, my conclusion is that, despite its massive profile and incessant growth, new information technology remains, amongst young people, the prerogative of a privileged minority. Further, it is often an under-used resource by those who do have access to it and make use of it. It is also – possibly – an overstated essential for the future. Old traditions and aspirations, and cultures, still retain a firm grip, even in some of the most technologically advanced countries within Europe.

One has to accept, nonetheless, that new information and communication technologies do present enormous potential but, even after this symposium, we still cannot be sure exactly how or why.

We need better evidence of the distribution and types of usage by which kinds of young people. We need to understand more about both its leisure and educational potential and its social implications. We need to understand why a significant number of young people are not connected (not interested) despite its presence and availability. We need to understand its limitations. As Duravka Vrgoc observed, Croatian youth will not manage to set up links with Europe via the Internet alone. Technology is embedded in the social world.

Many contributors to the symposium have testified to the enormous value of new technologies – in the shaping of identity, assisting transitions, developing skills and competencies, and in providing new forms of leisure and lifestyle. There may a few technophiles and even a few luddites amongst us but I am confident that most of us would agree that an initial task for the development of a "youth policy" dimension to the information society is to identify those elements which will establish the "social envelope" within which we can build what Conny Reuter referred to as "appropriate information and communication architecture" in order to fulfil socially integrative objectives.

I hope that this synthesis has struck some kind of balance to the arguments which have been circulating during the symposium. As a technological novice, I remain with an open mind – concerned about the deep divisions in the social condition of young people, which may in fact be worsened by the information society, but simultaneously optimistic that new information and communication technologies may also offer renewed hope for re-connecting and confirming the connection of young people to the societies in which they live.

During the symposium, there have been a number of references to roads and to maps, even to roadmaps. Ilse Trapenciere illustrated how the road to accessing information technology in Latvia progressively narrows; Claude Baltz talked more theoretically about how we now need to look at the world differently if we are to make sense of the new map of the world before us. Roads and maps are useful metaphors when discussing youth transitions. We can argue about destinations, starting points, the vehicles available for use and the obstructions along the route. New technologies represent part of the vehicle, though it appears that at the moment those young people in the fastest and best-maintained vehicles are also gaining the added advantage of technological assistance. But, whatever vehicle they are in, few young people have a firm grasp of the terrain they are having to navigate. These thoughts brought to mind an old friend who was responsible for reconnaissance for the British Battalion during the Spanish Civil War. He would crawl to the top of a hill with a notebook and pencil and draw what he could see. On that evidence alone, his unit would plan its military strategy. And each day the terrain changed – requiring a new "map" to inform a new strategy. It was the best they had.

The information society presents equally new terrain and, it seems to me, equally primitive map-drawing. The critical question is whether we have the capacity to produce a more accurate map and to build the necessary social, educational and technological superhighway to ensure that most young people are able to reach their destinations retaining optimism about their futures and experiencing as little hardship as possible along the way. Tom Wylie, now the Chief Executive of England's National Youth Agency said as much ten years ago in a paper entitled "Opportunities for Europe's Youth". The varied maps we have produced at this symposium are tentative and, quite possibly, inaccurate. They are not yet the basis upon which an effective strategy may be constructed, but they represent a start.

Dr Howard Williamson
School of Social and Administrative Studies
University of Cardiff
Wales
United Kingdom

Statements by Mr Conny Reuter, representing the non-governmental youth organisations, and Ms Erzebet Kovacs, representing the European steering committee for intergovernmental co-operation in the youth field

Statement by Mr Conny Reuter on behalf of the non-governmental youth organisations

Having thanked the general rapporteur and expressed pleasure that someone from Southern Europe was able to speak at the symposium, Mr Reuter made the following points:

– He restated the importance, in the research sector of the Council of Europe Youth Directorate, of a "trialogue" with researchers, political decision-makers and youth workers/youth organisations working together to define fields of research and to conduct the actual research. This work was of interest to the NGYOs because of the scope for encounter, debate and speculation among researchers, officials responsible for youth questions and representatives of NGYOs who thus participated in ascertaining what Europe meant for young people today.

– Referring more specifically to the symposium on "Youth in the information society", he noted that it was important to secure and promote access for all (youth included) to the new information and electronic communication technologies. He wanted youth organisations to be still more active in this field. Via the new communication technologies, it was certain that the concepts of culture, identity and participation were under challenge. These new technologies could be productive but at the same time destructive, with an equally structuring and destructuring effect on youth. Challenges therefore confronted both the individual and the community, from the local to the European level.

– Furthermore, it was pointless to deny the challenges raised, or the deepening rifts between young people and the new communication technologies, caused by geographical differences (differing opportunities for access in Northern and in Southern or Eastern and Western Europe and in urban and rural areas), and by economic and social inequalities as well as gender inequalities.

– In such a context, it was essential to discover pathfinders who might blaze the trail: youth organisations, educational institutions, young people already conversant with the new technologies, and researchers. It was important to foster and support co-ordination and interaction among these various partners by developing relevant research, promoting the widest possible access and training (to be construed in inter-generational terms), and supporting existing arrangements. This could also lead to other forms of association for young people and new organisational methods in that regard.

He concluded by calling upon all symposium participants to stimulate new ideas, make new proposals and suggest new approaches, all aimed at securing general access to the new communication technologies.

Statement by Ms Erzebet Kovacs on behalf of the European steering committee for intergovernmental co-operation in the youth field (CDEJ)

Ms Kovacs stressed the importance of the symposium for the entire Council of Europe Youth Directorate, particularly through the "trialogue" in which researchers, officials responsible for youth questions and youth organisations were involved and which she would like to be established at national level as well.

– With specific reference to the symposium, she said that it was vital for the Youth Directorate to take account of the cultural differences existing in Europe with regard to the information society, and to allow for the distinctiveness of the central and eastern European countries. The result should be to strengthen solidarity among all European states and to determine common fields of interest in a spirit of partnership. Youth organisations and youth workers should be committed to this endeavour, thereby expressing the steering committee's concern for the participation of young people. The symposium had opened up new prospects in that regard.

– It should be possible to enlarge on the specific question of young people and the new information technologies by means of specific programmes. For that purpose it was important to sustain the synergies with other Council of Europe directorates, with the Congress of Local and Regional Authorities of Europe, and with the European Union. Likewise, the questions relating to new communication technologies should be incorporated into the current programme on evaluation of national youth policies.

– In this context, the European youth centres had a part to play whether through publications or by aiding young people's access to the new technologies. They were capable of giving the question substance, and must do so. Ms Kovacs concluded by thanking all present at the symposium.

Visions of the information society

The postindustrial information society: history and perspectives

The most important and still valid concepts and models of the information society had been introduced in powerful ways in the early 1970s by social scientists like Daniel Bell and Marshall McLuhan (Bell 1973, McLuhan 1964).

Bell's first concept was "the postindustrial society", where the production of commodities would be followed by information as the core of societal production. Bell was for a long time perceived as conservative sociology's attack on marxism, while he has later been "rehabilitated", also among radical sociologists who have cultivated ideas about postmodernity.

The changes from an industrial to a postindustrial information society have a long range of implications and consequences, but here we will only indicate a few of them. Industrial production is characterised by some basic relationships between man and thing (objects), while the basic relationships in the information society are between man and man, or between human beings. Instead of capital and labour in economic circulation, we find technology and knowledge in social circulation. Bell is speaking about a transformation from "an economising mode" to "a sociologising mode", and by "mode" he refers to the marxist term of "mode of production".

The whole idea behind this kind of theorising on the general characteristics of society is the necessity of conceiving the time we are living in. The correct time is necessary for the correct diagnosis and medicine for what is going on. In the industrial society we have a social order based on the relationships between capital and labour, between employers and employees. A chaos in this mode of production could be an unintended lack of qualified leadership in family-based enterprises, or an intended chaos caused by politics and revolutions – but nevertheless a new order of capital and labour was necessary to (re)establish as long as we were living in an industrial society.

Chaos in the information society is chaos of information. Our entrance into the information society means leaving circumstances characterised by the Norwegian Gudmund Hernes as rich in human experience and poor on information, and entering a mode of poverty of human experience and overloading of information. An easier version is the distinction between a society with scarcity of information and a society where we are drowned in aggressive information flows. However, the main point is that chaos has to be avoided by knowledge, technology, science, education, skills, intersubjectivity, mutual confidence, etc. as the "filters" for efficient selection of relevant and non-relevant, essential and non-essential information. The "good learner" in Freudian terms and therefore also industrial terms could be compared to the steam engine, the individual balancing emotional development (steam) and skill achievements – not becoming disturbed by body, parents and/or "too much" information. In the information society the "good learner" is a cybernetic information system, where we can compare the individual with the personal computer (PC) in a network.

The further implications of these distinctions between the industrial and the information societies have to be elaborated during the coming days.

Cybersociety is coming – are you prepared?

We will try to take you a bit closer to the relationship between the information society and youth. We will try to give you some ideas about why the digital media or rather the computer-mediated communication (CMC) should attract youth. And if it does attract youth, we will argue that it should be used much more systematically as an instrument in youth work.

Basically Internet includes enormous amounts of information that interests young people and is relevant for them. Everything from their favourite rock artists to finding a vacant job is there. Internet is also a natural medium for youth, "The Wired Generation". Why should it not then be used as an instrument in youth work?

In addition there is also a deeper cultural reason for promoting digital media as a pedagogical instrument. The reason comes from a general analysis of postmodern youth. The Dutch sociologist Manuela du Bois-Raymond has maintained that during the postmodern era "political, moral and ideological citizenships" are losing their relevance among youth. It may be hypothesised that they are being replaced by "membership in cultural and electronic communities". At the same time institutional education (the school, parents, church, youth organisations, etc.) and representative democracy will be more often replaced by non-formal education (peer group learning, cultural activities, use of digital media, etc.) and direct forms of participation, perhaps virtual democracy and disobedience.

The changing contexts of socialisation seem to anticipate the coming of the cybersociety – a society with new means of growing up and new forms of participation.

The changing contexts of growing up: Cybersociety is coming – are you prepared?

The Context	*The Means*
From moral, political and ideological citizenship ...	Institutional education; parents, family, school, church, work, youth organisations, etc. Participation; representative democracy

| ... to membership in cultural and electronic communities | Non-formal educational settings; cultural activities, peer group learning, use of digital media. Participation; direct participation, virtual democracy |

"Reality sucks – get virtual!"

Mondo 2000

Of course, there are hundreds of reasons for young people to be fascinated by the modern media. To take an example, it has been suggested that today's young people who lack value horizons, norms and the motivation to go to school and work rather drift into any virtual world than stay in the meaningless reality. Cyberpunks are examples of young people who seem to be highly fascinated by the virtual worlds. Cyberpunks are people who like to live in the world of electronic nets – in a world which is sometimes called the cyberspace. It is indicative how cyberpunks themselves define this highly controversial concept called "cyberspace": "An online metaverse that's now realler than what's outside your window" (*Cyberpunk Handbook*, The Real Cyberpunk Fakebook, 1996, p. 45).

In addition to cyberpunks, nerds and OTAKUs – the Japanese versions of netsurfers – there are countless other types of young people living in the electronic cyberspace. They all seem to suggest that we should show more understanding to the constructivist conception of truth; truths are relative to the particular point of view.

"The medium is the message"

It is amusing to observe in the 1990s how an obscure and marginal idea from McLuhan from the early ages of modern media has become extremely popular, this slogan about "the medium is the message".

We shall use his contributions to our modern understanding of new media with a certain awareness of his contemporary context of meaning. This was in the middle of the 1960s, during the Beatles and Merseybeat revolution of how young people spent their school and leisure time. It was also prior to Woodstock and 1968 student riots at universities worldwide. And these occasions brought old social scientists like the "Frankfurt School" and the student rebels on to the same agenda.

There are some good reasons to recall history. The main contradiction in McLuhan's slogan was directed against the enlightenment tradition. The 1960s should be perceived as a decade when young people were the conquerors of an autonomous right to self-enlightenment. And from an old history of Jewish and Marxist social sciences struggling with fascism, emigration to USA, and a new postwar era in Germany, came the enlightenment people par excellence – Marcuse, Adorno and Habermas – into the meeting with the restlessness of the students. There are many lines and internal oppositions within this history, but at least Marcuse's position as an admirer and seducer of the students could be studied with many benefits even today. However, the main point here is that despite very differing viewpoints on methods, the new youth cultures, student rebels and the Frankfurt School shared a very optimistic, traditional perspective on the impact of enlightenment: transparancy and insights into the rotten repression of the capitalist system, would lead the intellectual vanguards to the politics of social change.

From this position all of them would go directly to the new media and handle them as schoolmasters, conceptually. While the position of McLuhan was that "sorry friends, but you did not understand anything". In the age of television and visual communication we are moving from the direct message to the meta-message, we are moving from the story to the performance, or even worse: As the television is not a radio with pictures and the man on the screen is not a teacher with improved technical equipment, we are facing quite a new communication order where all old truths are false. At this precise point, no real progress has been made since the observations and viewpoints of McLuhan.

The easy version is that the old storyteller cannot tell the same story on all stages. Bertold Brecht was one of the few contemporaries who understood this problem with the theatre, and he tried to manipulate in an experimental way the relationships between the audience, stage and text. In cinema films we have seen Woody Allen as a very conscientious follower of Brecht, in his combinations of a very traditional oral storyteller, and an intensive experimental manipulation of the cinema genre (in many of his films, like "The Red Rose of Cairo", or "Zelig").

The more developed and elaborate media appear, the more they are self-referring. Visualisation means aestheticism, and aesthetics are a quite different normative code than for example the ethical code. We believe in reason and rationality, but we are not sufficiently aware of how changes of codes imply changes of reason. When the priest moves from his church to a TV transmitted (divine) service, there is a shift from a textual to a visual message – and the ability to be convincing and persuading depends suddenly on the performance – not the content.

Jürgen Habermas has in his "theory of communicative action" (1986) emphasised three historical domains of justification of knowledge and reason, which could also explain McLuhan in a better way. He discerns between science, morality and aesthetics, and then also between the justifying principles of verified truth, of ethical right actions, and of beautiful expressions. One of the recent examples of the importance of these codes of justifications could be demonstrated by the Gulf War (1991), when the US Armed Forces had developed a controlled media concept where all news about the war were presented as a "clean" computer game for the press. Here they showed all their learning from the history of Vietnam, where the aesthetic code dominated by radical opposition (pictorial press) against the war was the winner in comparison with the ethical reason of "better dead than red". In the Gulf War we could not see any civil (or military) suffering, only very precise missiles with heat-seeking noses finding their targets – like a perfect computer game. This is an adaptation to "the medium is the message", even if some ethical and scientific norms are still present on the agenda (Saddam Hussein as "the evil", etc.).

There is no hope for traditional enlightenment people in the information society. But anybody who understands that there is progress in a better balance between the true, the right and the beautiful can survive.

Electronic communities – genuine or fake?

The preceding chapter raised the question whether the medium has become more important than the message or the contents of it. How about electronic networks, the Internet? Are they important only as a medium or can they communicate "real" content:

In Internet young people discuss with each other in a virtual state (IRC = Internet Relay Chat), send e-mail messages, surf in the data banks and web pages. Participants form more or less casual relationships, but do these relationships form real, human communities, or, further, are these communities socially or pedagogically useful or acceptable? Are these not just impersonal, pedagogically empty, ethically and morally questionnable activities which rather split one's personality than construct it? What is the pedagogical meaning of staring at the screen, reading the time schedule of the London metro, looking at pornographic pictures or learning how to construct a plastic bomb? The american psychiatrist Sherry Turkle, who in the 1980s said that computer games deteriorated the moral standards of the players, has now discussed whether surfing on the net furthers the splitting of one's personality. And what about the Japanese phenomenon of OTAKU, young people who seem to use the net just to escape (so-called) reality. The OTAKUs surf on the net without any specific purpose or meaning. They just drift around. The researchers call them part-time drop-outs and wonder whether they will later turn out to totally drop out from the (so-called) "real world" to the (so-called) "artificial world" of electronic nets.

On the other hand, there are arguments that maintain that electronic communities can truly promote one's social growth and that Internet can be "a truly interpersonal mass medium".

– First of all, CMC provides a possibility to choose the community to join. In "the real world" one is "forced" to join the communities which are socially acceptable or even induced and geographically feasible. In the Net geographical situation is not a problem and the rules and practicies of social acceptability do not apply.

- Secondly, virtual communities may be used to enrich existing communities. As an example there is an empirical study (Bradd, 1993) on GayNet (gaynet@athena.mit.edu), an Internet discussion list, to serve the needs of lesbian and gay persons on college campuses. The list included lively discussion, debates, lots of queries, announcements, reports and administrative material. Bradd concludes that GayNet served well to disseminate information, promote activism and provide personal support for participants.

- Another similar example is the Finnish Netforum for feminist research, which has proved to be a very active, topical and multifaceted means to enrich the community of list participants.

- Thirdly, the peculiarity of postmodern identity is that identities are multiple and that they are constantly being developed and experimented. The cyberspace of Internet provides a natural forum for this kind of postmodern identity search. Net researcher Denise Dalaimo writes: "Cyberspace is the ultimate environment for the nourishment of the fragmented, multiphrenic, contradictory postmodern self. Visual anonymity and lack of social status cues allows the user to experiment with different aspects of selfhood, as well as to "disguise" him/herself completely." (Dalaimo, Denise, 1995)

- Additionally, net communication is often criticised because it lacks face-to-face contact. Of course this is true (so far), but we should add two comments. Firstly, one could ask why should face-to-face communication serve as an ideal? This ideal seems to be prevalent because we associate it with Gemeinschaft-type community with intimate personal contacts, but there is no reason why other forms of communication should not be as effective or as "human". In fact, the effectiveness of virtual communication provides more time for physical encounter and virtual communication also makes possible an encounter which is not physically possible (for instance because of geographical distance and overlapping time schedules).

- Finally, there are young people, who dislike face-to-face contacts with adults and prefer other forms of communication. An Insurance company found out that young motorbikers were not interested in their insurance. They developed a possibility to obtain insurance via a computer. The method was a great success. Young people responded in mass by taking out insurance policies because it did not involve a face-to-face contact with an adult. This suggests that many young people would prefer electronic communication instead of face-to-face communication.

- Despite these small pieces of evidence, our knowledge of the nature of electronic communities is lacking. There is a need for much research in this field. Steven Jones in a recent book on *CyberSociety* (1995, 12) argues that "Conspicuously absent is an understanding of how computers are used as tools for connection and community".

The specific youth mode: youth culture and new concepts of learning

The steps from industrial to postindustrial society, and from message to medium, are general observations without any specific significance to young people or youth matters. Nevertheless, there are lots of reasons for the close relationships between youth research in general, and issues like postindustrialism, postmodernity and a variety of media analyses. This is mainly due to an essential role of young people in processes of social change, repeated many times in social history and in the reflections of social and human sciences.

But it is also necessary to come closer to a more specific reality, to more specific ways of conceiving youth and the information society. Otherwise we should leave the whole topic to the engineers and the nerds (or Bill Gates and Microsoft). As a mal-apropos, we shall take note of the impressive and surprising fact that the chief nerd Bill Gates in his *Highways to the information society* never pays a second of attention to the power of his early creativity, namely the fact that his business adventure started in his early teens. At the age of 40, he is not able to see this youthfulness as a significant and specific power in his life, that of others, or that of society. If this is not a smart way to smuggle away a secret business concept, we will have very sad prospects for the future of Gates and Microsoft.

In a youth research context there have been specialisms on youth cultures for decades, and they might be summarised and synthesised for the purposes outside the world of Gates. It is possible to make an introductory exercise by looking back to the 1960s decade, and a springtime country by country in the western world of amateur shadow bands. Guitars, youth clubs and music waves joined forces, and in Oslo alone in 1969 there were one thousand bands. Four years later there were only four bands. I wonder what the figures would have been for Liverpool or London? But if we tried to find these thousands of individuals today, we would find that most of them had careers in emerging branches of music studios, entertainment, advertisement, broadcasting and television, etc. Mostly without qualifications from their schooling, but from their leisure pursuits. It is a pity that we do not possess more detailed empirical studies on this occupational and vocational history, because it now appears to be repeated in the expanding recruitment of writers and drawers for Internet publishing.

There is nothing sensational in these observations, seen as the history of technology – and some laws about generations. I was a child on a farm in the 1950s, at a time when the number of tractors exploded (and the old horses went to the slaughter). At the age of 6 to10 years we were the best tractor drivers, and you could see from the clumsy bodies of our parents on the tractor seat that they had been used to walking with horses.

These memories are only helpful when I look with envy at my children's simultanuous use of the walkman, reading a cartoon, watching television and playing a computer game – when I am only able to do one of these things at a time. But there are more specificities to understand and explain about the affinities between youth (cultures) and the media – or the information society.

I think we can approach these questions along two lines, one concerning language, and one concerning time and space.

The "youth" period is distinguished by intensified spurts of physical and intellectual growth, and of intense comparisons, competitions and collaborations with peers. When we look closer at the content and form of peer groups and the wider youth culture frames, we can characterise these excercises as stiff training of linguistic and communication skills or competencies. To some extent we can point towards a continuity from childhood, where all forms of playing also can be seen as training of communicative competence. But the specific, secret or hidden curriculum of language socialisation among young people is a certain dimension of language. Not the language of newspapers, school books or teachers, which we will call the digital dimension, but the analogue dimension: Body motion language, visual, symbolic or ceremonial representations, sometimes called codes of meaning – about how things are not what they appear to be, but the meaning we create for things. Youth culture is a combination of conflicting views. It is a struggle to come to terms with correct clothing and to be sure that you are not wearing yesterday's fashion or using "slang" of a group other than that to which you wish to belong.

The digitalisation of linguistic skills and communicative competence among young people is one of the essential reasons for the affinities between youth and new media – especially visual, symbolic and/or virtual media. But if we demystify these affinities, we shall remind ourselves that the baseline of this communicative competence is the classical school on "who is now saying what to whom, and why?" We should also demystify all ideas about digitalisation as a threat for mathematics and reasonable speech – even if there are (early) youth phases of "silence and dead faces": there are logical interactions between these two poles which mean "more digitalisation". Teenagers making video films write more text than ever, being good in music means writing notes for your own compositions, running for last news in computer graphs means to be very quick on the "zero-one" language of the computer.

Internet in youth work – the example and propects of the city of Helsinki

Working with computers can promote your qualifications in many ways. One could even maintain, that media qualifications, or rather the ability to use CMC, should be seen as a basic civic skill. Of course millions of people in the world do not even know how to read and even in the most advanced Internet countries like Finland the majority do not use it. Still, about fifteen years ago Ken Olssen, the managing director of Digital, the huge American computer company, said that personal computers would never enter the household! Considering the pace of development, things can change unexpectedly quickly.

At the moment (autumn 1996) 26 per cent of young people in Finland aged 18 to 20 years have recently used CMC and 71 per cent of boys and 57 per cent of girls expect to use it in the near future. Finland tops the ratio of Internet users per inhabitant. The city of Helsinki has moved on quickly to apply modern information technology. Most of the public libraries have an Internet access as a free basic service for library users. Most of the schools are connected to the city's fibre cable net and the Internet. Also a majority of the city's sixty youth clubs also have Internet access. If an increasing proportion of Internet-connected home computers are added to these facilities, the CMC is relatively widely available for the young people of the city.

But how can Internet be used as an instrument of local youth work? Examples of current activities and activities which are planned to be carried out in the future are as follows:

Providing a possibility to use Internet as a free basic service of youth clubs

– The basic philosophy of the city's youth clubs is to offer versatile and pedagogically meaningful leisure-time activities to any young person for free or at a low cost. These services provide the possibility for a daily access to CMC.

CMC courses for "media drop-outs"

– The youth clubs organise courses and guidance to "read the nets". This includes technical guidance, as well as studies in specific knowledge skills and the ethical questions concerning the net. The idea is to contribute to the state's (and European Union's) aim that young people should not be divided into those who have media qualifications and those who do not. For example, in many of the youth clubs young people, with a large proportion of youth at risk, have become acquainted with Internet by designing web sites for their own youth club (see http://www.hel.fi/nk/koti.html).

Youth information services via Internet

– The youth information unit of the youth department is developing its own interface on the Internet to provide easy-to-get hypertext access to the most often needed information. Information on vacant jobs in Helsinki, youth exchange programmes, events, cinemas, etc. and around Europe, rooms to let, information on drugs, rock concerts, sports events, etc.

Internet and the learning organisation – how to generate, apply and disseminate knowledge of youth projects?

- The electronic networks can be used to improve organisational capacity. It is a natural instrument to be applied in an organisation which is based on teams and networks. The youth department of the city of Helsinki explores how a flexible structure of teams and networks with the help of electronic media works.

Typically youth projects are carried out in isolation from similar projects in other parts of the city or projects in other cities. This effectively excludes the main dynamics of project development; exchange of ideas and experience of the project workers. Secondly there is a lack of proper evaluation of the projects. Thirdly the experience and knowhow of the projects tend to stay at the project level and do not mature into general policy measures to be made available at a higher level of management in the city's youth field. Fourthly the knowledge and the results of the projects should be more efficiently disseminated among people working within the youth field. To summarise, there is a lack of communication structures between the projects, a lack of research input, isolation of top management from both the shop-floor projects and insufficient dissemination of information on the projects. The organisation of the work into teams supported by efficient information structure (the electronic net) seems to be a promising possibility.

Towards Europe – using Internet to become acquainted with European youth

– CMC can be used to facilitate international co-operation between youth groups in various ways. By way of example: at one of the youth clubs a group of young people decided to travel to England next summer. First they had to find out how to raise the money: they plugged in to Internet and found the web pages of the local organisation responsible for YFE III and also obtained a reply to their indidual request via the net. Secondly they went on to look for partners in England and are now in communication with a school class. Further, to make better use of the travel they needed more general information on their target city, which was also available on Internet. Now they are planning to develop on a personal level – of course via Internet – conversational relationships and probably will be able to sort out lots of details before the actual journey.

Monitoring youth – a model of a constant survey of aspirations and conditions of young Helsinkians

– One basic problem of (local) youth policy and youth work is to be able to somehow follow the changes of young people's aspirations, expectations and their social condition. One standard solution is to carry out research, maybe to draw a sample of five hundred young persons and to send out a questionnaire, preferably twice a year to follow the changes. But this takes time and money. Let us look at the case of Helsinki, where the sixty youth clubs around the city are electronically linked. A random sample of ten young people in each of the clubs will make a total sample of five hundred who can be asked any questions which are then handled by the server (central computer) of the youth department. Using the software (similar to the Norwegian local youth surveys developed at the UNGFORSK in Oslo) any youth worker in the department can easily get the results or time span he or she individually wants. This way you can very easily, quickly, and in fact cheaply follow any changes of young people's lifestyles, desires or life conditions.

The Netiquette – taking responsibility

– Cyberspace – the world of electronic nets – is a huge largely uncontrolled world of its own. As a different world it also has its own moral and ethical rules of communication which the newcomer has to learn. Secondly the cyberspace, like the streets of a city, includes pedagocically undesirable areas. There have to be guidelines as to where one should not go. The city's youth department has published its own Netiquette, a compilation of rules of communication and conduct of the cyberspace, with which every-one using the city's Internet services has first to become acquainted.

Time and space, and some pecularities of youth cultures today

To relate youth cultures and peer group socialisation belongs to basics. And to form a "we" based on similar tastes, the needs of alliances towards "stupid" adults like parents or teachers is also something we teach in our introductory courses. Many of these community or tribal formations of youth have always been related to cultural trends, and also repeated "moral panics" in the surrounding societies. The dangerous things young people could do have always been described as threats to their physical and mental development. Before 1890 the bicycle caused moral panic, because of the lack of natural position for the body and the unstable minds due to free transport out of the community at church time on Sundays. Ten years later the cinema was new and dangerous for the body and the mind, in the 1920s and 1930s ballrooms were discussed with the same arguments as drugs and drug addiction fifty years later. This historical analysis was made at the begin-ning of the 1980s, as a comparison to the debate on video recorders. But today we are worried about the hackers and the nerds for the same reasons and also with the assumption that they are male and will forever be male.

These reflections can help us to see some continuity of peer groups and youth cultures shaped by the necessity of producing socially the boundaries between the young and the adult worlds. This concept of "worlds" could sometimes be called "life worlds", sometimes "territories", just to underline that youth research has been effective in the observations of the space dimension of youth worlds. The needs of discriminating between "us" and "them" have for a long time been sufficient conditions. But we are at a time when we need to elaborate and refine our concepts and ideas.

We can see that the dynamics of youth cultures are not so strongly related towards the adult world(s) – and what is today "adult"? But instead we can see how the internal distinctions within the youth cultures are more and more important – between the "us-us" and the "us-them", that is to say, the horizontal instead of the vertical distinctions. And we can also see that cultural trends develop in new ways in today's media and on the Internet. Some decades ago the only trend lines were from the cities to the suburbs: From London or Paris, via our local capitals, and slowly rock and roll also appeared in rural areas. Today Manchester United supporters come from everywhere to see a match against Juventus in Turin. Latin broadcasting for a worldwide circle of Latin speakers comes from a radio station in Finland. And Björk is an Icelandic, international star. New phenomena can start anywhere, but perhaps more often from the suburbs than the "dead cities".

From these observations we can come to some new "platforms", where we can see that the old rules about space and time as something dividing or separating young people from each other, have reached another dimension. My peers as my "we" were not only those similar to me in a spacial meaning, but also as my contemporaries in the meaning of time. This was for sure also present in an abstract sense at the time we knew that other people worldwide were "digging" the Beatles – and we called this a "reference group", but there is something else going on with kidlinks and global youth dialogues on the Internet. Here you find your Greenpeace mates, and here the local rock composer is "picking down" tune sequences from a friend in San Fransisco, and a lot of more unusual special interests are identified between contemporaries. To be peers means to be the same age, but now there is more and more emphasis that we also belong to the same time – simultanuously.

These particular phenomena lead one to speak about the information society as a continuous globalisation. To some extent this is obviously true, but this truth also meets its limits when others describe this as "hyperreality" and a "global village" where we use a smaller world to concentrate on the royal marriage of Charles and Lady Di. I think it is easier to finish this introduction of some useful concepts to work on by contrasting the globalisation concept with local "flexibilisation" as the interactive process. This means that a smaller, more accessible world does not lead to increasing similarities of the human beings – or youth, but to increasing cultivation of peculiarities, particularities, etc. in a cultural meaning. In this globalised community it is much easier to be a local teenager who is against rock music and appreciates Mozart than it was twenty-five years ago. Instead of one youth culture, the information society implies a rapid increase in the subculturisation of youth.

The age of "technophiles" and "luddites"

Probably we all are divided into two opposing camps in terms of our rela-tionship towards Internet. One camp thinks Internet has great potential for human progress and will change our ways of thinking, the other feels that it is a backlash of progress – just a by-passing (masculine) toy or a device to control people or a purely commercial marketing method, etc. To categorise, the first camp can be named "technophiles" and the latter "luddites".

Techno-optimists like Alvin Toffler, Marshall McLuhan, Yukio Masuda, Jacques Attali, and all the spokesmen of the computer industry think that the development of media technology helps us solve our societal problems and take us to "the electronic cottage" – a revival of the traditional family com-munity via electronic facilities (Toffler), "the global village" – a new form of cohesion between electronically-linked people around the world (McLuhan), "the computopia" – a utopian society run by intelligent citizens and com-puters (Masuda) or to "an emergence of new nomad communities" – a new global network of communities of computer-connected enthusiasts.

"The luddites" refers to bands of rioters who broke machines in England in the 1810s. They thought that the new industrial technology was the reason for their unemployment. Later the term became to denote resistance to progress and technological development. In that sense modern-day luddites are those who feel like breaking down the computers, modems and Internet servers, because they are thought to destroy human communication; face-to-face contacts, emotions, one's sense of reality, the content of communi-cation, etc. Media researchers like Neil Postman warn us that modern media technology has joined the global entertainment industry "to amuse ourselves to death"; he thinks that entertainment will take over education and offers us only "edutainment" (education + entertainment). Theodore Roszak (1988) strongly criticises the mysticism and the magicians inherent in the information technology. People are brainwashed to believe that computers and Internet are sacred and should not be criticised. Julian Stallabrass in *New Left Review* (1995, p. 32) studies the concept of "cyberspace" – the world of Internet. He maintains that cyberspace is "... merely a literal expression of ... business people and their camp followers (engineers and intellectuals) spinning universalising fantasies out of their desire to ride the next commer-cial wave. This wondrous but specious technology threatens to act as ano-ther curtain between those who consume it and the condition of the world; as the poor are excluded from the cyberspace, and will appear on it only as objects, never as subjects with their own voices, there is a danger that they recede even further from the consciousness of the comfortable. As the real world is left to decline, the air once again becomes full of phantoms, this time digital, promising at the last moment to pluck utopia from apocalypse".

Coming back to the case of Helsinki on the prospects of using Internet as an instrument in youth work. At the moment the major obstacle to carrying out the plans at the youth department is the resistance of youth workers to apply

CMC. It is often felt to be a menace to the traditional forms of youth work and specifically what is called "contact work". Here we come back to the phenomenon of the luddites:

"Technophiles are taking us all on an utterly reckless ride into the unknown"

Unabomber: "Industrial Society and the Future", 1995 on http://vip. hotwired.com/special/unabomb

The unabomber is an American anarchist, who since 1978 has planted or mailed sixteen package bombs that have killed three and wounded twenty-three, most of his victims being in universities or airlines. (Hence the initials "un" and "a"). In his manifesto unabomber points out that "Technophiles are taking us all on an utterly reckless ride into the unknown". Unabomber is a pathological phenomenon, but expresses in a highlighted manner a more widespread resistance to technological change. During quick changes people and cultures have problems to relate development to their past and adapt themselves to new circumstances. This is a human cultural reaction, already expressed in the disbelief of the heliocentric worldview (which we still have not accepted in the sense that even today we think that in the morning the sun rises and in the evening it sets). Change is experienced as a threat to one's present position and competence (McMurdo, 1996). Among youth workers Internet is experienced as posing a risk to "the basic task of youth work", which normally refers to personal encounter with young people. From the viewpoint of the Helsinki experience one major obstacle to find out how CMC can be used as a tool in youth work is attitudinal, the attitude of the unabomber. To what extent the people with whom we work, the people we represent and we ourselves are mental unabombers – or is that what we should be?

Lasse Siurala, Ola Stafseng

References

Bell D: *The coming of post-industrial society: a venture in social forecasting*, New York Basic Books, 1973

Bradd L: *Virtual communities: computer-mediated communication and communities of association* (telecommunication), Indiana University, 1993

Cyberpunk Handbook (The Real Cyberpunk Fakebook), 1996

Dalaimo D: *The simulation of selfhood in cyberspace*, Dissertation. University of Nevada, December 1995

Habermas J: *The theory of communicative action*, Polity Press, Cambridge, 1986

Jones S: *CyberSociety*, Thousand Oaks California, Sage, 1995

McLuhan M: *Understanding media: the extensions of man*, New York Signet Books, 1964

McMurdo G: *Stone Age Babies in Cybespace*, Journal of information Science, 1996

Roszak T: *The cult of information: a neo-luddite treatise on high tech, artificial intelligence and the true art of thinking*, Berkeley University of California Press, 1988

Stallabrass J: *Empowering Technology: The Exploration of Cyberspace*, New Left Review, 1995

Unabomber: *Industrial Society and the Future*, http://vip.hotwired.com/special/unabomb, 1995

Post-Fordist possibilities for lifelong learning[1]

> "The widening reach and impact of information technologies, the gathering momentum of globalisation and trade liberalisation, the ageing of the population, growing cultural and ethnic diversity and the changing nature of work are combining to create new opportunities in a context in which knowledge and skills will play a more significant role." OECD *Lifelong Learning for All* (1996).

A new international consensus has identified the quality of a nation's human resources as holding the key to prosperity in the global economy. Within this consensus, lifelong learning, knowledge, information, and technical competence are seen as the new raw materials of international commerce:

> "Knowledge itself, therefore, turns out to be not only the source of the highest-quality power, but also the most important ingredient of force and wealth. Put differently, knowledge has gone from being an adjunct of money power and muscle power, to being their very essence. It is, in fact, the ultimate amplifier. This is the key to the power shift that lies ahead, and it explains why the battle for control of knowledge and the means of communication is heating up all over the world." (Toffler, 1990: p.18)

Although such statements exaggerate the importance of knowledge in advanced capitalist economies, the quality of a nation's education and training systems has become a key element of economic competitiveness. In academic circles this debate has centred on the failure of western nations, including the United States and Britain, to modernise production in ways that overcome the debilitating consequences of "Fordism" (Piore and Sabel, 1984). This is because the Fordist inheritance has been identified as a source of inefficiency in uncertain and rapidly changing market conditions.

It is suggested that organisations now need to apply "entrepreneurial principles to the traditional corporation, creating a marriage between entrepreneurial creativity and corporate discipline, co-operation, and teamwork" (Kanter, 1989: p. 9-10). A related argument is the claim that bureaucratic organisations are no longer appropriate to the conditions of the late twentieth century:

> "Bureaucracy thrived in a highly competitive, undifferentiated, and stable environment, such as the climate of its youth, the Industrial Revolution. A pyramidal structure of authority, with power concentrated in the hands of few with the knowledge and resources to control an entire enterprise was, and is, an eminently suitable social arrangement for routinised tasks. However, the environment has

---

1 This paper is a revised and extended version of "Post-Fordist possibilities: education, training and national development", in L Bash & A Green (eds.) *Youth, Education and Work*, London: Kogan Page, 1995.

changed in just those ways which make the mechanism most problematic. Stability has vanished." (Bennis, 1972: p. 111)

In this article we will assume that "Fordism" is being undermined in western capitalist societies, although its global significance has remained undiminished as the mass production of standardised goods and services is transplanted in the newly industrialising nations (NICs), especially in Asia and South America (Lipietz, 1987; Dicken, 1992). We also believe that a massive process of organisational restructuring is occurring in western economies in an attempt to breakdown the rigidities of bureaucratic and Fordist paradigms (Brown and Scase, 1994). The same process of restructuring can be seen in public as well as private sector organisations, and in medium as well as large enterprises. There is no doubt, for instance, that the introduction of new technologies has expanded the range of strategic choice available to employers and managers. However, this has exposed increasing differences, rather than similarities, in organisational cultures, job design and training regimes (Lane, 1989; Green and Steedman, 1993). There are few guarantees that employers will successfully exploit the potential for "efficiency", precisely because they may fail to break free of conventional assumptions about the role of management and workers, and cling to the established hierarchy of authority, status and power.

As Harvey (1989) has recognised, new technologies and co-ordinating forms of organisation have permitted the revival of domestic, familial, and paternalistic labour systems given that:

> "The same shirt designs can be reproduced by large-scale factories in India, co-operative production in the 'Third Italy', sweatshops in New York and London, or family labour systems in Hong Kong." (p. 187)

This should alert us to the fact that the shift towards "flexible accumulation" does not necessarily lead to changes in the nature of skills and involvement which are required in order to compete in "high value" production. The interests of employers seeking to maximise profits and workers seeking to enhance the quality of working life and wages remain an important source of cleavage given that it is still possible for companies to "profit" from low-tech, low-wage operations. There is no invisible hand or post-industrial logic which will lead nations to respond to the global economy in the same way, despite the fact that their fates are inextricably connected. Indeed, we would suggest that the universal consensus highlighting education, training and lifelong learning as holding the key to future prosperity has obscured fundamental differences in the way nations are responding to global competition.

Therefore, while recognising that some of the key elements of Fordism in western nations are being transformed in the global economy, it is important not to prejudge the direction of these changes which must remain a question of detailed empirical investigation (see Block, 1990).

For analytical purposes it is useful to distinguish two "ideal typical" models of national economic development in terms of neo-Fordism and post-Fordism (see Figure 1). Neo-Fordism can be characterised in terms of creating greater market flexibility through a reduction in social overheads and the power of trade unions; the privatisation of public utilities and the welfare state, as well as a celebration of competitive individualism.

Alternative, post-Fordism can be defined in terms of the development of the state as a "strategic trader" shaping the direction of the national economy through investment in key economic sectors and in the development of human capital. Therefore, post-Fordism is based on a shift to "high-value" customised production and services using multiskilled workers (see also Allen, 1992).

Figure 1:
Post-Fordist possibilities: Alternative models of national development

Fordism	Neo-Fordism	Post-Fordism
Protected national markets	Global Competition through: productivity gains, cost-cutting (overheads, wages) Inward investment attracted by "market flexibility" (reduce the social cost of labour, trade union power)	Global Competition through: innovation, quality, "value added" goods and services Inward investment attracted by highly skilled labour force engaged in "value added" production/services
	Adversarial market orientation: remove impediments to market competition. Create "enterprise culture". Privatisation of the welfare state	Consensus based objectives: corporatist "industrial policy". Co-operation between government, employers and trade unions
Mass production of standardised products/low-skill, high-wage	Mass production of standardised products/ low-skill, low-wage flexible production/niche markets blue chip and sweatshops	Flexible production systems/small batch/ niche markets; shift to high wage, high-skilled jobs
Bureaucratic hierarchical organisations	Leaner organisations with emphasis on "numerical" flexibility	Leaner organisations with emphasis on "functional" flexibility
Fragmented and standardised work tasks	Reduce trade union job demarcation but little move to multiskilled workers	Flexible specialisation/multiskilled workers.

Mass standardised (male) employment	Fragmentation/ polarisation of labour force. Professional "core" and "flexible" workforce; (i.e. part-time, temps, contract, portfolio careers)	Maintain good conditions employees. None "core" workers receive training, fringe benefits, comparable wages, proper representation
Divisions between managers and workers/ low-trust relations/ collective bargaining	Emphasis on "managers right to manage". Industrial relations based on low-trust relations	Industrial relations based on high-trust, high discretion, collective participation
Little "on-the-job" training for most workers	Training "demand" led/little use of industrial training policies	Training as an national investment/state acts as strategic trainer

In the "real" world the relationship between education and economic development reveals examples of contradiction as much as correspondence.

Moreover, although it is true to say that countries such as Germany, Japan and Singapore come closer to the model of post-Fordism, and the USA and Britain approximate neo-Fordist solutions, we should not ignore clear examples of "uneven" and contradictory developments within the same region or country. It also highlights the fact that there are important differences in the way nation states may move towards a post-Fordist economy with far-reaching implications for democracy and social justice.

Nevertheless, these models represent clear differences in policy orientations in terms of the dominant economic ideas which inform them and underlying cultural assumptions about the role of skill formation in economic and social development (Thurow, 1993). Here we will argue that those nation states which have adopted New Right "market" reforms in education, training and the labour market, gravitate towards the neo-Fordist route to national development, whereas the shift towards post-Fordism will require a fundamentally different response based on the struggle for collective intelligence.

Fordism and national development

Antonio Gramsci (1971) used the term Fordism to describe a new system of mass production introduced by the American car manufacturer Henry Ford. Gramsci recognised that the introduction of mass production also required a new mode of social regulation "suited to the new type of work and productive process" (p. 286). Ford's rise to prominence at the time stemmed from the market success of the Model T motor car which was launched in 1916. The system of mass production enabled him to capture 55 per cent of the US market in the early 1920s by selling the Model T at a tenth of the price of a craft-built car (Braverman, 1974; Murray, 1989).

Fordist mass production is based on the standardisation of products and their component parts. Many of the tasks previously undertaken by skilled craftsmen, such as making door panels or parts of the car's engine "by hand", can be mechanised by designing jigs, presses and machines able to perform the same operations hundreds, if not thousands of times a day, with the use of a semi-skilled operative. The Fordist production line is also characterised by a moving assembly line, where the product passes the workers along a conveyer, rather than the worker having to move to the product as in nodal production.

A further feature of "Fordism" is a detailed division of labour, within which the job tasks of shop-floor workers are reduced to their most elementary form in order to maximise both efficiency and managerial control over the labour process. Hence, Fordism is based on many of the principles of "scientific management" outlined by Frederick Taylor in his analysis of pig-iron handling in 1911. In this work, Taylor suggests that it would be possible to train an intelligent gorilla to become a more efficient pig-iron handler than a human (p. 40, quoted in Gramsci p. 302).

The importance of Taylor's ideas in the development of Fordism was that he offered a "scientific" justification for the separation of conception from execution, where managers monopolised knowledge of the labour process, and controlled every step of production.

Although some writers have restricted their definition of Fordism to refer exclusively to the system of mass production, others have emphasised that Fordism is a label that can equally be applied to Keynesian demand management in the postwar period (Lipietz, 1987; Harvey, 1989). In other words, Fordism is used to refer to the expansion of mass consumption as well as mass production. The rapid improvement in economic efficiency which accompanied the introduction of mass production techniques necessitated the creation of mass markets for consumer durables, including radios, refrigerators, television sets and motor cars. In order for economic growth to be maintained, national governments had to regulate profits and wage levels in order to sustain the conditions upon which economic growth depended.

In this broader use of the term, the development of the welfare state in western industrial societies is seen to reflect efforts on the part of national governments to maintain the Fordist compromise between employers and organised labour. The role of the education system was assumed to be vital to this enterprise. This fact was clearly recognised by Henry Ford who stated when making a donation of $100 million to an institution which he called the School of the Future:

> "I have manufactured cars long enough to the point where I have got the desire to manufacture people. The catchword of the day is standardisation." (quoted in Cooley, 1993)

Fordism, bureaucracy and education

Despite Ford's desire to "manufacture people", the rise of mass schooling has never resembled a simple correspondence to the requirements of the economy (Green, 1990). The education system throughout the twentieth century has been shaped less by Fordist production techniques than by the principles of bureaucratic organisation (Brown and Lauder, 1992a). Indeed, the growing importance attached to systems of education has partly been a result of the need for a formal system of "socialisation" and "selection":

> "The bureaucratisation of the high school is ... a manifestation of the general trend toward the rationalisation of daily activities in all spheres of contemporary life. With the progressive differentiation and special-isation of functions in modern society, we expect an intensification of attempts to maximise the efficiency of identifying and developing the talent within the population." (Cicourel and Kitsuse, 1963: p. 139)

The development of education systems in industrial societies has, therefore, been premised on a set of rules, procedures and practices which conform to the principles of bureaucratic organisation. Weber described the characteris-tics of bureaucracy in terms of a "... form of organisation that emphasises precision, speed, clarity, regularity, reliability, and efficiency achieved through the creation of a fixed division of tasks, hierarchical supervision, and detailed rules and regulations". (Morgan, 1986: pp. 24-5)

Weber also argued that "if these principles of bureaucracy are followed it is possible to attain a high degree of efficiency and an organisational structure which is superior to any other form in its precision, stability and reliability". As well as providing a social technology which can create a set of predictable outcomes, bureaucracy is intimately related to the idea of a "meritocracy" because it treats individuals according to "objective" achievement criteria. In education, individuals are treated according to ability rather than on the basis of ascribed characteristics such as social class, gender or race. The organis-ation of formal educational systems according to bureaucratic criteria there-fore provided a rational means of social selection for expanding public administrations and capitalist corporations. School and college credentials provide a useful screening device for employers who are concerned that future employees should be inculcated into the appropriate forms of rule-fol-lowing behaviour, as well as having the appropriate knowledge and skills for their place in the technostructure. However, given the demand for large numbers of low-skilled workers with little room for individual autonomy, the educational system has had to confront the problem of offering greater equality of opportunity whilst limiting the aspirations and ambitions of the majority by defining them as academic failures. This contradiction at the heart of bureaucratic education – of seeking to promote a "talented" few while attempting to "cool out" the majority – has consistently presented a problem of legitimation and resulted in various forms of working-class resis-tance (Brown and Lauder, 1992).

Education and the demise of Fordism

The demise of the bureaucratic/Fordist paradigms of organisational efficiency and their implications for education and training systems, cannot be explained in "technocratic" terms. There is as we have noted no internal "logic of industrialism" or "logic of capitalism" which has set western nations on the path to either neo-Fordism or post-Fordism. The direction of change will crucially depend upon the outcome of political struggle, which in most western economies currently centres on the role of the nation state and the free market.

New Right proponents of the free market assume that the reassertion of market disciplines in social and economic institutions will lead to improvements in both efficiency and productivity (Gamble, 1988). However, we will argue that the most likely outcome of attempts to "get the state off people's backs" (as Ronald Reagan once expressed it), through an extension of market competition will lead to the development of neo-Fordist economies, characterised by low skill and low wages for the majority of the workforce. We will also suggest that the appeal to "self-interest" and "free enterprise" serves to mask the political interests of the most privileged sections of society. Indeed, the very notion of a national system of education is called into question as professional and elite groups secede from their commitment to public education and the ideology of meritocracy upon which public education has been founded.

Market reform and political interests

The New Right interpretation of the Fordist "crisis" is based on what we call the welfare shackle thesis (Brown and Lauder, 1996). In the nineteenth century it was the aristocracy and the ancient regime in Europe who were blamed for "shackling" the market and free enterprise. In the late twentieth century it is the welfare state[1]. The New Right argue that the problem confronting western nations today can only be understood in light of profound changes in the role of government during the third quarter of the twentieth century. They assert that there is no coincidence that at the same time western governments were significantly increasing expenditure on social welfare programmes, there was high inflation, rising unemployment and economic stagnation (Murray, 1984). Western societies have run into trouble because of the extensive and unwarranted interference by the state. Inflation, high unemployment, economic recession and urban unrest all stem from the legacy of Keynesian economics and an egalitarian ideology which promoted economic redistribution, equality of opportunity and welfare rights for all. Hence, the overriding problem confronting western capitalist nations is to reimpose the disciplines of the market.

---

1 The Feudal Shackle is discussed by Hirschman A, in *Rival Views of Market Society and Other Essays* (1986), Viking, pp. 105-141.

71

According to the New Right the route to national salvation in the context of global knowledge wars is through the survival of the fittest, based on an extension of parental choice in a market of competing schools, colleges and universities (Ball, 1990). In the case of education, where funding, at least during the compulsory school years, will come from the public purse, the idea is to create a quasi-market within which schools will compete (Lauder, 1987). This approximation to the operation of a market is achieved by seeking to create a variety of schools in a mixed economy of public and private institutions. In some cases they will aim at different client groups such as the ethnic minorities, religious sects, or "high flyers". This "variety" it is argued will provide parents with a genuine choice of different products (Boyd and Cibulka, 1989; Halstead, 1994).

Choice of product (type of school) is seen to be sufficient to raise the standards for all, because if schools cannot sell enough deskspace to be economically viable, they risk going out of business. Moreover, the economic needs of the nation will be met through the market, because when people have to pay for education they are more likely to make investment decisions which will realise an economic return. This will lead consumers to pick subjects and courses where there is a demand for labour, subsequently overcoming the problem of skill shortages. Equally, there will be a tendency for employment training to be "demand led" in response to changing market conditions (Deakin and Wilkinson, 1991).

In response, it can be argued that the marketisation of education serves the interests of the highest-paid professional workers among the middle classes as well as ruling elites. And that their interests are intimately related to the changing nature of the global economy where the conditions have been laid for transnational executives and highly paid professional workers, what Reich (1991) calls "symbolic analysts", to secede from national systems of education, health and welfare. Their high income and geographic mobility means that they have less allegiance to a national system of education and a greater concern to buy "quality" through private education.

Brown (1990; 1994) has argued that the transformation of western capitalism since the early 1970s has led to increasing competition for academic and professional credentials. The intensification of global competition, economic recession, unemployment, the privatisation of public utilities, and the restructuring of private and public sector bureaucracies into leaner, fitter and more flexible organisations, have all contributed to making job insecurity an endemic feature of employment, irrespective of socio-economic status. This has heightened the competition for credentials because it has become necessary to "stay fit" in both the internal and external markets for jobs, as the security associated with incremental progression within bureaucratic "career" structures is being undermined.

Critics of the marketisation of education therefore argue that the introduction of choice and competition provides a mechanism by which the middle classes can more securely gain an advantage in the competition for credentials. This is because not all social groups come to an educational market as equals (Collins, 1979). Cultural and material capital are distributed unequally between classes and ethnic groups. In particular, it is the middle classes which are more likely to have the cultural capital to make educational choices which best advantage their children (Halsey et al., 1997). In consequence, the introduction of parental choice and competition between schools will amount to a covert system of educational selection according to social class as middle-class children exit schools where there are significant numbers of working-class children. The consequence will be that the school system will become polarised in terms of social class and ethnic segregation and in terms of resources. As middle-class students exit from schools where there are working-class children they will also take much needed resources from those schools and effectively add to already well-off middle-class schools.

What evidence there is about the workings of educational markets suggests that they are far more complex than its critics suggest (Lauder et al, 1994). Nevertheless, the evidence so far confirms the prediction that choice and competition tend to lead to social class and ethnic polarisation in schools (Willms and Echols, 1992; Lauder et al, 1994). In nations like Britain, the overall effect will be to segregate students in different types of school on the basis of social class, ethnicity and religion. The net result will again be a massive wastage of talent as able working-class students again find themselves trapped in schools which do not give them the opportunity of going to university (Halsey et al, 1990). If this is the overall effect then it can be argued that the marketisation of education, while appearing to offer efficiency and flexibility of the kind demanded in the post-Fordist era, will in fact school the majority of children for a neo-Fordist economy which requires a low level of talent and skill.

Given these conclusions, it is not surprising that to critics the ideology of the market sounds suspiciously like the political mobilisation of a doctrine which serves the interests of those who have most to gain from asserting primacy of individual interests over those of the community or nation. Moreover, by seceding from national systems of education the state loses the most articulate "clients" of education and hence a significant voice in maintaining educational standards. Of course, the impact of such a loss will vary from nation to nation depending on the strength and prestige of existing private systems. Arguably, the secession of this group in Britain would be little noticed, however, the impact might be far more significant in France or in the nascent private systems in Scandinavia.

What is more significant, however, is their impact on the ability of nation states to compete in what may be termed the global auction for inward investment and jobs (Brown and Lauder, 1996). Although multinational organisations are always on the lookout to reduce their overheads, including labour costs, investment in "high-value" products and services crucially depends upon the quality, commitment and insights of the workforce, for which they are prepared to pay high salaries. The problem that nation states now confront is one of how to balance commercial pressures to reduce labour costs and other overheads whilst mobilising an educated labour force, and maintain a sophisticated social, financial and communications infrastructure. This problem has been exacerbated by the fact that the low-skill, high-wage jobs associated with Fordism in North America and Europe are either being transplanted to the NICs where labour costs are much lower, or leading to a significant deterioration in working conditions and wages in the west.

In the context of the global auction, the market reforms in education are likely to leave a large majority of the future working population without the human resources to flourish in the global economy. Here the link between market reforms and neo-Fordism is barely disguised in countries with New Right governments such as Britain, until recently. The principle objective of economic policy is to improve the competitiveness of workers by increasing labour market flexibility by restricting the power of trade unions, especially in order to bring wages into line with their "market" value. This led to a refusal to sign the "Social Chapter" as part of the Maastricht Treaty among member states of the European Union. The Social Chapter was rejected by the British Conservative Government because it was argued that the introduction of a minimum wage and protective legislation relating to working conditions would undermine Britain's competitiveness in terms of inward investment from global corporations, despite the low wages and inferior working conditions which this inflicts on employees.

In contradistinction, market reforms in education and the economy have ensured the conditions in which highly-paid middle-class professionals and elite groups are able to give their children an "excellent" (sic) education in preparation for their bid to join the ranks of the "symbolic analysts".

A different critique, albeit coming to the same conclusion, can be mounted against the introduction of market mechanisms in post-compulsory education and training. A key area of the post-compulsory sector for a post-Fordist economy is that concerned with the education of skilled tradespeople and technicians (Streeck, 1989). The New Right has argued that the introduction of market mechanisms into this area will ensure a closer matching of supply and demand for trained labour and hence greater efficiency in the allocation of skilled labour. The argument rests on the assumptions that individuals and employers should bear the cost and responsibility for training. It is assumed that individuals gain most of the benefits from such a training and that they should therefore bear much of the cost (Lauder, 1987). Moreover, since they are paying substantially for their training they will choose to train in an area in which there is market demand. Insofar as employers should help bear the cost of training and the responsibility for the type of training offered, it is argued that employers are in the best position to assess the numbers of skilled workers required and the kind of skills they should possess. Underlying this observation is an appreciation of employers' interests. Given the assumption that they "know best" what the levels and nature of skilled labour there should be, it follows that they will be reluctant to pay taxes or levies for training undertaken by a third party, such as the state.

While this view, as with other New Right views, is plausible, it has come in for sustained critique. One of the most cogent is that of Streeck (1989, 1992). He argues that under a free labour contract of the kind found in liberal capitalist societies which gives workers the right to move from one firm to another, skills become a collective good in the eyes of employers. This is because the rewards of training individuals can easily be "socialised" by the expedient of trained workers moving to another job while the costs of training remain with the original employer. Since employers face a clear risk in losing their investment they are unlikely to invest heavily in training. Streeck argues that, as a result, western economies are likely to face a chronic skill shortage unless the state intervenes to ensure that adequate training occurs.

Moreover, unless there is state intervention employers will reduce the training programmes they do have when placed under intense competitive pressure and/or during a recession. Streeck (1989) notes that in the prolonged economic crisis of the 1970s, western economies, with the exception of Germany, reduced their apprenticeship programmes.

In Germany government and trade union pressure ensured that the apprenticeship programme was extended. Two consequences followed: the apprenticeship system helped to alleviate youth unemployment and it contributed to the technical and economic advantage enjoyed by German industry in the early 1980s.

There are further criticisms that can be made of a market-determined training system. From the standpoint of the individual, it is unlikely that those who would potentially enter a skilled trade or technical training, working and lower middle-class school leavers, could either afford the costs of such a training or take the risks involved. The risks are twofold: firstly, given the time lag between entering a training programme and completing it, market demand for a particular type of training may have changed with a resulting lack of jobs. In the competitive global market, such an outcome is all too likely. If the training received were of a sufficiently general nature to produce a flexible worker that may be less of a problem. However, in an employer-led training system the pressure will always exist for training to meet employers' specific and immediate needs. The consequence is that such a training system is likely to be too narrowly focused to meet rapidly changing demand conditions. Secondly, a further point follows from this, namely that the industries of today are likely to be tomorrow's dinosaurs.

As a result, employer-led training schemes may not contain the vision and practice required in order to maintain the high-skill base necessary for a post-

Fordist economy. Clearly the structure of Germany's training system offers an example of an alternative which can begin to meet the requirements of a post-Fordist economy. This, as Streeck (1992) notes, involves a partnership between the state, employers and trade unions. It is a system which ensures that employers' immediate interests are subsumed within a system concerned with medium and longer-term outcomes.

Towards an education system for a post-Fordist economy

The implication of this critique of market-led education and training systems is that the question of who should fund and provide education and training for lifelong learning, the state or the market, is not just a technical question of weighing up the merits of the two types of delivery. Rather what is at stake is the question of whether the political interests which have been unleashed by the creation of the new global economy can be sufficiently reconciled to create a social settlement which reflects the national interest rather than the sectarian interests of the middle class and social elites. Nations which fail to achieve such a settlement will effectively implode into civil knowledge wars as different social classes and ethnic groups compete for educational advantage with the consequence that, at best, they will produce an education system commensurate with a low-skill, low-trust, neo-Fordist economy. A nation's ability to successfully shift towards a post-Fordist economy will require a radically different set of political tools and to begin with cultural assumptions far removed from the New Right's glorification of "rugged individualism".

In what follows we will argue that the development of "collective intelligence" will need to be an integral feature of a post-Fordist society.

Collective intelligence as the foundation for lifelong learning

We have argued that the education systems in most industrial societies have been based on the bureaucracy paradigm. This includes the idea that there is a limited "pool of talent" in a sea of mediocrity which ignores the important ways in which intelligence is collectively structured by the form of production (Kohn and Schooler, 1983). Moreover, the low-discretion and low-skill work roles which confront large numbers of workers in Fordist organisations have generated low-trust responses including worker resistance, minimum level of commitment, high rates of absenteeism, wild-cat strikes, etc. (Fox, 1974). These responses have traditionally been interpreted by management as a manifestation of the feckless irresponsible nature of most workers. Indeed, managers have typically recognised these responses as a justification for the use of surveillance and the threat of sanctions in the control of the workforce.

Our conception of collective intelligence involves a fundamental re-evaluation of these ideas which are outlined in Figure 2.

Figure 2:
Human ability and motivation

Fordism	Post-Fordism
Intelligence is a scarce resource, but can be "scientifically" identified among children at an early age	Unfolding of human capacity limited by social hierarchy and cultural attitudes
The organisation of education and employment corresponds to the normal distribution of talent	The capacity to exercise imagination, ingenuity, creativity, etc., is widely distributed in the population
The average human being has a dislike of "work" and will avoid it if possible	The expenditure of physical and mental effort in "work" is as natural as play or rest
People must be coerced, controlled, directed, threatened with punishment to fulfil organisational goals	People will exercise self-direction and self-control to fulfil aims to which he/she is committed
Most people avoid responsibility, have relatively little ambition, and above all want security	Under the right conditions most people will both accept and seek responsibility

There is an urgent need to jack-up the normal curve of human intelligence. Given the right motivation (which is socially determined), at least 80 per cent of the population are capable of achieving the intellectual standards required to obtain a university degree in adult life. This view is supported by comparative evidence which shows significant differences in the proportion of students from different advanced industrial societies participating in higher education. Such differences need to be explained in terms of the social, cultural and institutional differences between nation states. We do not, for instance, subscribe to the view that the Germans, English or Americans are innately less intelligent than the Japanese! We are also struck by the ever increasing numbers of "mature" students who previously had few, if any, formal qualifications, but given a clear reason for undertaking undergraduate study (and the available opportunity), they generally prove to be able students. Hence, we concur with Sabel (1982) when he suggests that it is often "social hierarchy and the world views associated with it that restricts the unfolding of human capacity, and not the limitations of natural endowment" (p. 244). None of what we are suggesting need doubt the existence of innate differences in intelligence (although it clearly depends what you adopt as a measure).

What we are suggesting is that the vast wealth of talent has not been harnessed by current systems of education and training, and that it is nonsense to suggest that current levels of "academic" performance are a reasonable reflection of individual and collective capability.

The creation of a post-Fordist economy will need to continue to structure opportunity on the basis of individual effort and ability, but the "ideology of meritocracy" will have to be strongly reinforced. It has too often been a tool of "administrative convenience" for both teachers and employers to explain why some (usually from a middle-class background) make it, and why others (usually from a working-class background) do not.

Official assessments of this kind are extremely difficult to argue against as a student, or as a parent, because even if teachers are unable to produce a low IQ score as a "cause" of low achievement, they will point to the other half of the meritocratic equation, that poor achievement must be the result of a failure to work hard or as a consequence of poor parental motivation. The *coup de grace* of this form of ideological justification is reserved for those who prove the system wrong by achieving later as a "mature" student. These are imaginatively labelled the "late developers" on the assumption that had they been capable of earlier achievement they would obviously have done so. However, the growing need for knowledgeable and empowered citizens is heightening concern about a system which incapacitates and alienates large numbers of young people.

There is strong evidence to suggest that education and training systems must be organised on the premise that all rather than a few are capable of significant practical and academic achievements, of creative thought and skill, and of taking responsibility for making informed judgements. The role of education in this context must become one of nurturing this wealth of talent. We will need to redirect our attention away from the attributes of individual students as the cause of low ability systems of education, to the institutional context in which the learning process takes place.

Instead of pointing to the fact that their "failing" students are usually working class or black, teachers, trainers and employers would be forced to examine the institutional context and their professional practices for explanations of trained incapacity. This strategy would certainly help to generate a more integrated system of education and training involving teachers, students, parents, trade unionists, and employers.

From individual to collective intelligence

Intelligence, the ability to solve problems, to think critically and systematically about the social and natural worlds, and the ability to apply new skills and techniques, is usually seen as an attribute of individuals. However, there is a clear sense in which it is determined by forms of production and the social systems they create. Where societies have adopted Fordist forms of production it is not surprising to find a massive wastage of talent, precisely because the ability to act on the world is given to so few – the elite at the top of bureaucratic organisations who make all the key operational and policy decisions.

However, collective intelligence means more than simply increasing the pool of knowledgeable and technically competent people. It also needs to be understood as a measure of our ability to face up to the problems that confront us collectively and to develop collective solutions (Lacey, 1988: p. 94). Therefore, an education which does not examine the issues of the day, or help students to make connections between different aspects of their studies renders the latter less intelligent than they need be. A nation state, for example, which denies its youth the opportunity to examine issues concerning the causes and consequences of environmental pollution, the nature of HIV and AIDS, or offer political education is also symptomatic of a low-trust and low-ability society.

Equally, a new division of learning will be needed to support a new division of labour. Zuboff (1988), for instance, in her account of technological innovation in the USA, distinguished technology which automates from that which informates. Automation simply involves the replacement of the human body with a technology that enables the same processes to be performed with more continuity and control. In other words, it conforms to the principles of Fordism. Rather than decrease the dependence on human skills, technology which has the capacity to informate can enlarge job tasks and the room for individual discretion given that activities, events, and objects are translated into and made visible by information:

> "... an informated organization is structured to promote the possibility of useful learning among all members and thus presupposes relations of equality. However, this does not mean that all members are assumed to be identical in their orientations, proclivities, and capacities; rather, the organisation legitimates each member's right to learn as much as his or her temperament and talent will allow. In the traditional organisation, the division of learning lent credibility to the legitimacy of imperative control. In an informated organisation, the new division of learning produces experiences that encourage a synthesis of members' interest, and the flow of value-adding knowledge helps legitimate the organisation as a learning community." (p. 394).

In terms of education and training this raises important issues about the way employers and managers make decisions about how they deploy new technology in the workplace, and the need to breakdown low trust and low discretion relations which often existed in the past and which many managers seek to preserve (Scase and Goffee, 1989).

If we are to shape the future in ways which will facilitate social progress, formal systems of education and training will need to prepare a much larger proportion of workers/citizens to contribute to the decision-making process and to be more self-directed. Moreover, as Kanter (1984) has noted, single-skilled people are unable to function in the kinds of cross-disciplinary teams that produce innovation, and are less adaptable when circumstances change (p. 368).

Deschooling society

A further problem which will need to be challenged is the tendency for education and learning to be treated as synonymous to schooling. Large numbers of people have become alienated from any kind of formal learning because of its association with early childhood experiences of schooling, which is often viewed as irrelevant because it rarely connected with the experience of daily life, and because for many it involves lasting feelings of inadequacy and failure. We do not subscribe to the view that specialised institutions of learning, such as the school, should be abolished. No "educational" system in the late twentieth century can be successfully organised on an ad hoc basis (involving a free market or otherwise). However, students need to be "educated" and not "schooled". The state and professional educators must avoid socialising the vast majority of students to believe that they do not have the "brains" to benefit from formal education because far greater emphasis will need to be placed on empowering students to believe that they can have an impact on the world around them.

An education for empowerment must include providing students with the "power tools" of personal confidence and the intellectual skills required to interpret the wealth of information and ideological dogma to which we are all exposed, in order to make considered judgements in both the public and private spheres of everyday life. Indeed, given the trend towards shorter working hours and working lives the education system must seek to provide the intellectual and practical "power tools" needed to empower people to participate in all spheres of social life.

Therefore an important aim of education will be to provide students with the ability and creativity to make critical judgements and to develop alternative modes of thought. Clearly, given the current pace of technological change, there is little point in teaching students specific skills which are non-transferable and may rapidly become obsolete.

It is also necessary to challenge the increasingly instrumental attitudes of students and their parents to formal education because it is turning the "diploma disease" into an epidemic. Moreover, complying to school rules for long periods of time in order to get through examinations clearly contributed to the trained capacities of middle managers in bureaucratic organisations, but the potential demand for creative and innovative people runs counter to the dictates of an increasingly competitive pursuit for credentials, because the overriding concern with grades tends to inhibit rather than develop the power tools required in high-trust and innovative organisations (Kanter, 1984; Brown and Scase, 1994). This problem has serious consequences for the future and makes a nonsense of claims that educational excellence can be measured in terms of numbers of credentials. What employers thought they wanted in the past, and used certificates as a measure, may be precisely what they do not want in the future. The only way of reducing the severity of this problem is by adopting a broader view of educational excellence, and employers reflecting this broader understanding in their recruitment practices.

In search of excellence

In our view, excellence in education is best achieved through a state-provided comprehensive system. The fact is that education differentiated according to privilege and status would militate against the promotion of collective intelligence. Recent evidence would lead us to suggest that the better the social mix of schools the better the performance of the majority of students (Lauder and Hughes, 1990). In other words, far from a proliferation of school types in competition, what is required is a well-maintained comprehensive state system. Parents would have some choice of school, but the general thrust of policy would be to generate high-trust relations between teachers and parents, given that schools would become a truly community resource, used daily by people of all ages. In general selection for the various routes into employment would be delayed as long as possible in order to provide the greatest opportunity for students' intelligence and creativity to flourish. A corollary of the principle of delayed selection is that as far as possible there should be open access to all forms of tertiary education and training. This will become increasingly important given that formal learning is a life-long process involving periods of re-training for employment purposes and given a growing demand for self-development.

Underlying these principles is the aim of developing a common educational culture. If a general aim of educating for a post-Fordist economy is to foster teamwork and co-operation, then just as the hierarchies and differential cultures distinctive of Fordist production would have to be discarded, so would the differential cultures which undermine contemporary schooling. This can only be achieved by breaking down the class, gender and racial barriers within systems of education and training.

If we are genuinely concerned to produce the labour force of the future, the educational and training systems must break down sexist (and racist) practices which operate against both girls and boys and foster the development of narrow gender-specific occupational preferences and skills by, among other things, reinforcing the processes through which boys enter metalwork, woodwork and technical design courses, and the girls get channelled into home economics, childcare and office practice. The reason why these social inequalities require serious attention results from the fact that all educational and training innovations confront the real acid test of how they shape future life chances. Although there is nothing inherently superior about receiving a narrow and intensive "academic" education, it is favoured because it has the most "cultural capital" and "exchange value" in the school and labour market. It is for this reason that virtually all programmes of vocational education have failed to provide a "parity of esteem" because they deny access to the real vocational prizes (Watts, 1983; Kantor and

81

Tyack, 1982). There are consequently strong social and educational grounds for developing a broad-based curriculum of academic, technical and practical study for all students at least during the compulsory school years.

There is also a need to stop thinking about excellence in elitist terms. Excellence should be defined in terms of the collective skills, knowledge and knowhow which can be deployed within a society as a whole. To achieve the latter, it is necessary to end our obsession with the "great man" and "token woman" view of history. Sustainable economic growth will increasingly depend on the collective efforts of executives, managers, researchers, teachers, child carers, shop-floor workers, etc., because significant technological advances are rarely the result of the efforts and insights of any one person. It is, therefore, equally important to challenge the excessive individualism which is endemic in western countries, such as the USA and Britain, which among other things leads employers to be more concerned with poaching skilled labour from each other than developing a mutual social obligation to train.

Conclusion

In this paper it has been argued that the transformation of the global economy is having profound implications for western systems of education and training. We have attempted to describe these changes against a backdrop of bureaucratic/Fordist organisational principles. Out of the Fordist crisis have emerged post-Fordist possibilities for lifelong learning. However, the realisation of this potential appears remote in nations which have pursued free market policies as a route to economic salvation. Such reforms conform to a neo-Fordist strategy which will lead to increasing social and economic polarisation in education, training and the labour market.

If post-Fordist possibilities are to stand any chance of being brought to fruition, an altogether different political agenda will need to be defined and contested. In the final section of this paper we have been able to do no more than outline one aspect of this New Left agenda focusing on the struggle for "collective intelligence". What is already clear, however, is that the way nation states are responding to these new challenges will determine whether lifelong learning will become a reality in the twenty-first century.

Phillip Brown and Hugh Lauder

References

Allen J (1992) "Post-industrialism and Post-Fordism", in S Hall et al (eds.) *Modernity and its Futures*, Cambridge: Polity

Ashton D N, Maguire M & Spilsbury M (1990) *Restructuring the Labour Market: The Implications for Youth*, London: Macmillan

Ball S (1990) *Education, Inequality and School Reform: Values in Crisis.* An inaugural lecture, Centre for Educational Studies, King's College, London

Bennis W (1972) "The Decline of Bureaucracy and Organisations of the Future", in J M Shepard (ed.) *Organizational Issues in Industrial Society*, Englewood Cliffs: Prentice-Hall

Bernstein B (1975) *Class, Codes and Control*, Vol.3, London: Routledge

Block F (1990) *Postindustrial Possibilities: A Critique of Economic Discourse*, Berkeley: California University Press

Boyd W & Cibulka J (eds.) (1989) *Private Schools and Public Policy*, London: Falmer

Braverman H (1974) *Labour and Monopoly Capital*, London: Jessica Kingsley

Brown P (1990) "The 'Third Wave': education and the ideology of parentocracy", *British Journal of Sociology of Education*, 11, pp. 65-85

Brown P (1994) "Cultural Capital and Social Exclusion: Some Observations on Recent Trends in Education, Employment and the Labour Market" (forthcoming)

Brown P & Lauder H (1992) "Education, economy and society: an introduction to a new agenda", in P Brown & H Lauder (eds.) *Education for Economic Survival: From Fordism to Post-Fordism?*, London: Routledge

Brown P & Scase R (1994) *Higher Education and Corporate Realities*, London: UCL Press

Brown P & Lauder H (1996) *Education, globalization and economic development, Journal of Education Policy*, Vol.11, 1-25

Cicourel A & Kitsuse J (1963) *The Education Decision-Makers*, New York: Bobbs-Merrill

Collins R (1979) *The Credential Society*, New York: Academic Press

Cooley M (1993) "Skills and Competence for the 21st Century", paper presented at the IITD 24th National Conference, Galway, April

Deakin S & Wilkinson F (1991) "Social Policy and Economic Efficiency: The Deregulation of the Labour Market in Britain", *Critical Social Policy*, 11, 3: 40-61

Dicken P (1992) *Global Shift: The Internationalisation of Economic Activity*, London: Paul Chapman

Fox A (1974) *Beyond Contract: Work, Politics and Trust Relations*, London: Faber and Faber

Gamble A (1988) *The Free Market and the Strong State*, London: Macmillan

Gerth H & Mills, C W (1948) *From Max Weber*, London: Routledge and Kegan Paul

Gramsci A (1971) *Selections from Prison Notebooks*, London: Lawrence and Wishart

Green A (1990) *Education and Information*, London: Macmillan

Green A & Steedman H (1993) *Education Provision, Educational Attainment and the Needs of Identity: A Review of Research for Germany, France, Japan, the USA and Britain*, London: NIESR

Halsey A H, Heath A & Ridge J (1980) *Origins and Destinations*: Oxford: Clarendon

Halsey A H, Lauder H, Brown P & Wells A S (1997) (Eds.) *Education: Culture, Economy, and Society*, Oxford: Oxford University Press

Halstead M (ed.) (1994) *Parental Choice and Education*, London: Kogan Page

Harvey D (1989) *The Conditions of Postmodernity*, Oxford: Blackwell

Henderson A & Parsons T (eds.) (1974) *Max Weber: The Theory of Social and Economic Organisation*, New York: Oxford University Press

Kanter R (1984) *The Change Masters*, London: Unwin

Kanter R (1989) *When Giants Learn to Dance*, London: Unwin

Kantor H & Tyack D (eds.) (1982) *Youth, Work and Schooling*, Stanford: Stanford University Press

Kohn M & Schooler C (1983) *Work and Personality: An Inquiry into the Impact of Social Stratification*, New Jersey: Ablex

Kumar K (1992) "New theories of industrial society", in P. Brown & H. Lauder (eds.) *Education for Economic Survival: From Fordism to Post-Fordism?*, London: Routledge

Lacey C (1988) "The Idea of a Socialist Education", in H Lauder & P Brown (eds.) *Education in Search of a Future*, Lewes: Falmer Press

Lane C (1989) *Management and Labour in Europe*, Aldershot: Edward Elgar

Lauder H (1987) "The New Right and Educational Policy in New Zealand", *New Zealand Journal of Educational Studies*, 22, pp. 3-23

Lauder H & Hughes D (1990) "Social inequalities and differences in school outcomes", *New Zealand Journal of Educational Studies*, 23, pp. 37-60

Lauder H et al (1994) *The Creation of Market Competition for Education in New Zealand*, Wellington, Ministry of Education

Lipietz A (1987) *Mirages and Miracles: The Crises of Global Fordism*, London: Verso

McGregor D (1960) *The Human Side of Enterprise*, New York: McGraw-Hill

Morgan G (1986) *Images of Organisations*, London: Sage

Murray C (1984) *Losing Ground: American Social Policy 1950-1980*, New York: Basic Books

Murray R (1989) "Fordism and Post-Fordism", in S Hall & M Jacques (eds.) *New Times*, London: Lawrence & Wishart

National Commission on Excellence in Education (1983) *A Nation at Risk: The Imperative for Educational Reform*, Washington: US Government Printing Office

OECD (1989) *Education and the Economy in a Changing World*, Paris: OECD

Piore M & Sabel C (1984) *The Second Industrial Divide: Possibilities for Prosperity*, New York: Basic Books

Reich R (1991) *The Work of Nations*, London: Simon and Schuster

Sabel C F (1982) *Work and Politics*, Cambridge: Cambridge University Press

Scase R & Goffee R (1989) *Reluctant Managers*, London: Unwin Hyman

Streeck W (1992) *Social Institutions and Economic Performance*, London: Sage

Toffler A (1990) *Powershift*, New York: Bantam

Watts A (1983) *Education, Unemployment and the Future of Work*, Milton Keynes: Open University Press

Willms J and Echols F (1992) "Alert and Inert Clients: The Scottish Experience of Parental Choice of Schools", *Economics of Education Review*, 11, pp. 339-350

Zuboff S (1988) *In the Age of the Smart Machine: The Future of Work and Power*, New York: Basic Books

Information society and normative action

Some tendencies in the contextualisation of individualisation in modern society

"Information society" has become a new metaphor for today's society. However, what this metaphor stands for is not obvious. Maybe it points to a society where new groups have gained influence by access to information technology. Maybe it points to a society where opinions are made or exchanged in the media. Maybe it is another way of focusing attention on the actual technological accelerator of modern living. Or maybe it points to the idea that information is the new basic building stone of social contexts and modern living. Neither commodities, ideologies, learning or money make the world go around but information does.

Part of the idea of this modern living as it is described in the metaphor of information society might look like this:

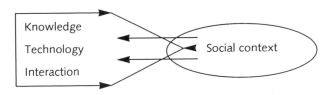

Knowledge, technology and social interaction are the tools of both the society and the individual and have become important in the construction of social contexts. And at the same time "social contexts" define or redefine the level and forms of knowledge, technology and interaction both at an individual and societal level. In this way our attention and reflections about the individual in the "information society" might point to new areas and to special ways of understanding the "contextualisation of individualisation" in modern society.

Diagram one: Sitting at home and watching the television

In the discussions of modern society we often look for changes in the relationship between the individual and the world. The argument sometimes follows the line of alienation. People have lost their authentic relation to the world, they only learn about life from the media. Media has placed itself as an information filter between the individual and the world. So, even though people know much more about the "global world" they have lost their own "local world". This pessimistic picture is sometimes criticised as having misunderstood or overlooked the perspective of global and local as not opposed but as defined and constructed by each other. And also it is criticised for having an old-fashioned or restricted theory of information exchange when information is seen as an interactive process in which messages are sent and received inside a specific media.

Today, however we might wonder if reality has not overtaken these theoretical discussions of information theory and society. We might even consider the value of the provocative position of McLuhan, who clearly challenged this understanding of information exchange by pointing to the opinion, that the media is the message. Without going into this debate it may seem that there have been some changes. Maybe the new situation of information society should mostly be understood as a "mixture of social contexts".

As an example we may point to the development of television. In recent years television seems to have invaded private homes in a new and provocative way. Television programmes such as "Jeopardy" or "Fortune wheel", etc. have created a total new situation. Television has become an expansion of the private living-room - or the private living-room an expansion of the television studio. We are not any longer concerned with sending information or giving information. We are concerned with "contextualisation of information". Not only has the media taken over the message, it has made the context of the media itself into the message.

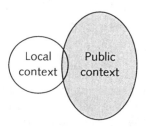

Diagram two: Peer learning

Another picture could be drawn from my own research in peer education. In Denmark peer education has increased in recent years. Peer education in Denmark should however not be seen as education or "informal education" as such. In the Danish version of peer education young people "teach" other young people to reflect on new areas and challenges of "youth life". They establish social contexts of common reflection, and they develop new ways of constructing modern life styles. In reflection on the youth situation young people point to the necessity of taking part in decisions and learning to take responsibility for their own lives.

In the interviews the young people underline that they often feel that adults want to teach them how to behave and not "why they should do something". So, they stress that they themselves want to find reasons for doing and to find out how things function. They want to become knowledgeable of what they do. And in this situation they often feel opposed to adult institutions and society.

In the peer education situation of developing new youth contexts and contextual understanding and reflection the youngsters feel frustrated. At the same time as participation is emphasised as necessary to modern development they feel that all "decisions" are moved further and further away from everyday life. For young people this situation of "alienated democratisation" seems strange. And they feel it to be a general situation including adults too. At the same time as participation and responsibility are stressed in society the serious decisions of future development are moved out of reach. They engage in the development of "modern democratic participation" at local level and their own lives, at the same time as they experience that influence, it has become limited as a result of "globalisation". In this way they become critical actors in modernity.

The first perspective

In 1985 James S Coleman and Thorsten Husén wrote *Becoming Adult in a Changing Society*.[1] The book was produced by the OECD as the theoretical part of a broad empirical project which should give information about the process of transition to adulthood as it took place in the member states.

One central aspect of this work is its focus on youth development as a transition and as a socialisation process. The book pointed to the different changes in society and in social institutions which caused the socialisation process to change, but mostly it looked at youth as more or less passive and conducted through "youth life" into adulthood.

In this way the book possibly could be seen as the product of an era in both "youth life" and youth research. The focus on norms and attitudes, on learning in socialisation and on the adaptive tasks of the different institutions, all point to the challenge of individual integration in social and adult life – or it pointed back to the hope for normative integration.

Though social integration is still of course the overall perspective of individual development, social integration has changed its focus from mostly normative adaptation, and "youth life" its character of "transition". Today youth development is not only a "transition". "Youth life" has developed its own perspective of individualisation as a quality in itself. Modern individualisation points to personal influence and participation in the developing of modern life as such and not only to integration as becoming part of an established society. Young people should not only become adults they should also develop their individuality.

---

1 Coleman, James S & Husén, T (1985): *Becoming Adult in a Changing Society*, Centre for Educational Research and Innovation, (Ceri), OECD Paris.

In this way, our understanding of social integration and youth development underlines the new aspects of participation and contextualisation. And one central aspect is that modern society integrates young people by the use of individualisation and "contextualisation".

Young people become "youth actors" in modern society. However, they are not "free" to do whatever they want. They have to learn the new rules of modern participation.

Challenges of modern individualisation

When we look at some of the challenges of individualisation in modern life they become visible in contrast to a, maybe too simple, picture of the lost world. Post or late modernistic theory points to very complicated and demanding perspectives of individual development. Inspired by the work of Giddens (Giddens 1987, 1991) we might draw this illustrative picture:

From: Traditional society	To: Modern society
Find one's place in time and space: Learn social rules	Live across time and space: Develop self-identity
Have confidence in expertise and authorities: Develop faith in authorities	Use different authorities and types of expertise: Develop reflexivity and self-assurance
Have confidence in everyday life: Live inside traditions and qualifications	Integrate in social life: Develop individual skills
Handle conflicts: Learn basic social skills and interests	Handle conflicts: Have ontological security

This general picture of modern individualisation tells that individuals today live in an open world. They move around and should develop activities and some sort of self-understanding which makes them able to reflect and become discursive about themselves, others and the way people refer to each other in a changing society. But, it also tells about the dangers of not being able to live up to the world. Individuals today are in danger of losing their self-understanding and their confidence in themselves.

When "youth life" of today is often described as increasingly complicated and demanding, this description may point to some of the demands which follow from the changes in individualisation. These changes, however, do not necessarily indicate that young people should be seen as individually "at risk" as formulated in more recent theories (Beck 1992, Furlang and Cartmel 1997). Individuals do not develop in an isolated or de-contextual way. They develop as part of "youth life", and "youth life" is a social and cultural context which is formed during this developmental process.[1]

---

1 Maybe the understanding of young people as being "at risk" follows from a traditional dichotomy in understanding the individual and society.

The question, then, does not seem to be whether individualisation has become more demanding. The question seems to be, how modern "youth life" as a social context fulfils the new demands and which sorts of problems have become important in this new situation.

When focus is set on individualisation in youth, a first picture of modern "youth life" may point to the following perspectives:

Because of the "function" of "youth life" as the time of life for young people to develop into members of a "modern individualistic society", "youth life" of today has become increasingly central to individual development. Also, the new demands on individualisation seem to have prolonged "youth life". Maybe to such a degree, that youth development "burst its borders" to fulfil its "function". Not only do young people become "young" earlier in their lives, but "youth life" is also prolonged. This prolongation creates new "youth life" styles and perspectives, as seen in the "young adults" concept.[1]

Challenges of individual development

Before we go into the discussion of the changes in modern youth we might draw some perspectives of theoretical and practical significance for the understanding of individual development. The first requirement for a new understanding of individualisation which takes account of its contextual basis is that it should overcome the traditional ways of focusing either on the individual or society.[2] To do this focus may be set on the activities which "make" the individual or create "the social self".[3]

If we look at individual activity and maybe think of youth at the same time, this simple model gives an overall picture:

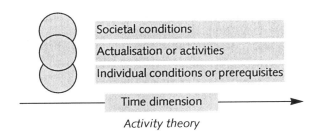

Activity theory

1 See Mørch, S (1996) Young adults. *Psychological Yearbook*, Tuskulæum, København and Walther (Hrsg) (1997): *Junge Erwachsene in Europa*, Leske & Budrich.
2 It has become more and more obvious that "the understanding of the individual" belongs to two different theoretical approaches in social psychology: a psychological social psychology and a sociological social psychology. See e.g. Graumann, C F: Introduction to a History of Social Psychology in: Hewstone, Stroebe, Stephenson(eds): *Introduction to Social Psychology*, Blackwell, 1996 (1988).
3 This "constructive position" is developed in many theories today. From Giddens to the constructionist. See e.g. Giddens, A: *The Constitution of Society*, Polity Press 1987 and Potter & Wetherell: *Discourse and Social Psychology*, Sage 1994 (87).

The model shows how activities and self-understanding should be seen as contextual construction or as "actualisation" of social and individual conditions in a specific situation or social context. This perspective might appear naive in social science if it is only understood as focusing on the "individual in society". However, its point is to overcome, on the one hand, the traditional psychological picture of the individual as an entity and individuals as "doing something" or maybe unfolding oneself in social situations, and on the other hand, the social determinism of much sociological thinking which, by looking at the individual as a "social actor", seems to disregard the real activities and intentions of the individual.[1] The difficulties of using this perspective seem to be, that we still might talk about the individual doing something in a society, but without assuming an individualistic or sociologistic perspective.

The meaning of actualisation with its dual function of using social and individual conditions active in the development of individual activity becomes more understandable when we look at its different aspects. On the one hand, people use societal conditions or acts inside conditions as possibilities and constraints of action. Conditions, then, should be seen as both rules and resources of action as they are developed in history and society. Conditions as historically developed possibilities and constraints on human activity are often contradictory and diffuse. For this reason the individual both uses and changes societal conditions in his/her activity. Societal conditions exist in social contexts, they are organised in and organise social contexts, for example in the case of the school system and school curriculum: school as a social context of youth in this way exhibits the possibilities and constraints of "youth life", but at the same time youth is part of the process of changing the school.

On the other hand, the individual uses his/her own previous experiences and personal capacities as his/her individual tools or conditions of action. In actualisation of societal conditions, the individual uses him/herself. He or she actualises his or her own potentialities in the situation and according to the conditions of the situation. Through this process, the individual develops him/herself and further capacities.

In actualisation, the way individuals understand both societal and individual conditions plays a central role.[2] To the individual, different aspects of both societal and individual conditions seem important or meaningful. And the particular conditions the individual finds important in the specific situation are crucial to the mastering of actual problems or tasks, and the conditions

1 See e.g. Potter, J & Wetherell, M: *Discourse and Social Psychology*, Sage 1994 (87), Sarbin, T R & Kitsuse, J I (eds.): *Constructing the social*, Sage, 1994. Mørch, S *Handlingsteorien* in Udkast, Copenhagen 1994.
2 The importance of individual understanding of social conditions in individual activity is stressed in *Critical Psychology*, (Holzkamp, K 1983, Tolman, C W & W Maiers 1991). Giddens' focus is more on the meaning of being conscious and the importance of the discursiveness of the situation (Giddens 1987).

the individual finds important in understanding his or her own life are important to the development of individual self-understanding.

The development of this self-understanding, however, takes place in the social relationship in the context. Social relations and social interaction are crucial in actualisation. In the development of activities it is important to be part of and belong to a social context.

So, the actualisation of societal conditions is the project of more involved individuals, and forms of mastering or actualisation exist in the social context. They are developed forms of activities according to the understanding of possibilities and constraints of social life. Youth cultures, for example, should be seen as such forms of meaningful activity patterns. Youth cultures are activities carried out by youngsters in mastering "youth life". Individuals learn from each other, they interact and they develop new forms of activities to overcome and solve contradictions in societal conditions.[1]

By taking part in social interaction in youth contexts individuals develop activities by the use of individual preconditions. The development of forms of actualisation, then, should not only be seen as being brought about by societal conditions but also influenced by individuals. Shared individual conditions, however, do not determine forms of actualisation in a simple way. Individual conditions should be seen as tools or means of actualisation and their influence should be understood in this respect.

The activity theory model now points to more conclusions. Individuals act within social contexts. In doing so, they share and develop experiences of social action, so, individuals and society should not be seen as basically "contradictory", as was often presented in the "critical theory" of the 1970s.[2] Contradictions exist mainly within or among societal conditions or within individual conditions, not between the individual and societal levels in a general way. Societal conditions and individual conditions are the tools of actualisation, and even though they sometimes seem far from each other, they are the rules and resources of actualisation.

Another aspect of this way of formulating an activity theory is that the individual, by being part of the social youth context, develops him/herself. He or she develops individuality as "tracks" of activities. Individuals build their own tracks in actualisation of societal and individual conditions.

---

1 This culture or youth culture perspective indicates that not only spectacular "cultures" should be considered. Youth culture represents plural activities (thinking and doing) which young people develop in mastering ordinary "youth life". School culture seems to be especially important. It also indicates that culture should mostly be seen as "cultural reproduction" in social contexts and not as "tradition".

2 This was the basic idea of the critical socialisation theory. Brücker, P: *Zur Sozialpsychologie des Kapitalismus*, Frankfurt, 1972, Vinnai, G: *Sozialpsychologie der Arbeiterklasse*, Rohwoldt, Hamburg, 1973.

A general model of youth development as development of youth activities and individual "tracks" based on societal and individual conditions may look like this:

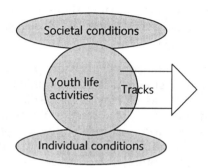

An activity model of youth development

As a consequence of this way of thinking, individuality of the young person is seen as a contextual construction made and changed by the use of different youth contexts. This explains both the similarities and the differences in young people. Youth contexts are common contexts for many young people but the way they participate in the contexts varies.

Individuals and individual tracks in modern living

Modern western and especially Scandinavian "youth life" in many ways has become bewildering. On the one hand we talk about youth problems and youth at risk. We point to modern family life as vanishing, to childhood as unprotected, to parents as missing or careless. Also youth unemployment, educational difficulties and adolescence come to the fore when youth is discussed.

On the other hand "youth life" has become "affluent". In a minor study of mine where I compared Danish and Siberian youth, one of the more astonishing facts was the different perspectives of "youth life". Siberian youth seemed much engaged in "youth life" as a transition to adult life. Danish youth seemed to like being young or experiencing "youthhood", but they seemed bewildered about their own life perspectives.[1] "Youthhood" had become affluent but undirected at the same time. "Youth life" seemed to have been a goal in itself for the making of an individual and affluent life, but it had become difficult to see it as a condition for adult life.

Some of the reasons for this "modern" development, which have made "youth life" a goal in itself, may be that "youth life" in many respects has

---

1 This perspective in "youth life" was developed in a comparative study of Danish and Russian youth. See Mørch, S (1993): *Dansk eller russisk ungdomsliv*, Psykologisk Laboratorium, København.

94

been democratised and made easy to enter. School life is accessible to all. And school curriculum, in the Scandinavian countries, has mostly been abolished in favour of supporting the youngsters' own interests and perspectives.[1] Also, youth has become the focus group of media, and particularly a steadily growing field of youth media. Youth has become the ultimate goal of late modern society. As also Giddens points out: the body has become central, and the body exposition is youth exposition.[2]

So in many ways we might be engaged in understanding some of these problems and forms of "youth life" as specific and obviously contradictory aspects of modern "youth life". And in some ways we might immediate analyse youth within these contradictions. Youth might be seen as both problematic and affluent.

However, to understand young people within the contradictions of "youth life" we should remember the broader perspective of societal individualisation. Contradictions should not only be seen as defined by "youth life" but as contradictions of modern life. It is not "youth life" in itself which has become affluent and contradictory, it is modern life as such. Modern "youth life" has become an established societal condition for modern individualisation, and this in itself explains its contradictions. "Youth life" has been subjugated by general social life and in this way subjugated its problems of modern social integration as based on an extreme individualisation.

This situation creates a challenge in "youth life". Individualisation has become contradictory. On the one hand individualisation seems to be the precondition for modern development and on the other hand it points to a private existence within "youth life". "Youth life" is the time for education and as such it has become central to social development. At the same time it has become a goal in itself and preoccupied with its own perspectives. This contradiction maybe is a part of the more general problem of a contradiction between modern integrative life and differentiation. "Youth life" has become a general condition of integration and differentiation to all young people. "Youth life" has become a unifying condition of individual differentiation.

The educational challenge of youth today

If we look at Danish society and the organisation of its educational system we find the basis of a new youth challenge which we may call the challenge of a contextual societal individualisation.

Since the 1960s, Danish "youth life" has become more or less uniform for all youngsters. To fulfil democratic goals, to get the intelligent working-class kids in front, and to meet modern technological requests, school has devel-

---

1 Mørch, S (1995): *Den sociale uredelighed*, Unge pædagoger vol 6. København.
2 Giddens, A: *Modernity and self-identity*, Polity Press, Oxford 1991.

oped its new goals as "equality through education". This means that most youngsters, both boys and girls, have been offered the same conditions of school and "youth life" and for this reason, in principle the same opportunities in work and adult life. This development is perhaps not the cause, but it is a central condition of modern "youth life". It shows that individualisation as an educational and societal development has become the main task of school life at the same time as school life has become "the same" for most youngsters. "Youth life" has become not only the time for "growing up", but the time for social change. And school and education have become the main tools and contexts for this change.

"Youth life" today no longer changes the child into a adult within the original social group or class. Today "youth life" both moves the youngster from childhood into adult life, and moves the youngster away from his family social position into new social positions. "Youth life" today has become a context of societal individualisation in a new sense, an individualisation according to new social positions. "Youth life" individualisation has become the principal institution of modern social mobility: Individualisation for a society based on educational qualifications.

The significance of modern Danish "youth life" may be shown like this:

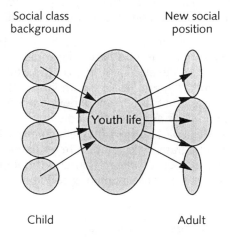

The modern youth challenge

The figure shows the "transforming" character of "youth life" at the individual level, and at the same time points to the general contemporary change of modern "class society" to a less class-based organisation of different income groups. This model shows how the period of "youth" has become not only an "individual transformer", changing children into adults, but a "social transformer" too: by use of the educational youth contexts the individual may be able to change his or her social position. "Youth life" has become the central means of social mobility. And social mobility both means to "go up" and to "come down".

The consequences of the creation of this "new youth life" are extensive. Firstly, young people today have become less dependent on social background and family conditions. The making of the future is their own responsibility. Secondly, "youth life" has become important for an individual's adult social position.

In this way, "youth life" has become fundamental and much more important to youth. The way young people engage and cope with youth conditions has become crucial for their future social position and adult life. Young people have to create their own social position through individual engagement in "youth life". For this reason "youth life" has become the central challenge in individual development. Youth success or failure has become part of "youth life". "Youth life" involvement governs young people's future much more than ever before. "Youth life" is not only a "transition", it has itself become an integrated part of social life.

This picture of youth is now part of a commonsense understanding which may be easily illustrated: thirty years ago, when a girl invited her new boyfriend home, her parents asked him about his father's occupation. Today the parents ask the boyfriend about his own education or involvement in "youth life". The interest is the same, only the question has changed.

This picture also shows why modern "youth life" has become "stressful". Individual success or failure seems to follow from individual activities in the educational system. This situation makes "youth life" into a competition and a problem for the individual. It causes youth problems. Obviously, the individual needs greater support to manage this situation, or perhaps he or she needs a prolongation of "youth life", which not only gives the individual more time, but supports individual development by offering a "new" structure of individual development. Before, "youth life" was part of a social class society, which made "youth life" "secure" for those who had one. Today "youth life" seems to have become an educational and individual battlefield.

The question in this situation seems to be: What happens to the group of youngsters which does not belong to or function in educational society?

New demands for understanding: modern "youthhood"[1]

"Youth life" organises some of the contexts as "steps" of individual societal integration. It constitutes "youthhood". And the individual develops his own personality and self-understanding by "stepping forward". In this perspective "youth life" and the individual life might be seen as a developmental

---

1 I propose the concept of "youthhood" as a parallel to childhood. As such the concept points to the time of adolescent development. Though the concept does not exist in the English language it is most common in Scandinavian languages.

career. In the making of an individual self we may talk about the individual "working on his/her track".

Concepts of individual development

In "youth life" understanding more concepts has become popular in recent years. Often they are seen as unproblematic descriptive and analytical conceptualisations of "youth development". Most well-known is the traditional concept of identity but other concepts have become competitors in youth understanding. Giddens concept of self-understanding and Bourdieu's concepts of habitus and cultural capital have inspired youth theory, too. When I propose to talk about tracks and social contexts I want to stress the aspect of youth development which to me has become most important: Youth today is mostly engaged in life course development as the continuous management of social contexts. And for this reason they themselves are aware of the making of the individual life course, the individual track.

The concept of track should be seen as an attempt to broaden the perspective of the trajectory concept used by Giddens. Trajectory points to the course of a projectile. In this way it may give the impression of a "life course". However, projectile trajectories may be predicted and calculated by ballistics. This makes the concept open to misapprehension. Though the concept points to the activity perspective it creates confusion. Individual life courses are not predictable. Giddens' trajectory concept either seems to point to a fixed "life course" in a "traditional society" or it seems to result from his emphasis on making early childhood a determining cause of the life story.[1] The trajectory metaphor may give the impression that individual life is "caused" and not "conditioned".

This does not mean that concepts such as identity, trajectory, self-understanding, habitus and cultural capital should not be used in youth research, but that they should be used according to the perspective they refer to in "youth life". They might be seen as descriptive and analytical concepts for underlining results of the basic involvement of young people in the making of their own track into adulthood. The way young people engage in their lives leads at the same time to the development of e.g. identity, self-understanding, a specific habitus and level of cultural capital in the individual.

Youth development, obviously, contains many goals or aspects. Some of the most important are: "Being", "knowing", and "doing". The question seems to be which aspects should be focused on youth understanding. Up to now "being", or identity, has been seen as basic to youth development.[2] Young people have been seen as fighting against family and parents to develop their own identity. Maybe the new or modern youth development has changed this situation. The development of young people today takes part in "public"

---

1 In Giddens' theory "the ontological security" seems to play a most important part in the future development of the child.
2 This seems most obvious when we think of the popularity of Erikson's theories even today.

youth contexts and not in "private" family life. Young people do not any longer primarily fight for their own identity. They fight for their place in youth contexts, they fight for the building of the individual "track". This maybe makes "knowing" or "doing" the most important aspects and challenge of modern "youth life" and the basis of the development of identity.

Youth making of tracks

The concept of track might be seen as pointing to the effort of the individual to making his best way into society. Tracks refer to both the making of one's own "route" as to the "trail" one leaves when moving. In talking about the interest in making one's own track we focus on the involvement of the individual in the making of his own life as a linked building of an increasing contextual integration into societal and social life.

The individual uses societal youth conditions in the making of his own track, his meaningful activities and self-understanding. This means that individual development as an individual track is a process of the individual him/herself, but it is made possible by the context of modern "youth life", of the existence of modern "youth life" as a sort of map or landscape. ·

This perspective might be made visibly by the theory of social reorganisation.[1] The model shows the basic idea of this theory. It illustrates that development is organised by societal contexts but is lived by individuals rethinking and rearranging their own lives as they move ahead. They develop activities and construct the meaning of their lives by looking forward. Or they construct the meaning of their lives by reconstructing their past according to the future. They reorganise past relations according to the future.[2]

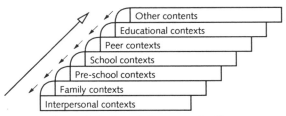

A model of social reorganisation

1 The theory of social reorganisation is formulated in Mørch, S (1990): *Ungdomsteori og intervention i Udkast 1*. The point in this formulation is to focus individual social development as a societal development. A parallel but more contextual perspective exists in modern constructionist theories about the making of the social selves, e.g. in Potter, J & Wetherell, M (1992): *Discourse and social psychology*, Sage, London or Burkitt, I (1991): *Social Selves*, Sage, London. A more psychological perspective on this relation between past and future of course exists in Erikson, E H (1963): *Childhood and society*, Norton, New York and later in Ziehe, T (1982): *Plädoyr für ungewöhnliches Lernen, Ideen zur Jugendsituation*, Rowolt, Hamburg.
2 The same perspective may be found in narrative theory as e.g. Mattingly, Ch (1991): *Narrative Reflections on Practical Actions: Two Learning Experiments in Reflexive Storytelling*. in: Schön, D A (ed): The Reflective Turn, Teachers College Press, New York, or Nicander, P (1995): *The Turn to the Text: The Critical Potential of Discursive Social Psychology*, Nordiske Udkast, København.

So, the point of the model is simple. Individual life development is the development of a contextual individual track as it is "organised by society", but it stays an individual challenge. When the individual moves ahead he/she has to re-reflect the past and future perspectives. When, for example, peer relations develop they help the individual to manage school and family relations. To be more precise the societal organisation of development makes it the individual challenge. However, combined with the above-mentioned individualisation and competition perspectives of modern life, new conditions do not only provide new individual developmental possibilities. At the same time they make individual life part of a societal differentiation. Often the individual, in the making of his own track, has to come to terms with social injustice in his own self-understanding - and maybe, because of the individualised world view, he feels social injustice as more or less caused by his own failure.[1]

"Youth life" of course is an individual challenge, but it is a challenge which is helped and directed by social and material conditions. "Youth life" is the frame or organiser of the individual track. And for this reason modern youth shares conditions and problems but not always their solutions. Young people today become diversified, not only because of the existence of diversified "youth life" possibilities, but by using individualised "youth life" conditions.

In this modern making of the individual track, democratic and associative participation by young people has become a central "youth life" condition. Not only as a passive condition but as an aid to reflect societal conditions and individual tracks. So, youth participation should be seen as part and partner in youth integration and development. It should help youngsters build their own tracks.

Learning from social science – norms or formulae

Should we transform this picture of modern individualisation to some more general challenges in modern "youth life" we might focus on what might be called the change in "youth life" from "normative youth" to "contextual youth" or from "learned norms to negotiated normativity".

The point in this description is to learn from the changes in modern sociology. If sociological theories are seen as historical constructs themselves, the development in sociological theory tells a story which maybe is more interesting than the story of the individual theories. We might focus on the change which has taken place from a Parsonian to an ethnomethodological and maybe constructionist position in sociology.[2]

Parsons' theory pointed to norms as the "cause" of action. Action was explained with reference to individual norms. For this reason Parsons' theory pointed to socialisation as the process for learning norms and the family as

---

1 This perspective seems to follow from the idea of "taking responsibility for your own life". If something goes wrong you only have yourself to blame.
2 Mørch, S (1994), *Handlingsteorien*, Udkast, København.

the place where this learning took, and should, take place. Ethnomethodological theory may be seen as a critical protest against this idea of "normative action". Ethnomethodology stressed that norms should not be seen as types of behaviour but as formulae of social activity. Norms only existed as the building "principles" of social contexts. This position seems to be even more elaborated in social constructionism, where social life is seen as mostly a social construction made by the help of common rules or formulae.

The development may be shown like this:

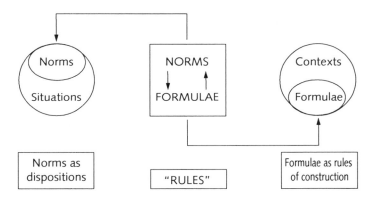

If we consider some of the changes which are understood and formulated in this development of modern sociology and use them to focus on youth development we might find, that modern youth individualisation points to the challenge of making youth the constructors of modern social life and individual tracks and not the followers of parental normative expectations.

In my view some basic aspects of this change in modern "youth life" could be characterised as a change from a normative "creation" of youth by family, school teachers, and youth workers, to a social contextual and individual self-development of youth.

This change started in the western societies in the 1960s but has become a global change which influences local youth development. It has followed the development in the educational systems towards more equal or democratic educational patterns and also the commercialisation of "youth life".

The main changes of this situation may be formulated as:

– a growing individualisation in "youth life" (a challenge to solve social position problems by individualisation);

– a change from learned normative behaviour to negotiated normativity (a change of behavioural rules from "normative values" to "formulae of construction").

These changes have, on the one hand, made young people more involved and responsible for their own lives. Young people have become participants in the making of individual "youth life" and tracks and in this way formulating modern global "youth life" as a local project.

On the other hand, the demands concerning the making of their own lives in combination with the extreme individualisation have created challenges and problems for young people. This second perspective has become most popular in modern youth theory as it is, for example, formulated by Beck in the concept of "risk society".[1] With this way of thinking it seems obvious that if opportunities are difficult to use, they may turn to demands against the individual. In this way, the opportunities of modern youth individualisation create youth problems and problem youth. More and more young people become losers in the competition of modernisation. They need skills for participation and they become isolated from peers. We may talk about a political and ideological making of individualised and drop-out youth.

Though this perspective perhaps contains some truth it does not give the whole story. At the same time as "youth life" has become an individual challenge, it has also become contextualised in new forms. The individualisation process is not necessarily an "individual" matter. Young people are individualised in the making of tracks in "youth life" contexts. The problems for young people perhaps stem from the marginalisation of young people, which today has become part of youth contexts. Before young people were made to be different because they came from different social classes. Today they are differentiated within school and educational contexts.

These problems are not easy to overcome. Individualisation and becoming the individual maker of one's own life is a necessary and demanding process in modern "youth life" even if it does not necessarily have to be an individualistic process.

"Youth life" as the path

Without going into a broad analysis of the history of youth development, it is possible to draw a simple, overall picture of "youth life" today as it exists as the condition of individual development. Youth conditions today exist within social arenas or social contexts. This model shows the principal organisation of modern "youth life":

---

1 See Beck, U: Risk Society. Towards a New Modernity, Sage, London 1992, Furlang, A & Cartmel, F: Young People and Social Change, Open University Press, Buckingham, 1997. Also Giddens focus on individualisation tells the same story. See Giddens, A: Modernity and Self-identity, Polity Press 1991.

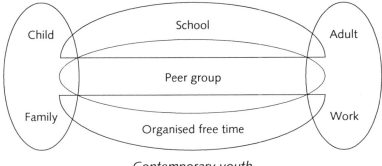

Contemporary youth

In the development of "youth life", school life is – still – the fundamental developer and organiser. But today several other contexts organise conditions of youth development. They offer conditions for the development of different forms of competence or qualifications for adult life.

Primary and secondary schools were originally separated into different institutions. In this way children and youth were defined within the school system. Today this has changed. Danish children, for example, go to the same school from the first to tenth grade and the school develops the difference between children and youth within its curriculum by the way the teachers deal with the children/youngsters. To be a child or a young person has become a contextual social construction defined and redefined in the situation.[1] This difference between a child and a young person could perhaps be conceptualised as a difference in developmental goals. Children are expected to develop active self-management while young people are expected to develop qualified self-determination.[2]

So, school life organises the development of the pupils according to the curriculum of the school which is established as "the way to become a grown-up" in contemporary society. In this way school organises developmental conditions for the development of qualified self-determination. And as it has already been shown this process also differentiates children according to futher developmental steps.

As more and more children have stayed on at school, leisure time has developed. From the beginning of this century leisure time has become the object of several political and pedagogical interventions. Leisure time activities

---

1 The separation of children and young people in the school system was supplemented by a separation of boys and girls. It would be interesting to use this perspective to analyse how gender differences were and are constructed in everyday school life, and how youth and gender are constructed together – perhaps some contradictions exist in the field!

2 The change between being a child and a young person as organised in school environment might be shown by the use of project work. Children are expected to learn from the teachers, young people are expected to be active partners in the learning process by taking part in deciding the content of education.

should support young people and prevent youngsters from posing a problem. Today most young people in Denmark join "youth clubs" for a period, and youth clubs have become the context of "informal teaching" or development of social skills. Scout movements, sports and pedagogical work all offer possibilities for "youth life". Historically, these organised parts of "youth life" have focused on the social development of youth. In recent years the goals of individual social development have particularly been democratic social participation.

In Denmark, since the end of the 1950s, the youth group or peer group has become more influential. The peer group came into existence as "youth life" became accepted by adults and the young people themselves. Youth had to become a "broad" and accepted phenomenon to make a "free" "youth life" acceptable. However, as described, the peer group today is gaining influence in the lives of young people. In the peer group, youngsters may learn forms of activity to master "youth life" and they learn to co-operate and become part of a social group.

The overall picture of youth today is that "youth life" conditions exist as a possibility for all youngsters. However, "youth life" as actualisation of youth conditions varies. "Youth life" today is open to all, but it is actualised in different ways by different youth groups.

Problems of "youth life"

Until now, "youth life" has been described in its basic construction and development. "Youth life", however, is not only harmonious. "Youth life" contains contradictions, which cause it to vary and become a serious challenge to young people. "Youth life" contradictions also create varied "youth life" actualisation and in this way make "youth life" change. If the contextual organisation of "youth life" is focused upon it may show some of these challenges to modern "youth life".

"Youth life" as a time of societal individualisation and as a transformer between family and work life is sensitive to modern development. The more family life and work life become separated in time and space, the more difficult the change from child to adult becomes. No other period in history or in individual human life demands such a change of personality as we see today. The extension of "youth life" seems reasonable merely due to this fact. The prolongation of "youth life" seems necessary to make personality change and development possible. To become competent in the modern world, more and more young people are placed in educational systems for longer and longer periods of their lives. For this reason they stay young, or they are defined as young people in terms of adult occupations. They are partly considered as youth and partly as adults. They will become "young adults":

104

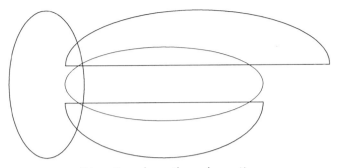

Educational youth prolongation

Naturally, "youth life" in an organised, professional social context has changed in this process of modernisation. The school and educational system have changed. School has developed its curriculum and pedagogical methods, and leisure time possibilities have developed accordingly. The difficulties of "youth life" have been given better support. But at the same time the expectations of adult life have become increasingly demanding, creating pressure on "youth life". "Youth life" is in many ways becoming more and more difficult for the individual to manage, and demands on motivation, involvement and understanding become crucial for the individual's own development.

Contemporary "youth life" also encounters other serious problems. Due to unemployment and limited possibilities for further education, "youth life" does not always look as we may expect. To many young people, no adult life possibilities seem to be open. They will have no further education and no job.

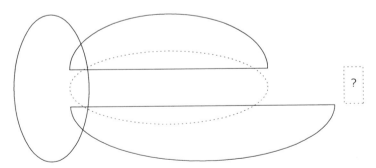

Youth with short education and without a future

To young people in this situation, involvement in organised "youth life", in school and organised leisure time activities poses a problem. It is difficult to see any perspectives or goals and for this reason involvement in youth educational contexts does not perhaps seem "worth the trouble". This explains the fact that for many young people, "youth life" is seen as an obstacle to adult development, so they leave school, education and pedagogical youth activities.

In this situation the peer group may be the only social context for the youngsters. Within the peer group, young people may find a social life which they themselves can make meaningful, as is shown in this model:

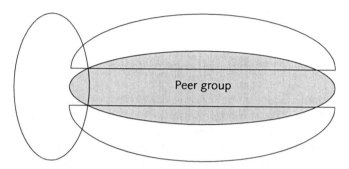

The peer group youth

The peer group may be important for social youth development, and often "youth life" and projects develop from this "modern" "youth life". But the isolated use of the youth peer group often develops into a problem situation. If young people do not use the broad social youth contexts such as school and youth clubs they may face developmental problems. Often they feel rejected from educational contexts and the peer group becomes the only path to adult life. In this situation they will experience problems in getting a job in the modern "educational world".

The "container youth" situation

The problem of offering further education and jobs to young people has caused a change in "youth life" as a societal, organised time of adult development. More and more young people leave school without any possibility

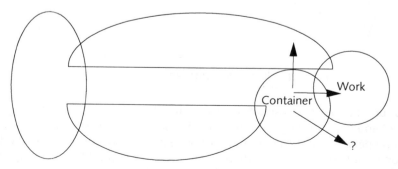

Container youth development

106

of further education or career directions. They become young unemployed. The official answer to this situation may be the making of youth unemployment projects of various kinds. In this way a new "youth life" is created – "container youth" – a context for young people for whom no other possibilities exist:

The interesting aspect of this situation is however that "container youth life" involves youth with very different life perspectives. Although they are all seen as "unemployed", they themselves may have different perspectives in their lives. Some hope to return to education, some hope for work, and some have no adult work plans. What is common to "container youth" is that they are kept young or as "young adults" in the sense of not being admitted to the adult world.

So, several varieties of "youth life" exist today. These diagrams, may be sufficient to show some of the basic problems of modern "youth life".

Consequences for "youth life" empowerment and intervention

Youth projects

"Youth life" has become a project for young people in the sense that they should develop their tracks in a situation with many unknown conditions and perspectives. But because "youth life" has been "created" it is possible to influence this "creation". Maybe not so much in changing the general youth contexts as such, but in supporting the individual in the making of his or her own self or track. The youth project may be supported.

Youth projects in their broadest sense – as organised activities planned to develop goals for young people – should be seen as contexts for youth support. They should empower youth in the making of modern "youth life" and in the development of the individual tracks. Youth projects in youth clubs, schools, youth organisations, etc. may help young people to build their own "life project" but at the same time help them to overcome some of the privatisation and individualisation of individual development. Youth projects should be planned to help individual tracks to develop inside the overall possibilities of societal development.

Youth activities and projects should establish "paths" for adult life or "maps" in which young people may be helped in developing their own track.

To do this we should develop more knowledge about possible mappings and a greater awareness of "means to an end" thinking in everyday life. At the same time the planning process should be "open" to discussion to make the participants themselves part of the making of "youth life". Activities should be reflected to develop a more discursive understanding and reflective actions.[1]

---

1 See Schön, D A: *The Reflective Practitioner*, Basic Books. N.Y. 1983, Argyris, C et al: *Action Science*, Jossey-Bass, San Francisco, 1985.

The point of planning activities as "projects" is exactly this necessary reflection which makes the individual discursive about youth goals, means and results.

The main requirement for project planning is that it ensures that the project activities or "interventions" are developed as appropriate "actions" to the problems we wish to tackle, and that they bring about desirable consequences. The basic elements of a project, therefore, are the problem definition, the activity planning, and the development of goals or results according to the specific youth group or individual young person. The activities should be regarded as the means that could be chosen to further the goals of the project, and for this reason attention must be focused on the relevancy of activities or means to the problem of the target group (planning action strategies), and the relevancy of activities or means to goals or results (planning for results).

It is possible to set up these requirements as a list of items for the project plan. During project planning it is necessary to ensure the following:
– clarify the problem that we mean to deal with;
– clarify the goals to be attained;
– develop the means, interventions or activities to be applied;
– go through with the activities as planned;
– create consequences or results;
– evaluate consequences as relevant to the project and target group development.

In project planning a very important kind of knowledge should be used: knowledge of modern "youth life" and tracks (youth theory) and knowledge about intervention planning (pedagogical knowledge).

One way of combining the requirements of project planning has been developed in my "project model". It stresses the planning requirements in the development of youth projects:[1]

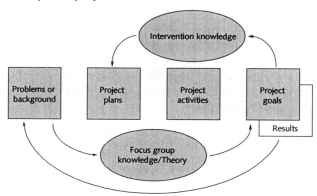

The project model

1 The model has been developed as a planning and evaluation model for Danish youth club projects. See Mørch, S (1993) *Ungdomsprojekter*, Rubikon, København (English version: *Youth projects – A guide to planned youth work*, Psychological Laboratory, Copenhagen), Mørch, S (1993) *Projektbogen. Teori og metode i projektplanlægning*, Rubikon, København.

When using the model, problems and goals should be developed together. General "youth" goals should be made specific project goals of the focus group. And when project goals are developed, they should be made specific (operationalised) according to focus group results. The specified goals should be used to point to any possibilities of planning helpful activities or interventions. In this process, professionals should use pedagogical experience to plan activities which will assist the focus group to attain its goal.

It is important to stress that no direct connection exists in the model between problems and plans of the project. An important aspect of the model is to make youth workers and other professionals aware that they must not "jump" from problems to plans. To go directly to planning activities in a project often confuses the problem understanding. Problems in this situation are defined according to practical intervention possibilities, what people usually do, or want to do, and not according to the real developmental interests of the focus group.

An important point of the model is to make decisions open and necessary and to organise discussions and decisions in the project group so that problems, goals and means of the focus group are all interconnected. It both shows how it is possible to work in more "traditional" projects, aimed to help some specific problem group, and in situations where professionals or initiative groups themselves want to do something. The basic point of the model is that the project should be planned in the interest of the development of the focus group members.

For this reason, it is most important to develop the understanding of the problems of the youth group according to general youth developmental goals: the making of useful tracks for the individual. Youth problems in the project should primarily be understood as problems of youth development.

This project planning model organises the planning of activities as "action strategies" to obtain results or consequences. At the same time it is a useful tool for "action research" and evaluation. If projects are planned according to the model very close connections can be made between problem identification, goals, activities and results which will make it possible to develop experience about youth work as support of youth development. In this way it may become a model of action research in youth work.

Consequently, a central point of the model is that it plans projects for evaluation. It makes decisions open to discussion, points to intervention as planned activities for bringing about results and makes goals and results the visible objectives of planning and evaluation.[1]

In this way it is a practical example of an action research model. It makes it possible to develop knowledge about activities or practical experience. It

---

1 See Mørch, S (1995): *From Evaluation to Participation in Youth life*, Nordiske Udkast 2, København.

gives help to test action theories such as: if in situation S activity A brings forward consequences C. It makes it possible to develop interventions and to research whether or not interventions produce results.

Conclusion

The necessity of project work in more varied forms would seem essential to allow modern "youth life" and tracks to develop. Youngsters today should be able to take part in the construction of their own lives. For this development it is not sufficient for young people to learn social norms as the basis of activities. The modern world is changing all the time and norms might not guide behaviour itself. However, this does not mean that norms in the meaning of values of social activities are useless. In the construction of social contexts "normativity" as "rules of social responsibilities" plays a very important role among other formulae.

In youth project work this aspect becomes most important. The key words in current youth projects show this awareness and interest. Democratic decisions and participatory planning and evaluation have become most important.

The challenge in this situation, however, seems to be not to confuse methods and goals of the projects. If this happens effective support of "youth life" would be sacrificed in the interests of ideology. The general goal of youth projects should be made known to help individual trajectories develop which both integrate and develop the individual youngster.

Sven Mørch

References

Argyris C et al. (1985): *Action Science*, Jossey-Bass, San Francisco

Beck U (1992): *Risk Society. Towards a New Modernity*, Sage, London

Brücker P (1972): *Zur Sozialpschologie des Kapitalismus*, Frankfurt

Burkitt I (1991): *Social Selves*, Sage, London

Coleman, James S & Husén T (1985): *Becoming Adult in a Changing Society*, Centre for Educational Research and Innovation. (Ceri), OECD Paris

Erikson E H (1963): *Childhood and society*, Norton, New York

Furlang A & Cartmel F (1997): *Young People and Social Change*, Open University Press Buckingham

Giddens A (1991): *Modernity and Self-identity*, Polity Press, Oxford

Giddens A (1987): *The Constitution of Society*, Polity Press, Oxford

Graumann C F (1996): Introduction to a History of Social Psychology in: Hewstone, Stroebe, Stephenson (eds): *Introduction to Social Psychology*, Blackwell (1988)

Holzkamp K (1983): *Grundlegun der Psychologie*, Campus, Frankfurt

Mattingly Ch (1991): Narrative Reflections on Practical Actions: Two Learning Experiments in Reflexive Storytelling in: Schön, D A (ed): *The Reflective Turn*, Teachers College Press, New York

Mørch S (1990): *Ungdomsteori og intervention i Udkast 1*, København

Mørch S (1993): *Dansk eller russisk ungdomsliv*, Psykologisk Laboratorium, København

Mørch S (1993): *Projektbogen. Teori og metode i projektplanlægning, Rubikon*. København

Mørch S (1993): *Ungdomsprojekter*, Rubikon, København (English version: *Youth projects – A guide to planned youth work*, Psychological Laboratory, Copenhagen)

Mørch S (1994): *Handlingsteorien*, Udkast, København

Mørch S (1995): *Den sociale uredelighed*. Unge pædagoger vol 6, København

Mørch S (1995): *From Evaluation to Participation in Youth life*, Nordiske Udkast 2, København

Mørch S (1996): Young adults. *Psychological Yearbook*, Tuskulæum, København

Nicander P (1995): The Turn to the Text: *The Critical Potential of Discursive Social Psychology*, Nordiske Udkast, København

Potter J & Wetherell M (1994): *Discourse and Social Psychology*, Sage 1994 (87)

Sarbin T R & Kitsuse J I (eds.) (1994): *Constructing the social*, Sage

Schön D A (1983): *The Reflective Practitioner*, Basic Books, New York

Tolman C W & Maiers W (1991): *Critical Psychology. Contributions to an Historical Science of the Subject*, Cambridge University Press, Cambridge

Vinnai G (1973): *Sozialpsychologie der Arbeiteerklasse*, Rohwoldt, Hamburg

Walther (Hrsg) (1997): *Junge Erwachsene in Europa*, Leske & Budrich, Opladen

Ziehe T (1982): *Plädoyr für ungewöhnliches Lernen, Idseen zur Jugendsituation*, Rowolt, Hamburg

European information society and citizenship

One or several information societies?

The idea of constructing an "information society" is prompted by the desire to find a new form of economic growth. The idea was first formulated during the crisis which took place at the beginning of the 1970s. At the time, a Japanese research institute, the JACUDI, recommended that the government should introduce this kind of society since it considered it to be the most realistic social project. Given the problems with pollution, it did not consider the pursuit of an industrial society to be a desirable objective; a more social model or a leisure-based society did not seem possible given the problems with funding. The idea was again floated in 1993 in an American report on "the national information infrastructure" and in the statements made by Vice-President Al Gore who presented the information superhighways as the new frontier of the twenty-first century. The American initiative, perceived above all as an attempt to relaunch the economy by taking the lion's share of the new markets, was to be followed by other initiatives of the same kind, including one proposed by the European powers.

Apart from the economic benefits, the opportunities offered by the information superhighways and the general introduction of digital systems seemed such that they will bring numerous advantages. For example, in an official French report on the subject we read:

"The revolution which will take place in the year 2000 will be one of information for all. Comparable in its technical scope to that of the railways or electrification, its effects will be wider reaching since telecommunications networks are now the nerve centres of our societies. It will also be much more rapid because technologies develop more quickly than they did a century ago. It will fundamentally alter economic structures, methods of organisation and production, the access of all to knowledge, leisure, working methods, and social relations".

The new technologies are presented as being intrinsically beneficial. They will by themselves provide economic prosperity, more active democracy and better education. The process is supposedly irreversible and all-pervading. Those who adapt first to the new digital age will benefit from the advantages it offers and will continue to have every possible chance of winning the economic competition.

This vision of an information society offering only benefits invites criticism. This is so because such a society also implies new risks. Thus, an American media specialist who considered that it is better to contemplate possible hurdles before coming up against them, cited seven major sins heralded by the new digital age: a new form of inequality between those with a plentiful supply of information and others, the stultifying effect on the vast majority of people generated by game shows and commercial campaigns, the threats to privacy resulting from data stored in computer memories, the disintegration of the community through the segmentation of the general public, the distortion of democracy by instant referendums, the tyranny exercised by the largest communication enterprises as the guardians of programmes, the loss of the values of public service and social responsibility which have been deliberately cast aside in the construction of the electronic superhighway. This other less euphoric manner of considering the information society has the virtue of opening up the debate and of demonstrating the ambivalent nature of all things technical.

The sphere of application also has a role to play and a technology cannot by itself impose the best or worst possible results. There is no such thing as a ready-made information society which would automatically set us on an upward or downward path. For all that, technology is not a neutral force: it determines the scope of possibilities, imposes constraints on its users, encourages certain types of behaviour and implies changes in scale.

Democracy is an important consideration in the construction of a European information society, as shown by the recent adoption of a directive on the protection of personal data. Respect for privacy is indeed an essential condition of a democratic system. Democracy also requires active citizens and in addition to the defensive approach embodies in the expression of freedom of protection, it is necessary to promote the expression of freedom of participation. In other words, through the development of new information technologies, the participation of the largest possible number of people in the affairs which are of direct concern to them should be facilitated. It is on these two fronts, one defensive and the other participatory, that efforts towards citizenship training must focus as a matter of priority.

Controlling information or being controlled by it?

The notion of a control society is perhaps the hidden corollary of the notion of an information society. Increasingly frequent recourse to computers and to the new information and communication technologies has brought about substantial growth in the storage and processing of information on individuals. Faced with such a large-scale phenomenon, it might be wondered whether the advent of computerised systems does not lead directly to a control society in which more and more decisions on individuals are taken on the basis of information gathered on them without them being aware of it or having the opportunity to intervene. The development of information technologies can undoubtedly enhance the development of control technologies. Digitalisation, the information superhighways, sensors such as video cameras, portable computers and observation satellites enable the amount of information gathered on individuals to be increased considerably.

Under a political system mindful of the expression and preservation of individual freedoms, the control of information which leaves people ignorant of the procedures and manipulations which are however of direct concern to them, is unacceptable. All the more so since, following the computerisation of personal files and identification of dangers in the 1970s, most democracies have adopted legislation designed to defend the right to privacy. With the advent of computerised systems, such a right has assumed considerable importance. It is a reactive right which was previously taken for granted and did not need to be formalised in legal terms. It is very significant that the first declarations on human rights do not contain any references to it. In the face of aggression strengthened by a previously unknown technological force, democratic society responded by re-affirming the freedoms to which it recognised its members as being entitled. After all, what we seek to preserve is minimal personal independence which is one of the essential conditions for life in a democracy. Private interests are not on the fringes or at the border with public interests. They are the basis thereof and it is on that basis that general interests can be evaluated. Milan Kundera expresses the same idea with great force:

"The personal and the public are essentially two different worlds and respect for this difference is a *sine qua non* if a man is to be able to live as a free being. The partition which separates these two worlds cannot be violated and those who break down such partitions are criminals ... It is a matter of the survival or the disappearance of the individual."

Everyone, be they strong or weak, must be able to cultivate their secret garden, free of all interference. It is not a handful of privileged people who should enjoy the protection of their innermost secrets but in fact the whole of the population.

As regards information on individuals, there now exist a number of rules with which anyone responsible for computer files and data processing must comply. The European Directive of 24 October 1995 on the protection of individuals with regard to the processing of personal data and on the free movement of such data presents the view that images and sounds are affected by these rules in the same way as traditional text-based data. A certain amount of sensitive data such as those on ethnic origins or political opinions should not be recorded. Other information can be recorded, subject however, to compliance with a number of principles. An essential point concerns informing those concerned. As soon as data are collected, they have the right to be informed in advance about the existence of processing and, if they so desire, can be informed of its main characteristics. Through these provisions, it is intended to give greater transparency to a mechanism which thus far has been secret and enable an individual to re-assert control over personal information so as to re-invest him or her with the status of a subject compromised by control technologies. Major efforts at promoting information and education should be made through an "open files" day or week for example, in order to explain the point of such new rights and to explain the relevant practical arrangements. Prior to this explanation, it is clearly desirable that people should be made aware of the dangers inherent in the files. In a work published in 1988, (A Vitalis et al., *L'ordinateur et après* ("The computer and beyond"), ed G Morin and Eska), the following exercises were proposed with a view to making people aware of the dangers of computerised files.

1. You have to produce an individual registration form for some kind of activity (a group dynamics course, day-care centre, sports event and so on):

   Make a list of the items which you consider necessary.

   When this has been done, the group must decide whether the information requested is relevant and identify what is missing.

2. You are asked to provide a form issued by an organisation (loan application, request for assistance, admission to an institution, enrolment and so on). What are the main items on the form and to which aspects of personality do they apply?

   Are all the items justified by the purpose of the form? Are they objective?

3. What are the main forms which you have filled in in the past? Were you obliged to do so?

   What is the difference between filling in a form during a census or to order a journal?

4. You have to draw up a computer profile based on the information contained in the different files in which you appear. Starting from your birth, note the different particulars recorded about you.

a. What do the following know about you:

   your employer? or the national education authorities?
   your bank?
   the tax authorities?
   the town hall?
   the social security services?
   the family allowance authorities?
   the police?
   the electricity board or the water company?

b. Which files contain the most sensitive personal information?

c. Is the information held on you by such organisations comparable to what is known about you by your caretaker, your neighbours or your work colleagues?

d. Does this computer profile resemble you? What does it say about you?

5. Explain the difference between manual and computerised files.

   Give the names of the files which you know to be automated.

6. Which files contain your social security or identification number?

   Do you know the number by heart?

7. For what reasons is a file automated?

   When a manual file is automated, for what reasons do the number of items of information recorded generally tend to increase?

8. Should financial data on individuals be kept secret?

   What should be made of the combined use of tax files (income, immovable or movable property) for the purposes of combating tax fraud?

9. Exactly what information can be gathered on a prisoner?

10. How true is the following bald statement: "Files are not created as a means of assistance, but assistance is offered in order to create files?"

11. What is meant by "normal", "maladjusted", and "handicapped?"

12. What are the particular features which people do not like others knowing about them?

13. Comment on this statement: "Statistics are the subtlest form of lies."

14. Would you agree to consult a databank whilst knowing that a record is kept of all the consultations you make?

15. If you were "interviewed" by a market research institute, would you agree to give your name to the interviewer?

16. Can the television programme you watch every evening be identified from a distance?

New information practices to enhance expression and participation?

By offering new information carriers and instruments, new technologies can enable broader participation in democratic life. Democracy is scarcely imaginable without effective means of communication. For example, some consider that non-specialised television channels now contribute to maintaining a non-binding social link. News bulletins talk in terms of citizens as members of a political society. Through the televisual media, the area open to the public has become more visible. The largest possible number of people are offered a continual insight into the way negotiations are conducted and the confrontations between the major players, and sometimes they are offered assistance in understanding the terms of the debates in progress. Interactive networks allegedly herald even greater transparency in the future. These communication networks supposedly facilitate the flow of information from the top downwards but also from the bottom upwards and between the different decentralised communities. On the basis of these new means of communication, we can even imagine direct democracy or at least an increase in electronic surveys designed to take decisions on the major issues confronting society. The active construction of a personal viewpoint through multimedia and the information super highways can contribute to the emergence of a different kind of public area no longer based on the receipt of information but on its processing. Such an area would no longer be dominated by the all-embracing culture of television for the masses but would promote other forms of exchanges and social links.

Although the technical new deal does actually offer new opportunities, it is in no way certain that these opportunities will be properly used. Training must focus on learning how to use new tools so that they are not reserved for a small number of insiders. The efforts made towards technical training are insufficient and must be complemented by a demonstration of the benefits and shortcomings of the new instruments. In this connection, distinctions must be made in order to evaluate the situation correctly and to avoid taking at face value the "technological bluff", to use the words of Jacques Ellul to describe the continual exaggeration of the possibilities offered by technology.

Thus, confusion is too often generated between the information carrier and the information itself, the container and the content, the medium and the message. An essential point is forgotten: in order for information to make sense, there must be human intervention; without this intervention, the most sophisticated technology possible can, by itself, in no way be considered as a means of promoting knowledge and communication. Information is not a commodity. It is the combination of sign and meaning. All information is based on some kind of sign or form: this is a necessary condition but is not sufficient. In addition, if a meaning is to become clear, it is necessary to have a means of interpreting the form. Information implies relating sign to meaning. A voice on the radio is nothing more than airwaves if there is no ear to listen to it; if there is no eye to read them, this book or that terminal is merely a series of characters or a screen emitting light signals. Information as such does not exist. It exists only on the basis of an interpretation, or efforts to assimile, integrate and digest. A mental and/or ideological structure must filter, monitor and place in context what is presented as information. Such a structure provides more or at least as much as the signal which is transmitted. Nowadays too much attention is paid to a signal which can be produced and processed industrially. The provider of meaning has continued to use traditional methods. There is a fundamental diversity between the industrial production of messages and the traditional reception of meaning. A larger number of signals does not necessarily imply more information. By contrast, an abundance of messages can deprive the individual of the time needed to assimilate them. In such conditions, more and more "information" can generate less and less meaning. Eventually the sovereignty of the individual over information may be impaired. Interactive networks now provide the individual with a much more active role as a producer but the force of the means available is, to a very large extent, greater than his or her capacity for communication. It is not possible to communicate with the whole world and while I am communicating through a terminal, I am not communicating with my neighbour.

Other distinctions need to be made with regard to information carriers. Each of those carriers has its advantages and disadvantages. In a world of multimedia, it is essential to consider the specific features of each individual medium. The carrier is never something neutral. It is just as important to be aware of the possibilities for storage, processing and transmission offered by each carrier at which the content of a message is directed as of the content itself. Such awareness should convince us of the specific features of each instrument and of the need to use them selectively. There is no general-purpose carrier for information and communication, even if efforts are made to convince us that the opposite is true as far as the new instruments are concerned. Thus, for example, consulting a databank may prove very useful for ascertaining the state of the market or the different properties of a metal. However, it is of little or no use in developing a qualitative or critical viewpoint. Images, traditional written forms, oral expression and computer data cannot provide the same services. There is obviously a difference in character between the information conveyed by a car's dipped headlights, that gathered from reading a daily newspaper, listening to a quartet or watching a television programme. A whole spectrum may be drawn up ranging from the sternest, most functional and formalised types of language to the most ambiguous and emotionally coloured forms. In more complex terms, several levels of information can be distinguished: the level of cybernetic information linked to action, semantic information where the processing of knowledge is important and finally, that of information based on relations which is accessible only to a human being as the heir to a particular culture and someone with the capacity for sensitivity and intuition. Another fundamental distinction to be made concerns digital and analogue representations. Whereas the first group, including the spoken word or a written text, has only a conventional relationship with the object represented, the second group seems to represent reality directly. Owing to the absence of the arbitrary nature of a signal, an image holds a particular fascination and great power of conviction. Through the introduction of digital systems, the image has become a ubiquitous means of writing and must no longer be considered as an end in itself. We must learn to read virtual images and to maintain sufficient detachment to avoid being misled by falsifications and manipulations of all kinds.

André Vitalis

Information society: a new source of inequalities

Two years ago Korea held a conference on the subject of young people and the globalisation process – a high ambition and an extensive programme. Confronting young people with this process was indeed like opening Pandora's box. If even the most solid experts are shaken when the horizon of human possibilities and challenges recedes before their eyes, the spiritual effect on the young students taking part in this world conference must have been disastrous. For an entire week they heard an assortment of messages as utopian, idealistic as could be imagined – even romantic in a way. These had one point in common, the myth of the global village; the world being, or becoming, a village; history nearing its end with levelling of differences and interlocking/integration of the world's component parts into a unified planetary fabric. A few dissident voices were raised here and there, drawing attention to the dangers and perils of this rampant one-worldism. Some bold or foolhardy spirits went so far as to recall that this ongoing internationalisation was nothing but the march of capitalism in a new guise; the market extending its dominion worldwide; a further intensification of the production process not only making socio-economic systems interdependent but also levelling their differences. On the whole, however, this self-proclaimed elite of the new generation were united in their perception of the new **globalisation** creed.

The same theme is apparently under discussion at today's seminar if Krishan Kumar's recent book, *From Post-Industrial to Post-Modern Society*[1] is any indication. In fact this writer, and many others besides, consider it possible to analyse not only the changes now occurring in modern societies, but also the challenges facing them, via three closely interconnected avenues: the information society, post-Fordism and postmodernism.

The common denominator of this corpus of analyses lies in the various propositions made concerning the development of the information society; their appearance on the academic scene cannot be dated because speculation is in full swing. Authors like Reisman and the lonely crowd, McLuhan and Fiore with their theorisation of the media society and Alvin Toffler, who heralded a completely altered society under his evocative book title *Future Shock*, drew everybody's attention to the tremendous upheaval brought about by the advent of a society with three principal traits: prodigious growth in the volume of information, acceleration of its circulation, its altered nature, and particularly its rapid obsolescence.

---

1 Krishan Kumar: *From Post-Industrial to Post-Modern Society*, Blackwell, Oxford, UK, 1996.

While these prophets, experts or enlightened analysts painted perhaps an impressionist picture of the changes in progress, others went on to measure their impact on the social structure. Here again, one cannot venture to name the first to point out the transformations of labour demand and their effects on the social pyramid. Unskilled jobs are fast disappearing; the pursuit of increased productivity entails the introduction of new technologies, and this raises a sustained demand for highly skilled or managerial posts. Professionals, planners and managers have their finest hour in a society where knowledge is in ever greater demand. This aspect was heavily emphasised by John Goldthorpe, who applied the term "service class" to the phenomenon. Kraft 1987, Perez 1985 and Baran 1988 then envisaged the possible future shape of modern societies with a small group of decision-makers and researchers at the top, a growing mass of clerical workers and low-skilled manual workers at the bottom, and in between an expanding class of people engaged in the work of handling and processing information.

The advent of the information society is a colossal phenomenon that concerns and affects all social strata without, however, causing homogenisation of society around the "middle classes" as some predicted. Divisions persist, if only with regard to employment; the figures even prove that they are hardening.

New light is cast on this aspect by the contentions relating to post-Fordism. The analysis has the same starting-point as before: growth in the demand for professionals associated with more acute need for the introduction of new technologies into the production and consumption cycle (home automation is admittedly invading the private sphere too). However, this assessment is bound up with a socio-political analysis of the transformations affecting the way the market operates. As its name suggests, neo-liberalism marches onward under the banner of a new dogma, that of deregulation. The state relinquishes its controlling power and places in unseen hands the task of balancing the market for the greater benefit of all concerned. The direct outcome of this option is increased flexibility in various possible directions including working time, technology and company organisation. One cannot but echo Robert Boyer's conclusion, in a book already a good fifteen years old, that most European countries have chosen the worst possible of these solutions as far as the workers are concerned: flexible use of the manpower generated by segmentation of the labour market. The diversity of social status mentioned in the preceding paragraph is thus compounded by diversity of job status. Life-long permanent employment consisting of the old familiar full-time job on a contract of indefinite duration continues to be the norm although it is becoming rarer in a new recruitment pattern dominated by fixed-term, temporary and part-time work, plus of course the host of artificial or sheltered jobs lacking any real connection with the labour market and created by governments and official agencies merely as a misguided, superfluous form of welfare provision for unemployment. Delivered into the hands of market forces alone, the neo-liberal economy produces casualisation, unemployment, poverty, and social exclusion at the end of the line. This process has undergone very close analysis by economists and socio-economic pundits, so it requires no further comment except to reiterate that the very sure economic recovery in most of Europe's industrialised countries is not labour-intensive, that far less added value is generated by labour than can be extracted from circulation of money, and that in certain countries such as the United States unemployment is no longer the prime factor of poverty as some working people are much poorer than those drawing unemployment benefit. It is not an ineluctable tendency, rather an economic policy choice in favour of a neo-liberal philosophy, made by the richer countries, the big financiers and the main international financial institutions such as the World Bank and the International Monetary Fund. Yet the preponderance of this choice in most wealthy countries determines the restructuring of societies; it has been said that they were once geared to integration (Parsons T) but now work on the principle of exclusion (Castell R). The frames of reference within which our societies are organised may well have been transposed as Alain Touraine suggests. Modern postindustrial societies may be discarding the principle of vertical stratification founded on a traditional class structure in favour of a horizontal stratification hierarchically graded into the settled, the insecure and the excluded. A working hypothesis of this kind has the merit of drawing attention to the bipolarisation of society as a whole into ins and outs. It has the advantage of highlighting a "relatively" new phenomenon: the wholesale sidelining of part of the population. However, it should not lead us to believe, as is sometimes suggested, that the present growing distinction between the integrated, the insecure and the excluded replaces or is about to replace stratification according to social class. More than a relationship of substitution, it is a nexus between these two dimensions of social structuring. This interpretation is premised by the significance attached in the analysis, even where it concerns post-Fordism, to the implications of the "Third Italy" phenomenon. Indeed, not everybody is a victim of the current restructuring; some can gain by it, not least those who live and subsist by placing the sale of their labour on a contractual footing. Even though the primary effect of this increasing flexibility is to casualise part of the workforce, other flexible devices are seen to be emerging at various points of the production apparatus. One is the sub-contracting system which enables big companies to farm out some of their production by handing the work over to small advanced technology enterprises with highly skilled staff. Computerisation, electronic communication networks and new information technologies overcome time and distance, allowing work to be performed at what were once impossible locations and production costs to be significantly reduced.

Who gains by this new-found flexible economy? Those who not only possess the requisite knowledge, skills and technical flair to employ the new instruments but are also flexible, mobile and adaptable enough to keep up with the fluctuations of the market, for who else could derive profit from this new form of decentralisation? Toffler (once again) in his book *Future Shock* drew attention to the close correlation between these two types of ability. The more culturally endowed are in fact the most mobile and capable of adapting to current change. Knowledge enhances mobility, and vice versa; as a case in point, a beneficial dynamic that privileges the privileged is generated by the mere possession of information on the scope for mobility offered by a constantly changing worldwide employment market for professional staff.

In a remarkable presentation given at the London School of Economics in 1996, Professor Ian Angel portrayed the tendencies pervading modern societies like this: there is a handful of top managers and very highly qualified people capable of using new technologies and creating new ones in a relentless productivity drive imposed by the neo-liberal economy which all countries seemingly hanker for, and a growing mass of outsiders (the cruel realism of this observation is borne out by Julius Wilson's United States research on the hyper-ghettoisation process in black residential areas). He ended by remarking rather mischievously that if your children cannot join the elite, they must join the police force, the army or the private militia because the demand for security financed by individuals, neighbourhood associations and firms is unlikely to stop growing. Nor is the social fracture, complacently spoken of by politicians at election time, likely to last forever without arousing some reactions from those denied a share of the prosperity. Here again, the United States blaze the trail with their residential areas for the rich enclosed by walls and barbed wire, under permanent video surveillance monitored by a squad of private security guards. Florida provides a fine example of this situation, and the black riots in St Petersburg, Florida give a fair indication of the type of reaction to be expected. It will be a violent, nihilistic rebellion by those deprived of hope. Yet the coloured underclass cannot be expected to commit mass suicide by drug-taking, alcoholism, banditry or membership of sects. Other countries than the United States are caught up in this process too; lagging far behind perhaps but taking shape nonetheless is a comparable situation in the United Kingdom with the emergence of a genuine underclass, whatever the terms used to designate the phenomenon. In France, with a fifth if not a quarter of the population excluded, as in most European countries, signs of a similar process are readily discernible.

Thus the restructuring of the environment of social classes takes place against a background of social exclusion. Classes do not disappear but are reconstituted according to the crucial alternative of integration or exclusion. During the boom years 1949-75 in France, class rating determined status in the social pecking order but still took place essentially within an integrated system, so that individuals, irrespective of their status, means and possibilities were members of social groups and of society as a whole. Today, class rating is directly linked with acknowledgement as a member of society.

The final explanation for the current changes refers to the arguments about postmodernism, but postmodernism is all about the uncertain and the unknown. The accumulation of studies on the subject already gives the first glimmerings of some solid food for thought, most of it foreshadowed in the two theories described above. Postmodern societies are on the move, being transformed by leaps and bounds; the indicators are plentiful. No more full employment, no more security, no more protective State; instead, development of the neo-liberal economy, of new technologies and of the information society, resulting in higher demand for skilled staff, professionals and managers. All these elements are already embodied in the theories stated earlier, but the arguments about postmodernism turn the spotlight on another component of the current changes, **fragmentation of society**.

The founding fathers of sociology regarded society as an aggregate whose components, dimensions and spheres of activity were all interlinked and incorporated into one system. The current changes ushering in postmodernism invalidate this type of presentation. Instead of being semi-integrated, the various components of the social system are seen to take on an extremely varied pattern. The fields of cultural activity lose their self-sufficiency; the realm of culture is no longer separate from the social sphere. Business and culture merge and consolidate each other. The systematisation of modern industrial societies gives way to a melting-pot where shades of difference are waning. The "globalisation" process may no doubt be regarded as the chief vector of this phenomenon in which a single movement affects the economic, cultural and social aspects alike (cf. Malcolm Walters). Nation states are on the way out, national cultures are in decline, and above all the growth of new forms of economic production breaks up the elementary communities in which individuals used to forge their group identities.

Postmodern societies become more and more **pluralist** through the interconnection of different cultures, but that is not all; they increasingly incline towards individualist values. The traditional contexts of socialisation have broken down, society's controlling institutions are no more, the ideologies, doctrines and frames of reference which used to regulate community life have lost their legitimacy, and the elementary communities (residential, occupational and recreational) have also ceased to exist; as a result, postmodern societies have freed the individual from his former constraints. Man becomes central to his own destiny, free to choose and responsible for his acts as well as for the trajectory along which he is propelled.

Here, theory relies on plentiful statistics or statistical observations pointing in the same direction; fewer marriages, more divorces, more widespread loneliness among the young and not so young, breakdown of family relations and their reconstitution on radically new foundations, flexibility in employment, occupational and residential mobility, reduction of political or unionist commitment, distrust of the political representation system, lack of social involvement, etc. There is no shortage of evidence to back the theory that the traditional forms of social regulation are eroding. Anomy is in vogue, and the individual feels liberated as a result. He can **choose**, we are told, and become the master of his fate. Man is but what he does, as Sartre used to say, and the postmodernism theory assures us that the time has come for this ideal to be realised.

However, this liberation of the individual is utterly unequal and has altogether disparate effects. The fragmentation of the old society's regulatory forms mainly benefits those who hold the right cards to take up a position in the new game visibly being played, those who are properly equipped to employ the new technologies, decode the myriad signals conveyed by the channels of communication, able to choose, sort and digest what is fed to them. The managers and professionals, the upper middle classes are those who gain by the proposed or supposed "liberation" of the individual; the winners in socio-economic competition are unemployed one day and managing a business the next, as we heard only too often on the radio and TV broadcasts that covered the US elections. The rest are caught in a backwash and cling to traditional ways of life and lifestyles that are true and tried, known and assured, capable at least of providing landmarks and nurturing identities if not of effectively underpinning solidarities: marriage, family, community at neighbourhood or workplace level. Studies measuring the strength of weak ties demonstrate the reach of these informal linkages relied on by individuals unable to play their cards single-handedly, or if so with difficulty. But when the pressure is too strong, when the context is unpromising and the horizon irrevocably closed, clinging to traditional social forms becomes impossible and so anomy and disintegration set in. Being unable to take charge of their own social integration, and bereft of the essentials which used to provide them with a footing, foundation or support, individuals are relegated to a state of anomy. Thus Henri Coing in his day, analysing the impact of the rapid changes wrought in working-class communities by the advent of the consumer society, drew attention to the formation of a gulf between those in a position to take their chances and the others who find themselves isolated with no compass or bearings either. This is how the gulf appeared between these two classes of individuals, as it does today between the middle classes and the others. Such at least is the inference which anyone can draw from a review of the surveys made by Inglehart and Abrahamson on the development of materialism and post-materialist values, albeit with countless reservations – these writers had to admit that the rise of individualism was hampered by unemployment, lack of security, poverty and social exclusion. The relentless advance towards post-materialism which they have been predicting for twenty years is retarded if not halted. But it is also realised that these socio-economic risks are unevenly distributed and that certain groups are severely affected while others escape most of the ravages of time or are only superficially affected. The gulf is deepening; according to the views of these two writers, it is developing chiefly among the new generations which are split by differing social status, disproportionate backgrounds, future prospects bearing no comparison with each other, and consequently by attitudes, cultures and symbolic frames of reference that conform to largely conflicting systems of definitions.

Jean-Charles Lagree

Youth research in the information society

Introduction

There are two ways of looking at the effects of the information technology revolution – one is to see it as determining the shape of modern societies and the identities of the people who live in them – technological-determinist. The other is to see it from the point of view of social analysis – as a component of social change (Adamski, Grootings and Mahler, 1989). My approach starts with the former and ends up very much with the latter, in trying to define what the agenda for youth research in the information society should look like.

Let us start with a bit of history. Ten years ago along with colleagues from thirteen other eastern and western European countries, I took part in a Vienna Centre project, "Youth and New Technology" (Fürst Dilic, 1991). Cast your minds back to the situation then. Despite the loosening up of thinking and structures through *Glasnost* and *Perestroika*, Europe was still divided in terms of economics, ideology and political systems. There were also marked differences in access at the individual level to technological knowhow and equipment. Whereas in Czechoslovakia, (as it was then) and Bulgaria, for example, new technology might be defined as a colour television set or telephone, in the countries of North West Europe, especially Sweden, it was a computer in every classroom and in most homes.

Now the situation has changed. We share the same understanding of what is new technology, that most of what matters about it is its information technology components, and to see its manifestations in much the same physical and cultural products in all countries. We know what the Internet is, and find nothing strange about having an address on it.

IT Futures, a UK National Economic Development Office report written in 1987, presents what amounts to a geometrical expansion of IT from 1847 – the year of the invention of the telegraph – to what was predicted for the year 2000. If anything the predictions were conservative. The critical lift-off occurred when communications media and computers came together – the core of information technology (IT).

Access to, and competence in, the use of information technology has taken over as the defining feature of economic and personal advance. The differences with respect to access have not disappeared, merely shifted in geographical location. With the opening up of markets in all countries to much the same technological goods and services, their availability is present in theory to everyone. In reality, we see ever-widening divisions between north and south, rural and urban, and what is often referred to as the technological "centres" and "peripheries" of all European societies, in access both to information technology and even to work itself. The pervasive assumption spread by the mass media, and promoted by the political and economic interests that control it, is that everybody is participating in the information society. In reality, as with all forms of capital, ownership is concentrated in the hands of elites. There is no evidence to suggest that these elites are going to expand indefinitely. In fact as the demand for employees declines through modern production methods, work in the sense of employment, becomes an increasingly rare commodity. The restriction in purchasing power this implies, imposes severe limits on access to IT. In their book, *The Jobless Future*, Aranowitz and Di Fatzio (1994), paint a stark picture of this kind for the USA, estimating that even at the critical millennium year, 2000, only ten million Americans out of a population of over two hundred and fifty million will be fully "wired-up" to the information age.

But there are other signs of problems which, though only indirectly related to the information technology revolution, may be seen as new manifestations of tensions between the technological haves and the have nots. The replacement of the high cost welfare systems and unionised work forces of the post-war period by systems motivated by the dictums of "new right" market economics, move the emphasis from group solidarity to individual agency and family responsibility in the construction and maintenance of individual lives (Coles, 1995). This places ever heavier demands on personal and family resources in the interest of keeping "public expenditure" borne by taxation to the minimum. The periodic disruptions of street fights and riots from the Watts suburb in Los Angeles to housing estates on Tyneside in Britain, points to some of the simmering underlying social tensions.

It is ironic that a story that was dominating the English news media when I started to prepare this talk was of pupils who were so uncontrollable that the schools they attended could not function. Only if trouble-making children were expelled would teachers continue to teach in them. The debate has shifted now into the even more bizarre territory of whether re-introducing caning in to British schools will solve the problem. Children are to be seen as the causes of their alienation and punished for it rather than as products of alienating influences to which they have been subjected by the world of adults.

Isolated examples, do not make the case that fundamental social change has occurred, let alone that irreparable damage to the social, and moral fabric of society has followed in the wake of the IT revolution. But they do point to some old kinds of problem taking on new forms in the modern state. In this talk, I want to take a broad look at some of the consequences of technological change for young people attempting to negotiate their transition to adult life (Banks et al, 1992; Heinz, 1996). I want to use this review to identify the key components in a research agenda for the study of youth in the next century. A strong emphasis will be given to the practical and policy implications of what research finds out. An agenda which merely attempts to offer understandings without beginning to point to solutions is likely to fall on deaf ears.

Young people's situation in the information technology age

"Adolescents are facing demands and expectations, as well as risks and threats that are both numerous and more serious than they were only a generation ago. Millions are growing up under conditions that do not meet their enduring needs for optimal development. They are not receiving the careful nurturing guidance they need – and say they want from parents and other adults. They are yielding to social pressures to use drugs, including alcohol and cigarettes, to have sex, and to engage in anti-social activities at distressingly early ages. Too many are alienated from school and moving towards dropping out. Countless poignant examples exist of self-destructive, even violent, behaviour in the 10 to 18 year age group among both rich and poor."

This gloomy prognostication in a report from the Carnegie Foundation in the USA[1] makes the point that life is becoming increasingly difficult for young people in the modern world. Access to employment demands levels of education and acquisition of skills of a different order from those required in the past.

"They (adolescents) must cultivate enquiring and problem-solving habits of mind, acquire the technical and analytic capabilities to participate in the world-wide economy, and have the capability for lifelong learning and adaptation to changing circumstances. Further they must learn in our pluralistic society they must learn to live peacefully and respectfully with a wide array of ethnic, religious and cultural groups."

The massive expansion and extension of education and training can be interpreted as a response to the demand from employers for greater investment in "human capital" in the competition for jobs (Becker, 1975), i.e., the new kinds of jobs demand new kinds of skill and a longer period in education to acquire them. Alternatively, as social exclusion theorists argue (Collins, 1979), the increasing value placed on educational qualifications can be seen more as a means of rationing jobs in a situation of job shortage. Far from being creative and demanding, much modern computer-based employment is repetitive, alienating and mind numbing (Aranowitz and Di Fazio, 1994). Insisting on extensive education and credentials, as the preliminary to it, ensures that only the relatively privileged sections of society will get first refusal on the stimulating jobs that are on offer. The rest make do with the remainder of casualised part-time and partially skilled employment or face unemployment.

---

1 *Great Transitions*, Concluding Report of the Carnegie Council on Adolescent Development, Carnegie Corporation, New York, March, 1996.

A middle position is taken by Philip Brown (1996) who argues that the kinds of "charismatic" skills supposedly central to working in the modern company – team work and leadership, creativity, flexibility, adaptability – are precisely the kinds of attribute that middle class parents expect their children's schools to inculcate in them. Hence in the modern world the privileged, not only command access to the best opportunities on the basis of credentials, but actually have more of the skills that the modern workplace needs. On this basis US college education – with its emphasis on collegiality, generic competence, networking and sport – might be seen as the ideal form of vocational preparation for all (Bynner, 1996)!

But in reality, of course, education and training are not evenly distributed within countries, nor between countries. In many European states, where unemployment rates remain persistently above ten percent, and often exceed twenty percent, families simply do not have the means to enable their children to continue in education. Even if they did, many of the young people themselves would reject the pressure on them to postpone the individual and economic freedom that early entry to the labour market brings. The outcome is three features of modern societies, which have been identified in numerous policy analyses: polarisation, mobility and individualisation.

Polarisation is characterised by new forms of social exclusion (Virtanenen, 1996). These are not evenly distributed across societies, but tend to be concentrated in particular geographical regions (the technological peripheries) and in particular family backgrounds and demographic groups: single parent households, ethnic minorities, and families dominated by unemployment and poverty, for example (Heinz, 1996). In information societies, those that have the necessary access to education and develop the competencies needed for the forms of employment on offer, increasingly leave behind those without these opportunities.

Mobility reflects a phenomenon shared across the world: the migration of individuals and families towards the technological centres in pursuit of the prosperity identified with them. As the barriers between East and West came down at the end of the eighties, such pressures towards mobility increased, and will continue to be a source of tension between the host and new immigrant communities. Much of such movement is spearheaded by the young, who find not streets of gold in the affluent cities they re-locate to, but often joblessness, homeless, and subsistence living (Jones, 1995).

A vicious circle is thereby set in motion whereby a lack of a job or a permanent address reduces opportunities for training and employment even further. As was said recently by the chairman of a UK task force on Homelessness: "No home, no job. No job, no home".[1] Despite the British Government's "guarantee" of a training place for every young person who leaves the education system, large numbers are excluded because they do

---

1 Andrew Whittam-Smith, Fourth Albermarle Lecture, National Youth Agency, Leicester.

not have this key characteristic of a permanent address. Many do not even have the essential rudiments of basic literacy and numeracy skills that will give them access to education, let alone the advanced vocational qualifications and extended education that the changing labour market increasingly demands (Eksinsmyth and Bynner, 1994; Bynner and Steedman, 1995). A report on Dutch young people notes the tendency of young people to drift from one bad situation to the next.[1] As a report by a committee of the UK House of Lords in 1991 on *Young People in the European Community* poignantly put it: "All these factors combine to produce a revolving door syndrome ... no home ... no job ... no money ... crime ... increasing isolation and alienation from society ... imprisonment ... no home on release ... and so on ..."

The third feature of the information society, with a particular impact on young people, as discussed by German sociologists Ulrich Beck (1986), Martin Baethge (1989), and others is "individualisation" (see Furlong and Cartmel, 1996 for a comprehensive review). This manifests itself in a variety of forms. Most obviously, the fairly straightforward transitions from school to the labour market of the past, along well trodden career paths, no longer exist, except perhaps for those pursuing the routes to the professions via higher education. Increasingly there is risk and uncertainty at every point at which choices are made and next steps taken on the route to adulthood. In place of the career trajectories of the past, whereby such factors as family background, gender and ethnicity combined with local labour market opportunities to produce predictable locations in the occupational structure, young people now have to navigate their way through changing institutions and changing employment landscapes (Evans and Heinz, 1994; Evans and Furlong, 1996). The reserves of knowledge and skills they build up inside and outside the education system protect them against uncertainty, with qualifications serving as a kind of "vocational insurance" against the ever present risk of unemployment (Bynner, 1996). In this scenario the first transition from education may be no more than a testing of labour market opportunities before the route back into education or into some form of training is taken to build up more human capital first. This is a common phenomenon in Germany where many young people with the University entry qualification – the *Abitur* – opt to do an apprenticeship before going on to higher education. The process continues through life when individuals may expect to change their occupations several times in the course of a single lifetime (Gershuny and Pahl, 1994). The information society needs to become a learning society (Husen, 1989), in which the educational and training resources are on offer that will give individuals the opportunity to continue with employment through adult life.

---

1 *The State of the Young Netherlands*, a National Report on the Situation of Children and Young People in the Netherlands, Eberon, Delft, 1996.

On the other hand, the forms of employment themselves are changing, with much work conducted on a part-time basis, often more oriented to women than men and often taking place at home (Bynner, Morphy and Parsons, in press). The "feminisation" of employment is not so much that women gain the benefits of paid work, as that both men and women – not through choice, but through necessity – have to accept the poor terms of employment and working conditions that in the past were typically identified with women's work (Hakim, 1996). Writers like Baethge see further problems in what are increasingly individualised forms of work practice. Social relations between German *meister* and German apprentice, foreman and working group, give way increasingly to individuals detached from others working in front of computer screens, often at home. Thus one of the major means by which socialisation into adult norms and values occurred in the past, the workplace, no longer has the same significance. In place of it comes youth culture, as endlessly shaped and mediated through the mass media. Instead of the worker citizen we have the consumer citizen where adult identity is formed as much by patterns of consumption as it is by the experience of work (Jones and Wallace, 1994).

But the family, another major source of socialisation, is also under stress. The traditional transition from dependent child to family of one's own now takes place over a much longer period in a context of increasing family breakdown. The typical family of two parents living together with two children has been replaced by a variety of family forms in which single parent households become increasingly common, but far more in some EU countries than in others. For example, lone parent families with children under 15 years of age range from one in five in Denmark and the United Kingdom to one in twenty in Italy and Greece; yet with the exception of Italy, in every country over the period 1980-81 to 1990-91 the percentage increased (Eurostat/EPSC,1994).

The culturally bound and relatively self-sufficient routines of family life in the past are also now replaced at ever-earlier ages by pressures for the family to behave as media dictates. Financial dependency extends while individualisation and self-actualisation take on increasing importance at home as everywhere else. The countries of eastern Europe in the Youth and New Technology project noted that one of the elements in the breakdown of authority at home and at work was that the skills of modern living were effectively monopolised by the young. Computer literacy and keyboard skills, for example, are founded as much in leisure life as in the classroom. This challenges notions of how knowledge and skills are passed on from one generation to the next.

Transition, socialisation and agency

All these different facets of change in individual and group experience need to be seen in terms of the socialisation processes through which young people achieve adulthood. These occur in all the domains of life and include the developmental tasks to be accomplished, (Coleman, 1974; Hendry, 1983): e.g. the crystallisation of gender identity, motivated by the shifting focal concerns – sexual relations, peer relations and relations with parents. There is the transition from school via training to adult work. There are the transitions in leisure life from adult organised activities to casual peer group activities and commercial activities. There are the changes in family status from dependent child to independent adult. Although some of the sequences may remain fairly fixed and stable, especially those that are biologically based, those with strong social determinants, such as the means by which adult worker status is achieved, are much more malleable, with respect to timing and duration (Silbereisen, 1993, 1994). As education extends, for example, then marriage and family formation are likely to take place increasingly from positions of dependency or quasi-dependency, e.g. the university student. The consequence is radical re-structuring, or, as some German writers would have it (e.g. Gaisser and Muller, 1989), de-structuring and fragmentation of the life course. The forms and extent of these changes are not common to all young people, but vary depending on their location in the social structure – what Lynne Chisholm (1992) refers to as defining the contours of youth research. These range from such structural factors as family class, ethnicity, gender and locality, through systemic factors such as the institutional arrangements each country has in place for managing the transition from school to work – the German dual system, for example – to political, economic, moral, religious and technological transformation itself. All interact with each other in the socialisation processes that shape the individual (and group) identity.

Conceptualisation of this kind can run into the danger of seeing young people as relatively passive recipients of largely negative influences, which denies the role they themselves have in determining what their future will be like. Pessimism about the character of information societies, should not lead us to overlook their positive features. The German sociologist Walter Heinz (Heinz, 1987) makes the point that young people have not abandoned work values, merely have refused to take what is often unfulfilling work on any terms. Self-actualisation in all activities including work has simply become more important to them than it was in the past. But as we found in Britain, as ever, there is stratification process going on: the new (postmodern?) values are mainly to be found among the better educated (Bynner and Breakwell, 1991).

But perhaps the leading positive thinker in this area was the Romanian sociologist Fred Mahler (1991), whose concept of juvenology celebrated the benefits that extended education of young people in the information society would bring. Mahler's view gives pride of place to the role of personal agency in the social construction of modern realities. Thus he argued that the extensive exposure to education replaces on-the-job socialisation by anticipatory, or in his terms, emancipatory, socialisation into adult roles and responsibilities at work and outside. In this process, students and teachers learn from each other with the consequence that young people leave the education system with much greater power to change the world – including the world of work – outside. This dynamic between education, employment and the structure and processes of society, was seen by Mahler to be progressive and leading inevitably to wider benefits for all.

Mahler writing in the seventies and early eighties developed his ideas in the context of communist society – seeing the young as being the motivators of change within it but presenting this as a generalisation about the role of (educated) youth as an engine of change in all societies. He might well have been astounded by the success of his predictions, as least as far as the transformation of Eastern Europe was concerned. But the medium for change was maybe not quite what he anticipated. One of the conclusions from the Youth and New Technology project, which ended after the fall of the Berlin wall, was that universal youth culture borne by the mass media was simply too powerful to be resisted by the authoritarian state. As King (1992) points out, the media revolutions that have accompanied the growth of the information society bring common tastes and aspirations into every home. Once the closed system of norms and values is opened up through these means, then political transformation is inevitable. The Paths of the Generation Longitudinal Study conducted on young people across the Soviet Union (Saarnit, 1995), showed precisely such a value shift across the generations occurring, before the fall of communism, with respect to attitudes to work and materialism. Such dramatic upheavals in a context of accelerating technological change underpin much recent writing about the stage the modernisation process in western society has reached (Baumann, 1991; Beck, Giddens and Lash, 1994). In the postmodern world the forms and functions of society and the values underpinning them are under continuous (reflexive) appraisal. Not all agree, however, about the discontinuity this represents with the past. The British sociologist Anthony Giddens (1987) prefers to see the modern world as at the stage of late modernity, i.e. still very much responding to and developing in accordance with the social and political imperatives of the immediate industrial past.

Mahler's concept of juvenology raises broader questions about an over-arching issue so far stated only implicitly in the different areas of concern: citizenship. In the broad sense, as discussed by the British sociologist Marshall (1973), citizenship in the modern state means defining rights and responsibilities in the spheres of not just political life, but economic and social life as well. As commentators such as Jones and Wallace (1992), Coles (1995) and Chisholm and Bergeret (1992) argue, this defines a set of questions that need to be addressed if citizenship is to be satisfactorily achieved (Appendix). These embrace both youth problems in the societal as well as the individual sense and the resources needed to tackle them, including those available through the education system of each country and the youth service. The European Union's Targeted Socio-economic Research under the Fourth

Framework programme, focuses specifically on the education and training component of policy and the causes of social exclusion, especially unemployment. But youth research in the wider sense needs to go deeper than this in seeking understanding of the processes through which young people acquire their adult identities and how these are affected by the changing societal conditions in which they make the transition to adult citizenship. The title of a recent Finnish research programme on young people, *Youth and Life Management* (see Helve and Bynner, 1996), aptly pinpoints the young person's need for a critical bundle of skills, understandings and personal and social resources to survive in the modern world. The goal of discovering what these are gives us a lead into the new agenda for youth research.

Final reflection

In a lecture to Britain's Royal Society of Arts, the film producer Sir David Puttnam made the point that we live today not so much in an information society as an information economy. Demand economies of "the new right" kind are driven by fairly simple-minded principles of investment, profit and loss. They create opportunities for some and disadvantages for others. In the information economy such disparities are growing at an ever-increasing rate both between societies and within societies. Puttnam recites the story of a little girl who when asked in which countries elephants were to be found said it was a silly question because elephants were too big and intelligent to get lost in the first place. He uses it to exemplify the importance of new thinking of the kind that only young people can provide, if we are to convert the information economy into an information society. The older generation is in certain respects in competition with the younger generation about what the future will be like. Hence many manifestations of youth culture are seen as threatening and as signs of moral degeneracy rather than as new rays of light into a possible future. Youth problems are problems of a social and economic world created by adults. They need to be replaced by the opportunities provided by an information society created by the young. In Fred Mahler's terms society should leave the future open for every new generation to avoid its "colonisation" by previous generations. Let us hope that by the year 2000 the systems are still open and transformations to the information society will already be taking place.

John Bynner

References

Adamski W, Grootings P and Mahler F (1989). "Transition from School to Work: Introduction", in Adamski W and Grooting P (Eds.) *Youth, Education and Work in Europe*, London: Routledge

Aranowitz S and Di Fazio W (1994) *The Jobless Future*, Minneapolis: University of Minnesota Press

Baethge M (1989) "Individualisation as Hope or Disaster: a Socio-economic Perspective", in Hurrelmann K and Engle U (Eds.) *The Social World of Adolescents*, New York: Walter Gruyter

Banks M, Breakwell G, Bynner J, Emler N, Jamieson L and Roberts K (1992) *Careers and Identities*, Buckingham: Open university Press

Beck U (1986) *Risk Society*, London: Sage

Baumann Z (1991) *Intimations of Postmodernity*, London: Routledge

Beck U, Giddens A and Lash S (1994) *Reflexive Modernization: Politics, Traditions and Aesthetics in the Modern Social Order*, Cambridge: Polity Press

Becker G S (1975) *Human Capital*, Washington D.C.: National Bureau of Economic Research

Brown P (1996) "Cultural Capital and Social Exclusion" in Helve H and Bynner J *Youth and Life Management: Research Perspectives*, Helsinki: University of Helsinki Press

Brown P and Lauder H (1996) "Education, Globalisation and Economic Development". *Journal of Educational Policy*, 11,1-25

Bynner J (1996) *"The transition from School to work: New Routes to Social Integration and Exclusion"* paper presented to the workshop *New Passages from Education to Employment in Comparative Life Course Perspective*, Centre for International Studies, University of Toronto April 18-20

Bynner J and Breakwell G (1991) "New Technologies and Youth Attitudes: British Experience" in Fürst-Dilic R (1991) *European Youth and New Technologies*, Vienna: Vienna Centre

Bynner J and Roberts K (eds) (1991), *Youth and Work: Transition to Employment in England and Germany*, London: Anglo German Foundation

Bynner J and Steedman J (1995) *Difficulties with Basic Skills*. London: Basic Skills Agency

Coleman J (1974) *The Nature of Adolescence*, London:Routledge and Kegan Paul

Coles R (1995) *Youth and Social Policy*, London: UCL Press

Collins R (1979) *The Credential Society*, New York: Academic Press

Chisholm L (1992) *Young People in the European Community: Staking the Terrain for European Youth Research*, Paper presented to the British Sociological Association Conference, A New Europe, University of Canterbury, Kent

Chisholm, L and Bergeret, J-M (1991) *Young People in the European Community: Towards an Agenda for Research and Policy*, Report to the Commission of the European Communities Task force Education, Training and Youth, Brussels: European Commission

Ekinsmyth C and Bynner J (1994) *The Basic Skills of Young Adults*, London: Basic Skills Agency

Erikson H (1968) *Identity, Youth and Crisis*, New York: Norton

Evans K and Furlong A (1996) *Metaphors of Youth Transitions: Niches, Pathways, Trajectories or Navigations*, Paper presented to the Workshop on British Youth Research the New Agenda, Glasgow, July 26-28

Evans K and Heinz W R (1994) *Becoming Adults in the 1990s*, London: Anglo German Foundation

Furlong A and Cartmel F (1996) *Young People and Social change: Individualization and Risk in Late Modernity*, Buckingham: Open University Press

Fürst-Dilic R (1991) *European Youth and New Technologies*, Vienna: Vienna Centre

Gaiser W and Müller H U (1989) "The importance of Peer Groups in Different Regional Contexts and Biographical Stages", in Hurrelmann K and Engel U (eds) *The Social Life of Adolescents*, New York: de Gruyter

Gershuny J and Pahl R (1994) *Lifetime Employment in a New Context*, Paper presented to the conference on Challenges of Unemployment in a Regional Europe. Ljowert: Fryske Academy. Giddens A (1991) *Modernity and Self-Identity: Self and Society in the Late Modern Age*, Cambridge: Polity Press

Hakim C (1996) *Key Issues in Women's Work*, London: Athlone

Heinz W R (1987) "The Future of Work" in *The Factory of the Future and the Future of Work*, CEDFOP, Vocational Training Bulletin No 1, 13-19

Heinz W R (1996) "Status Passages and Macro-micro Linkages in life Course Research", in Weymann A and Heinz W R (Eds.) *Society and Biography: Interrelations between Social Structure, Institutions and the Life Course*, Weinheim: Deutscher Studien Verlag

Helve H and Bynner J (eds.) *Youth and Life Management: Research Perspectives*, Helsinki: University of Helsinki Press

Hendry L B (1983) *Growing Up and Going out*, Aberdeen University Press

Husen T (1989) "Integration of General and Vocational Education", *Education and Vocational Training*, CEDFOP, Vocational Training Bulletin No 1, 9-13

Jones G (1995) *Leaving Home*, Buckingham: Open University Press

Jones G and Wallace C (1992) *Family, Youth and Citizenship*, Buckingham: Open University Press

King E (1992) "The Young Adult Frontier and the Perspective of Continuous Change" *Comparative Education*, 28, 71-82

Mahler F (1991) "Transition and Socialisation", in Adamski, W and Grooting, P (Eds.) *Youth, Education and Work in Europe*, London: Routledge

Marshall G (1973) *Class, Citizenship and Social Development*, Westport: Greenwood

Paakkunainen K (1996) "Political Scepticism and Groupings among Unemployed youth: a Finnish German Comparison" in Helve H and Bynner J (eds.). *Youth and Life Management: Research Perspectives*, Helsinki: University of Helsinki Press

Saarnit J (1995) "Changes in the Value Orientations of Youth and their Social Context", in Tomasi L (1995) *Values and Post Soviet Youth*, Milano: Franco Angeli

Silbereissen R (1993) *Psychosocial Adversities and Adolescent Timetables: East versus West Germany*, Paper presented to the 101st Annual convention of the American Psychological Association, Toronto

Silbereissen R (1994) *Differential Timing of Vocational Choice*, Paper presented to the thirteenth Biennial meeting of the Society for the Study of Behavioural Development, Amsterdam

Virtanen P (1996) *The Making of a New Underclass among Unemployed Youth: Emerging Social Exclusion, the Mechanism for Integration and the Need for Active and Network-based Employment Strategies*, Labour Market Studies, No 150, Ministry of Labour, Helsinki

Appendix

Youth Policy Agenda:

i. social risks and casualties (including unemployment, homelessness, poverty, discrimination and disenfranchisement): what minimum "social guarantees" should there be with respect to employment and training, housing, social support and income?

ii. citizenship rights and responsibilities: what should they comprise, who should get them, in what contexts and at what age?

iii. intergroup-tensions and conflicts: how can social harmony and cohesiveness be achieved within a fully participative democracy?

iv. youth "culture" and its manifestations in lifestyles, consumption patterns and anti-social behaviour: how can it be influenced and its supposed harmful concomitants – drugs, alcohol, crime – be avoided?

v. general and vocational education and training: what should be its content and organisation and what accreditation should arise from it?

Socialisation for the information society

The question of identity
and on-line environments on the Internet

Over a period of more than a year I spent a lot of time in the computing lab of my university in Germany, observing different groups of students and talking to them about their use of the various Internet services. The computing lab is the only university building in Tübingen which can be accessed twenty-four hours a day by students, and the times when you do not meet anybody there are quite rare.

A collection of academic papers has already been devoted to virtual communities on the Internet. They mainly focus on descriptions of the life on-line. My own research, however, is primarily based on fieldwork off-line. I conducted qualitative in-depth interviews with students whose activities on the Internet seemed particularly interesting. These students did not only use their Internet account to send e-mail, to download software programmes and other files or to participate in various newsgroups. Their involvement went an important step further because they regularly engaged in synchronous, real time conversations with other users whom they had met only virtually and whom they addressed by fictional names. Under these circumstances on-line environments like multi-user role-playing games and the conversation channels of Internet Relay Chat open completely new spaces to manifest the self.

The question of identity is vigorously debated in social theory, and many voices proclaim a "crisis of identity". Due to the structural changes transforming modern societies in the late twentieth century, former stable notions like class, nationality, race, gender and sexuality, etc. have shifted and lost their explicitness. In the words of Stuart Hall the subject of late modernity is more than ever conceptualised as having no fixed, essential or permanent identity. He writes:

> "The subject assumes different identities at different times, identities which are not unified around a coherent 'self'. Within us are contradictory identities, pulling in different directions, so that our identifications are continuously being shifted about. If we feel we have a unified identity from birth to death, it is only because we construct a comforting story or 'narrative of the self' about ourselves. The fully unified, completed, secure and coherent identity is a fantasy. Instead, as the systems of meaning and cultural representation multiply, we are confronted by a bewildering, fleeting multiplicity of possible identities, any one of which we could identify with – at least temporarily."[1]

---

1 Stuart Hall: The Question of Cultural Identity. In: *Modernity and its Futures*, Hg.v. Stuart Hall, David Held, Anthony McGrew. Cambridge: Polity Press 1992, pp.274-325, p.277.

This general pluralisation of identity contexts seems to increase to infinity with the emergence of a new space of interaction – the virtual world of the Internet. Two major references for interaction and identity have ceased to be in force in computer-mediated communication. There is no being face to face any longer, no eye-witness, nor can any material, geographic space be experienced and measured. The human being is no longer physically, but virtually present. Former identification markers like outward appearance, sex, voice, body language, clothing, etc. do not apply any more. The same is true for the geographic and cultural context in which the subject used to be placed. In electronic networks identity is no longer dependent on visual markers. It solely manifests itself in words and text, without support from the body. To express this new quality Scott Bukatman has coined the term "terminal identity": it is "an unmistakably doubled articulation in which we find both the end of the subject and a new subjectivity constructed at the computer station or television screen".[1]

In my interviews I wanted to find out how these young people made sense out of their life on-line. How did they describe the relation between their virtual and their "real" persona? Which cultural skills did they develop for a successful presentation of the self?

In the course of this paper I will mainly tell three exemplary stories before trying to draw a more general conclusion at the end. The emphasis will be put on letting you listen to the users' "narratives of the self" by paraphrasing or quoting their interviews as closely as possible. But first I will introduce you to the world of fantasy games on the Internet.

There are more than six hundred multi-user role-playing games on the Internet, mostly known as MUDs. MUD stands for "Multi-User Dungeon", and follows in the tradition of American fantasy role-playing games like "Dungeons and Dragons". Those games are fantasy stories, imaginatively acted out in small groups face to face around a table. They are especially popular among boys who meet for several evenings or whole weekends to play them.

MUDs are similar to role-playing games except for the important fact that they are no longer face to face – they are on-line. This allows up to a hundred or more people to play simultaneously – regardless of where in the world they are sitting. The play does not have to end any more because there are always enough fellow players. Thus the routine of playing becomes much more part of everyday life. The game reality very often is not so much an alternative as a parallel life.

MUDs evoke fantasy worlds which parallel those of J R Tolkien's "Lord of the Rings", science fiction scenarios like "Star Trek", or "World of Darkness"

---

1   Scott Bukatman: Terminal Identity. *The Virtual Subject in Postmodern Fiction*, Durham: Duke University Press 1993, p. 9.

and horror settings with vampires and werewolves. None of the games I am talking about are graphic, they are purely based on text. MUDs rely on the imagination and creativity of their players who continuously expand the MUD world after having acquired the necessary programming skills.

The databases for these virtual, and in most cases English-speaking worlds, can usually be found on one of the many university computers in Europe or the USA. So far the majority of the players are college students, since most universities provide them with free and often unrestricted Internet access. However, the number of younger players, logging in from private accounts, is continuously rising. Personally I am not a player. I did, however, gain some experience in MUDs before I conducted the interviews.

Before I start with the stories of my interview partners, I will give you a short example of the fantasy world of an adventure MUD called "Nightfall". Its database can be found in Tübingen, Germany,[1] and at the moment its players stem from the USA, Canada, Mexico, Spain, the Czech Republic, Russia, Great Britain, Norway and Germany. The reality in the game, also characterised as "interactive fiction", might appear like this:

"How about a drink?" I'm startled. Suddenly, Ovlor, a member of the elf race, materialises in a puff of smoke right in front of me, grinning broadly. In his position as wizard he has powers at his disposal which I as a new beginner or "newbie" can only dream about. I have come to my favourite pub in Nightfall City to relax from the tough adventures of the day:

In search of a magic potion I had looked death in the face when two brutal orcs burst out of the woods, of course right when I least expected it. I only survived thanks to Sita, Ovlor's girlfriend, who arrived just in time to join me in the fight against them. Together we also succeeded in finally discovering the secret tunnel to the walled town of Lorinia. In the course of all this we got closer to the solution of an important quest and gained a couple of experience points. Our level of energy dropped dangerously, however, and we needed to take a flying carpet from Lorinia to the capital to strengthen ourselves with a huge T-Bone Steak.

Welcome to the fantastic world of "Nightfall"! I want to tell the story of Sita and Ovlor, the couple which was just mentioned. They met one day in this MUD, introduced by a mutual friend. Ovlor soon showed a lot of interest in Sita's life off-line. He wanted to know her real name and the place from where she was logged in. Sita, usually more reluctant concerning these personal questions, told him that she was called Amy, was 19 years of age and studied at a college on the American East Coast. She learned that Ovlor's real name was Klaus and that he was a 21 year-old computing science student at the university of Tübingen in Germany. When he asked her to be penpals she found the idea exotic and accepted. Before the exchange of the first

---

1 The address is: telnet quest.tat.physik.uni-tuebingen.de.

handwritten letters they had already solved a number of quests together and "talked" for hours and hours on-line on the Net.

At first Klaus was not a person for Amy: "He was this cool guy on the Net, Ovlor, and he was my penpal. He wasn't a person. I hadn't even associated a face with him." This changed when she received a first letter with his picture. Now she realised that he was a real person. But still: his face did not really belong to her college life but to the MUD world into which she immersed herself gradually more and more.

Unlike Amy, Sita was a happy, attractive and outgoing person, who did not hesitate to talk about any subject popping up and willingly shared her opinion with others. Apart from their mutual life on the MUD, Amy enjoyed the opportunity to tell Klaus about her problems with her boyfriend John in "Real Life", the term MUD players use to refer to the off-line reality. Amy remembers: "Because I *needed* someone to talk to. And I was in a place physically where I couldn't talk to anyone because everyone was our (i.e. John's and her) friends."

Amy felt safe on the Net. Nobody could look at her, nobody was expecting anything from her, nobody was judging her. As Sita she tested various possible reactions to the events on the MUD, trying to come to grips with conflicting aspects of Amy's personality. She found more acceptance from her fellow players than she had expected. In her everyday life, however, she felt stuck and lonely. Her MUD friends seemed to understand her better and somebody was always there for her at whatever time of the day or night. She mainly shared her worries with Klaus and tried to ignore the feelings growing inside her as well as she could: "It was very easy for me to say 'This is the Net. And this is real life.' It was very easy for me to say 'I can love this person all I want because he's four thousand miles away. He is Ovlor, not Klaus. And I am not Amy. I'm Sita on the Net.'" In the long run, however, she was not able to keep her "net feelings", as she called them, and her virtual life on the net separate from her real life existence. The desire to be Sita also in her college life eventually led to a break up between her and her boyfriend John. Amy found consolation among her MUD friends and spent even more time behind her terminal.

But then she slowly began to face the situation. For the first time Klaus and Amy listened to their voices over the telephone, and shortly afterwards they confessed to each other the intensity of their feelings. They longed to meet in person. Seven months after her first talk with Ovlor, Amy sat on the plane to Frankfurt, nervous about meeting Klaus. She was worried whether they would get along as well as on the Net.

But on the difficult path of reconciliation between Amy and her virtual alter ego Sita a few important steps were missing still, withheld from Klaus. Amy's converging with Sita was not yet complete. To put it another way: Amy had not managed to successfully emancipate herself from the fiction and ideal physical image of Sita yet. Her self still lingered in a transitional stage between virtual and physical culture, not quite prepared to meet Klaus in person: "That was very hard for me because Sita was not heavy. She was *thin*. And that was the one thing that I held on to so tight like when I finally became Amy, it was like I really have to hold on to this part because I can't like, I can't tell someone that I'm overweight."

Not surprisingly, her outward appearance and the fact that she had lied to Klaus became quite a burden for their relationship. So far Klaus had only seen her face in a picture but when he saw her for the first time in person, she did not seem to have much in common with the woman he had got to know on the Net. To their relief this changed in the following weeks and today, more than three years after their first encounter on the net, they live together in Germany. After two years of a long-distance relationship via regular talk-sessions on the computer, Amy finished college and moved over here. Looking back at how it all began she concludes:

> "If Klaus and I had met somewhere and had a really nice talk, I don't know if it would have gone any further. I don't think so. But I don't know. I mean, I don't think I was what Klaus was looking for in a girl-friend … like whole package wise. I think, I was in intellect. And that's what he was getting. So, I mean, that's why he was coming back because he liked what he was getting in what I was saying. And I think that was what he was attracted to."

The characteristics of computer-mediated communication – you deal with only a few elements of a person and enjoy a certain anonymity – proved to be favourable in Amy's case. Her story is fortunate because she did not only engage in Net life as a compensation for the difficulties in real life, but worked through important personal concerns and changed. In retrospect she tries to make sense out of the process she went through:

> "I think I used the Net as – I mean the MUD – as … 'This is who I really am.' And that made for difficulties in real life. Because I wanted to be this person in real life."

And on another, later occasion she said:

> "The character that I figured was who I wanted to be – who I thought I wanted to be – And then, the more I played it, the more I found that it was easier to be that person in real life. It's kind of like you have practice. And I mean, so I'm happier and … I don't know, maybe it's self-actualisation. It's closer to the ideal person that you have in your mind."

In Amy's case role-playing in the MUD context seemed to have had the same function as psychodrama in the context of therapy. She managed to successfully integrate her on-line persona with her sense of an off-line self.

147

The second story takes place in a quite different context. It is, however, another example of a successful attempt to come to grips with one's personal identity while facing problems in the outside world.

Jack is a 24 year-old American exchange student who came to Tübingen for one academic year to improve his German. He acquired an Internet account to stay in touch with his friends back home. Since the semester had not yet started and since his German was still rather basic, he found it difficult to make German friends at first. Thus he spent a lot of time in the computing lab exploring other services on the Internet.

One day he discovered the chat service IRC (Internet Relay Chat). IRC can be characterised as a kind of written telephone conversation. It offers hundreds of different virtual rooms or "channels" in which up to fifty or more users gather to discuss specific topics or just have fun and chat in their mother tongue. To join one of these channels one has to pick a nickname that should be original to avoid being mistaken for somebody else. This nickname together with the address of the computer from where one logs into IRC is the only information other users get about you.

Jack had learned that the German equivalent of his name was Hans. And since he studied air and space technology he picked the name "Luft Hans". He visited different channels, the majority being populated by Americans. One day he went on an English-speaking channel called "Russia", joining all kinds of people interested in this country. Before he could engage in the discussion he was already verbally attacked by another user logged in from Texas who called him a Nazi and insulted him with a couple of hateful swearwords. Obviously he had taken him for a German. Although this was no pleasant experience it turned out to have an interesting formative influence.

Jack became particularly aware of the implications of the label of nationality and learned how difficult it can be to speak from a German position in an international context. On American channels he often engaged in discussions about racism, nationality and the question of how to deal with the national history. Jack thinks that his opinion on these issues was a mainstream American one, shared by many other Americans but when he stated the same with his supposedly German background, he was met with a lot of opposition, also from other nationalities. He was angry about that because he considered it as one of his tasks as an exchange student to encourage people to be more open-minded about each other, especially with regards to his host nation, Germany.

On the other hand he realised that to be mistaken for a German could also be an advantage for him in other contexts. In his German surroundings in Tübingen Jack was immediately identified as a foreigner, even from afar. His outward appearance, the choice of clothes, etc. suggested his American identity. It was especially evident when one listened to his strong accent and noticed his difficulties with German grammar, that he had not been brought up in Germany. Jack was rather frustrated about that. He wanted to immerse himself into German culture as much as possible and not just watch everything from outside like on a window-shopping expedition. To a certain degree IRC gave him the opportunity to see the world through German eyes not only on an international but also on a national level.

Once he logged into IRC he lost his usual outsider status, for thanks to his German e-mail address most users took his German identity for granted. When some people still happened to ask him where he was from, he did not lie, but tried to avoid the question by merely saying that he was in Tübingen at the moment. The difficulty which still remained, however, was the language, since most channels populated by Germans use their mother tongue to communicate. On IRC you are not forced to participate but may prefer to lurk and just watch what other people have to say. And if you want to contribute something you can take your time and think about the exact formulation provided that the topic has not changed in the meantime. One usually sends only one sentence at a time which leaves more flexibility, too. The fleeting character of IRC communication parallels oral speech quite closely, so users do not usually worry about typos or spelling mistakes.

All these factors turned out to be quite helpful for Jack. While he still had problems following oral conversations, he understood a lot more when he saw them passing by in written form on the screen. Furthermore he felt less inhibited to contribute himself. To distract from his spelling problems he often made jokes about his supposedly bad typing ability. Jack is convinced that the majority of his chat partners did not question his German identity. Only when he met them in person at one of the regular IRC parties or went to visit his newly won friends in Berlin, they noticed his foreign background. IRC helped Jack to gain more confidence in his knowledge of German and to make friends in different parts of Germany. The fact that he felt equal on this medium allowed him to relax from his stressful life as a foreign student in Germany.

My last example leads back into a fictional world. Reina, 21 years of age, and Tracy, 20 years of age, were two other American exchange students that I met in the computing centre in Tübingen. During the last months of their academic year they used to spend nearly every night at their computer terminals, switching between three or four different windows, since they played several games simultaneously.

When Tracy described her weekly schedule she started like this:

> "Sunday night I would go spend all night in the computer lab, get home Monday morning about, hmm, leave the lab about 7.30-8.00 a.m. because that's when people start coming in to do work. And the net slows down because that's when all of Europe comes on-line to do actual business-type things. The Net slows down at about eight o'clock in the morning on weekdays. So I give up and go home.

Maybe I would go to the grocery store, get groceries, get food, go home, go to bed, sleep. Wake up Monday evening. Go back down to the lab ..."

The reason that both women primarily played at night, was not so much that the connection worked better, but that they needed to adjust their schedule to US American time zones. They preferred a special type of MUD called World of Darkness MUSH. MUSH stands for multi-user shared hallucination. Acting out mutually invented story lines with a horror theme is central to these games which are populated by vampires and other dangerous creatures.

This game type is not as widespread as the already mentioned adventure MUDs. Since the majority of the players are American so far, the game activity is particularly high during the evening hours. For Reina and Tracy, being physically situated in Europe, this meant the very early morning hours. Tracy explains:

> "See, I tend to stay really late because some of my favourite people don't log in until 9.00 or 10.00 p.m. their time, which is 3.00 or 4.00 a.m. our time. Which is kind of aggravating and I wished they would like loose their real lives and play in the afternoon or something! But you know that you accommodate people, since I have no real life!"

Tracy and Reina both had several parallel characters in the MUSH games which needed to be played differently according to their individual personality. They consider their characters on the one hand as their personal creation but on the other they also grant them a certain autonomy. This may even go as far as that the characters sometimes happen to surprise their own creator. Both agree that they learn a lot about themselves through role-playing and explicitly describe it as therapeutic. Reina says:

> "Yeah, I think I have learned quite a bit about what triggers certain emotions, responses in me ... no matter how real and separate my characters become from who I am, I can't really say that they were completely independent and so I do learn a lot about myself. And I think what I actually get to see is aspects of myself as they would develop had things been different maybe, you know. Different aspects of a theoretical life."

Unlike Jack they had chosen to give up in the fight with the German language and the foreign surroundings. After a half a year in Germany they had decided to primarily spend their time constructing lives in English-speaking horror worlds. These fantasy lives were more expansive than the ones they lived in physical reality. The events in a world of darkness setting are everything but pleasant, though, and both stress that they would not like to be their characters. They just enjoy the thrill of the action. Above all, playing within the MUSH reality gave them the satisfaction to be in control. Tracy said:

150

> "And you can make it all go away whereas you know like real life, I mean, I'm still trying to figure out the code in Earth MUSH here, there is no quit command. I can't quit and log out and go home and make the bad (go away). I can't, I can't close the book and say 'I don't wanna read any more right now.'"

Unlike real life, the game reality can be left whenever she wants.

Thinking in the MUSH frame, switching back and forth between player and character became so dominant, that it started to shape Tracy's perception of real life. She developed a way of thinking in which life is made up of many windows and real life is just one of them called "Earth MUSH".

To understand my last quote of her in this context, I will have to explain a few terms. A "wizard" is a person who has higher powers than usual players and is responsible for the administration of the game. Wizards are also the ones that take care of the programming side of the game. They "code" it. Finally, people speak of "lag" when the connection is bad and and everything slows down on the screen. Tracy said:

> "One of our references to real life is 'Earth MUSH: It's terrible, you can never find a wizard when you want one. It's badly coded and it lags all the time!' You know, just our reference to the real world. And sometimes I begin to think that Tracy Smith at Earth MUSH is just another one of the characters that I play."

I have told three boundary stories of virtual culture. All of them have to do with switching identities when moving between on- and off-line world. The last one could even be described as a reality-switch, given the fact that the two women even adjusted their sleeping hours according to the game schedule.

It is more or less coincidence that all examples are American. I could have presented a German student, too, who has a secret female character. Since a gender switch has similar learning effects as a switch of nationality, I decided to rather give an account of Jack's experience. In the framework of this European symposium I consider it more relevant.

These stories are exemplary for the diversity of ways young people may use their on-line selves. Some enjoy experimenting with personae very different from their real life selves. Others rather play out aspects of themselves that are not total strangers but may be inhibited in real life.

In their analysis of the characteristics of late modernity the German sociologist Ulrich Beck[1] and his British colleague Anthony Giddens[2] have described the self as a "reflexive project". In the so-called "risk society" young people

1 Ulrich Beck: Risikogesellschaft. *Auf dem Weg in eine andere Moderne*, Frankfurt/Main: Suhrkamp, 1986.
2 Anthony Giddens: *The Consequences of Modernity*, Stanford: Stanford University Press, 1990. Anthony Giddens: Modernity and Self-Identity. *Self and Society in the Late Modern Age*, Oxford: Polity Press, 1991.

are on the one hand released from the traditional life plans of the past and enjoy more liberties. But on the other hand these conditions also imply higher risks and insecurities because the future is less certain. Young people are not just free to decide but also obliged to do so.

On-line environments might possibly help to deal with these risks a little better by offering permission to play, to try things out.

Due to their unparalleled opportunity for such play, Amy Bruckman[1] and Sherry Turkle[2] from the Massachusetts Institute of Technology have called on-line environments like MUDs "laboratories (or workshops) for the construction of identity". Players experience identity as a set of roles that can be mixed and matched and whose diverse demands need to be negotiated. The Internet as an element of the computer culture has contributed to thinking about identity as multiplicity. People are able to build a self by cycling through many selves.

Whether MUDs are good or bad for psychological growth is difficult to answer. With regards to the problem of MUD addiction Sherry Turkle states:

> "MUDs provide rich spaces both for acting out and working through. There are genuine possibilities for change, and there is room for unproductive repetition. The outcome depends on the emotional challenges the players face and the emotional resources they bring to the game. MUDs can provide occasions for personal growth and change, but not for everyone and not in every circumstance."[3]

Of course, people can get lost in virtual worlds. And therefore I consider it as one of our tasks here to try to understand the dynamics of virtual experience, both to foresee who might be in danger and to put these experiences to best use.

I want to end by once more giving a voice to the users themselves. I read a passage from an e-mail that Tracy sent to me more than one year after her return to the USA:

> "I really enjoy my fantasy lives – all of them. Each different character is like a different version of myself: who I might be if I were in such a place and so a time under these or those circumstances. I like the freedom of anonymity: no-one has to know what I look like or how I speak to get to know me; I am judged solely on how I write. And to me that feels good. On the other hand, I sometimes think I should get out more, see more people in "Real Life", do more things in real life.

---

1 Amy Bruckman: Identity Workshop: *Emergent Social and Psychological Phenomena in Text-Based Virtual Reality*, MIT Media Laboratory, 1992 (ftp: parcftp.xerox.com/pub/MOO/papers).
2 Sherry Turkle: *Constructions and Reconstructions of the Self in Virtual Reality*, (ftp://home.actlab.utexas.edu/conferences/3cyberconf/selfinvr.txt).
3 Sherry Turkle: Life on the Screen. *Identity in the Age of the Internet*, New York: Simon & Schuster, 1995, p. 200.

But then I think, this is real life. The people on the other ends of the terminals, whom I call my friends, are real people, too. It's especially complicated with a long-distance romance. So I don't know. My feelings are mixed about it, and I guess that's about as much as I can say."

Anke Bahl

Young virtual travellers in and outside the Internet

Abstract

In my study of young leisure users of the Internet, I have so far conducted six interviews with girls (three) and boys (three) between 16 and 19 years of age. They all go to college, and except for one of them come from middle-class or upper middle-class homes with home computers.

Among these users I have found two distinct attitudes toward the use of the Internet. One of them I call "technical attitude" or "cyberearth attitude", and the other "cyberspace attitude".

Young people with a technical attitude stress the tool-like character of their use, the use for information value, and the control of the system. Their use of the Internet is often determined by real life factors, and their conduct on the Internet follows the same lines of thinking as in real life. Their use of various services is balanced, and the time spent on the Internet moderate, approximately five to ten hours per week. All of the cyberearth youth in my study are boys.

Cyberspace youth see the Internet as a distinct sphere of life and its action on the Internet is mostly social in nature. They appreciate the social character of the Internet: the possibility of meeting new and different people, the anonymity of the cyberspace; and use it for their identity work. They mostly use services which are social in character: news- and IRC groups and e-mail. There is a tendency in their use of services from those with a group character i.e. news- and IRC groups towards the more individual service of e-mail. They could be described as heavy users; time spent on the Internet is ten hours or more per week. All of the cyberspace youth in my study are girls.

I certainly still need to go on with my study. As for the cyberearth and cyberspace, the sharp distinction between the sexes may probably fade away. Moreover, the use of the Internet for "pure entertainment", especially the use of the www service for this purpose, cannot easily be conceptualised according to the above described scheme of action.

Introduction

In Finland, media publicity on the Internet is immense. Also, theoretical literature is starting to be available on the Internet and virtual reality. There is less empirical research on data networks, however, and the research carried out in Finland is dispersed into a number of fields, for example, information and communication studies, computer science and psychology. In general, surveys describing the frequency of use of various network services dominate the research settings. Most studies on data networks concentrate on the experiences of users with different available methods having their focus rather on the systems than their users. Moreover, the empirical data usually comes from business or university organisations (Savolainen, 1996). So, there is a need for studies on the leisure use of the Internet and for studies focusing on the meanings people give to it.

My starting point is in the context of youth research. The aim is to understand the use of Internet in this context; the meaning it has for its young users, the part it plays in their lives. The reason for asking how the young people understand the Internet and their own use of it, stems from the belief that people's actions are affected by the meanings they give to situations. In this meaning the reality is socially constructed. And its complexity, subtlety and constantly changing character calls for a position to be taken by qualitative reseachers, and for a need to see the researcher as a "human-as-instrument" as coined by Lincoln and Guba (See Maykut and Morehouse:26)

Young people have generally been considered as interpreters of our times and often seen as the pioneers of cultural change, and this is even more so, when we talk about the computer generation. Youth and Internet – both dynamic and changing – have a clear connection to the questions about cultural change and late modernity. And the study of young users of the Internet further offers the advantage that their use has not been influenced by university or work life. Therefore there is a certain fascination to be able to describe and understand it.

This type of a qualitative and emergent study is certainly not the best or easiest possible one to be presented in its middle stages of analysis. That is why I am not even trying to build theory here; it would be harmful to bind one's hands too much in the face of further conversations and analysis. Moreover, I try to use the language of my conversational partners as much as possible, and direct my attention to finding good questions to guide my further work.

Method

In theoretical sampling the decision on what data to collect next and where to find them is made on analytical grounds. This means that the process of data collection is controlled by the emerging theory (see Glaser and Strauss, 1967), whereby the important or salient dimensions in the phenomenon tell us who to contact or where to go next in our study. So far I have conducted altogether six interviews with girls (three) and boys (three) between 16 and 19 years of age. They all go to high school, and except one of them, to one of the best high schools in Helsinki. So, in most cases they come from families with well educated parents, and home computers; middle class or upper-middle-class homes.

The respondents were generally open and willing to talk. Most of the interviews lasted approximately two hours. The emphasis was on the active role of the interviewee in shaping the discussion; seeing interviews as guided conversations. The depth, detail, and richness I seek in interviews is what Clifford Geertz (1973) has called "thick description". I have tried to attain a congenial and co-operative experience, in which both interviewer and interviewee work together to achieve the shared goal of understanding. Rubin and Rubin (1995) suggest the term "conversational partner" to describe the parties of this type of guided conversation. I have a thematically organised paper with me in the interviews to help me to remember to take up all the important themes. However, I try to manage without it as much as possible; it has generally been at the end of the interviews when I have paid some attention to it.

Transcribed interviews are then coded using the protocol developed by Strauss (1987). The objective is to identify categories into which the data can be grouped and to determine connections between these categories. As the coding proceeds, particular categories become core categories and are used to guide later stages of analysis. As the theoretical saturation point (see Strauss, 1987: 35 or Strauss and Corbin, 1990: 188) has not been reached at this point of study, and the research process is emergent, following data collection efforts and analyses will probably alter the outcome.

Cyberearth and cyberspace

Machinery or space

So far I have found two profoundly different types of attitude towards the use of the Internet. It should be emphasised, though, that these types are meant to be taken as interpretative schemes, not as categories; the use of them as interpretative schemes is all the more important taking into consideration the current phase of my study.

One of these could be called technical attitude or technical interest. So, it comes as no surprise that in this study two of three of those young people belonging to this group also have computers as a hobby. However, as computers are a hobby even for people representing the other attitude, what remains is a certain attitude towards the Internet; an attitude which emphasises its tool-like character and its use as an information resource.

> "It gives you an easy and handy way of communication in the first place. That's what I've got. And I think it's the most important part of it, what it's most suitable for. And the next thing would be information." (Jaakko, boy 16)

> "I'm waiting when it (his e-mail) comes to use. I think these normal communication appliances are definitely much better, like, say, the telephone." (Petri, boy 18)

A study by Nissen (1993) on Swedish computer hobbyists finds two groups of these enthusiasts when it comes to their social lives: the ones are generally sociable and the others tell that they "never really were party people". The computer hobbyists in my study seem to belong to the group of generally sociable youth. They have other hobbies and they have good friends outside computer circles. They also use the Internet for communicating with other people and friends, as do the Swedish young people in Nissen's study by using Bulletin Board Systems, which existed before the Internet. Nissen finds that the use of BBS does not affect the boys' other types of contacts. He also sees that the system which he studied builds a community where traditions are held alive and changed. The boys often meet each other face to face, too. All this is similar to my findings. The Internet offers them a way of communication besides its other offerings. The emphasis, however, is on the information content of the Internet.

> "When you are there by the computer, you get excited to chat about it. I have never even tried to find anything else in there ... And then if I want to talk deeply, I talk somewhere else. I have another life as well, not just computers." (Jaakko, boy 16)

> "No, I don't get much out of it (talking about IRC). Say, for example now when we're talking: if you were asking me through a computer, wouldn't that be like, you wouldn't actually see at all, how I am." (Tommi, boy 16)

I call this attitude "cyberearth attitude" because of its earthliness, matter-of-factness, no-nonsenseness. Compared to the other attitude, which I call the "different world attitude", or the "cyberspace attitude", this point becomes clearer. For these users the Internet is not just any new medium, and it has little to do with computers as a hobby. Sociality plays a key role in their use of the Internet. There is plenty of life there.

> "There is always someone to talk to. Always someone new to meet. In the street it is much more difficult to go and talk to a person, in Finland, anyway. But there, there you could just go to a channel, and say 'Hi, is there anyone here who would have time for a little chat?', and so on." (Tiina, girl 19)

> "I didn't think it was the Internet that was so special, but the thing when I realised that I was not the ONLY one, who was interested in these toys. It was like "Oh, my God, there are other people in the world, I am not unnatural!" (Leena, girl 17)

> "Everyone can be who he or she wants to be, you're allowed to be yourself there. And then you can play with personalities, act a different character from what you really are."
> Question: "Have you tried this?"
> "Not yet: I'll have to do that, actually (laughs)!" (Minna, girl 16)

In contrast to cyberearth, cyberspace means action for its own sake for its travellers, or action which would be impossible to carry out "on earth". Cyberspace people appreciate the possibilities the Internet offers. For them the Internet is a distinct space with its own attractions, most of them social in character.

This attitude is far from technical interest; sometimes even in deep contrast to it as for example, machines may come to mind, when the life in cyberspace causes sorrow or trouble. A girl who was deceived by a boy in IRC and found out about it, tells about her feelings:

> "I was disappointed, thinking: "Well, I should have known really. After all, it's only machinery ..."

Controlling the Net and controlling life on the Net

Controlling the Internet is hardly a theme in conversations with cyberspace youth. This is in deep contrast to the cyberearth people, who understand the Internet more as a system and less as a distinct sphere of life. They continuously talk about controlling it, either how they can or cannot control it, or how it is uncontrollable and messy as a system.

> "Well, the thing doesn't really work. Even now the Internet is sticky and slow and everything like that. If even more things will be put in, then no-one will be able to control it, and it simply doesn't work. So that I hope it won't widen much more ... And that the quality would get better, too. Because you can find a lot in there, there're plenty of good things there, but then there is so much total crap as well." (Jaakko, boy 16)

> "And I've always been bothered by the fact that the system is really still in its infancy, they're selling a semi-finished product ... It's really rather tangled and slow, you know, and the information is really badly scattered there. If you sometimes go and try to find something, it's really difficult to catch. (Petri, boy 18)

Cyberspace youth in contrast are mostly not very interested in controlling the machine.

> "O.K. I'm interested in the Internet maybe, but I'm not so interested in technique. Of course, it is funny to know how it works or so, but I'm not like the people who count 'Hi there, I have Netscape version 3.0, which one do you have? Really: only the 2.5?', or anything like that. I think it is more of a medium, a tool, nice as such, and nice as a phenomenom, but not that it would be an end in itself perhaps." (Leena, girl 17)

> "Well, I still have a whole lot of things which I can't do, because my limits were there, what I learnt there and then, the couple of things,

which I necessarily needed to know, and then I used only them. I still don't know many tricks there." (Tiina, girl 19)

Even if Minna clearly counts as a cyberspace traveller, she is still very interested in being able to control the machine. However, as the cyberearth people seem to be interested in the control for its own sake, or for artistic purposes (demo-making, 3D pictures, etc), for Minna this wish for control stems from her wish to be able to control her own life and her life in cyberspace, and it also follows her use in time. Minna would like to learn to cover her acts on the Internet and to be able to deceive if needed:

"People are controlled all the time, day and night; wherever they go. It does annoy me quite a lot. And that's why I've grown interested in these privacy things ..."

"I like to make changes to pictures. See how far I can take it with my knowledge and capabilities. I got excited about it because there are these pictures in the so-called yellow papers, you see so many pictures which have been worked on. So, I grew interested in knowing if I could do it, too – mischief like that – well, not really – you know."

Cyberspace: anonymity and deceit

In his study from 1987, Myers finds two different types of leaders amidst the users of Bulletin Board Systems: system experts and social experts. Social experts dominated the system by what Myers calls "social context manipulation" and could dominate communication without much technical knowhow or control over the system. A major difference between these two groups was their attitude toward anonymity. Anonymity was more important for the social leaders, so important that they never revealed their real names to Myers (See Nissen, 1993). Nissen does not find this type of division; in his study the leadership seems to be a matter of time and energy.

My study would clearly seem to support Myers' findings, and also give some explanation for the reason for these differences. In the BBS which Nissen studied, conversations concentrated around everyday chat and computer matters whereas in Myers' study there were more messages with personal information, jokes, sexual matters and stories. So, it is probable that members in Myers' study were more heteregenous including people who in my study are called "cyberspace people".

Late modern times are times for individual identity work, and leisure time plays an important role in this process. (for example see Grundström and Siurala, 1991) Individuality is seen as the inner nature of human beings, and in an ideal situation the individual takes the initiative for action and makes the choice of her or his action her or himself, and is also able to account for it. There is a connection with courage and social abilities: even if individuality is natural for all, it is important to dare to put one's own individuality on show in differing social situations (Suurpää, 1996). The Internet would seem to offer a place for at least mock training these capabilities: the ability to jump into fast changing situations, come into contact with new people and ideas.

> "If you write true stories all the time, then you can't make such a long letter, when you go to school in the morning, come from school, do your home work, go to sleep, or are on the Internet in-between. When there are such days, you can't come up with a lot to tell them, and that's why you have to use your imagination then." (Minna, girl 16, cyberspace)

– "Sometimes I try out the boundaries everyday life in there. I come up with some stories, about what has happened to me or what has happened to a friend, or create my own characters."

– "Do you believe that the others do that as well?"

– "Yes, I think that they do, in some ways."

– "How do you mean 'in some ways'?"

– "Well, if they tell for example about their friends. I think that it is so, that what we deceive, is telling things as if they had happened to a friend. That it is easy to say that I have a friend who had this or that exprerience, easier than to say that it happened to me." (Minna, girl 16, cyberspace)

Earth rules and space rules

As cyberearth youth do not take the Internet as a separate space, but rather a continuation of their normal living, they also tend to take the oncoming situations very much like they would take them in their real lives.

> "I am just not interested in anything like that (talking about IRC). To someone I don't know at all, no, I wouldn't ... No, I don't think it is so REAL. So, I don't like it ... I want to see the person ... Say, if I were writing some real stuff to someone, I wouldn't know if he or she is telling the truth. That I may be here writing everything as it is, but he or she is telling stories to me, or something like that. No, I wouldn't, I want to see the person to whom I'm talking ..." (Tommi, boy 16)

> "I have commented very little. Normally, I just read the opinions of the others. It somehow feels so big, when you're there: from all over the world you have people writing and the discussion moves forward so fast, that you don't even bother to try. I've never got excited like that really. It's O.K. to go and read, though. I've written something to the Finnish areas, because they don't feel so big." (Jaakko, boy 16)

The attitude of cyberspace youth is very different. For them cyberspace creates – at least partly – its own life world, where prevailing rules are more or less different from those of real life. They can either follow and accept rules which totally differ, as for example in case of deceit, or they use the atmosphere of the space for acting more freely, as they would perhaps like to do in their real lives as well. They are also more enthusiastic about meeting different, weird, new and foreign people on the Net.

"It is that you can try out your limits, and no-one will mind, because everyone's doing it. Or, not everyone is doing it, but everyone has the same possibility to do it. So, somehow it's very interesting to see what happens when you act as someone else." (Tiina, girl, 19)

Question: "Are new relationships born there?"

"Yes, yes! We don't write only about these toys, but about other things as well. There are very interesting personalities there." (Leena, girl 17)

Cyberspace people often contact other news group or IRC members personally, and talk about personal matters.

"Or I ask for example 'Please, tell me your opinion about this and that'. Or then I send for him or her a message saying 'I think your story was this and that'. Or something like 'When you wrote about this and that last time, I thought: what an interesting thought, you must be an interesting person. I would love to know you better'. Sometimes they answer, sometimes they don't." (Leena, girl 17)

"Pretty often it was so that there was a guy I knew, and I wrote a message asking: 'How is your love life?' and that's how the chat begins then." (Minna, girl 19)

These relationships of the cyberspace youth have many features of what Giddens (1991) calls the pure relationship. They are friendships where the connection with the other person is valued for its own sake; it is sought only for what the relationship as such can bring to the partners involved. The pure relationship is focused on intimacy, and so are these meetings on the Internet. Intimacy brings the question of mutual trust to the surface. Tiina tells how she was once deceived by a boy:

"But still, those had been matter of fact discussions, and he had talked seriously about his own opinions. But then he had lied about some happenings, facts, things which he said had happened but hadn't. He had found these out because he had to come up with something more than the age and the name ... He is still one of my best friends. ... He said that he had just wanted to try it out, that he thought that it hardly will last longer than one night, that he just wanted to try it out, how well he can lie ..." (Tiina, girl 19)

Giddens sees authenticity in the sense of "being true to oneself" to become a fundamental value and a framework for self-actualisation in circumstances of late modernity. This is because of its value in the fight against personal meaninglessness, a fundamental psychic problem due to the separation of individuals from the moral resources needed to live a full and satisfying life.

162

To act authentically is more than just acting in terms of a valid self-knowledge; it also demands the discovery and fulfilment of one's "true self". However, additionally this process of self-actualisation is morally stunted. (Giddens, 1991) This importance of the "true self" is clearly seen in Tiina's reaction; in her relationship and discussions with this boy, the crucial fact was not the truth, but the authenticity of meaning:

> "He told his own real opinions, but told fictive sexual experiences. Which did not have such importance for me really, let him tell stories if it pleases him; anyway, a smart person, and was chatting genuinely – otherwise."

Cyberearth people also discuss personal and daily things, and sometimes get to know people really well over the Net. However, this seems to happen much more seldom, and the discussions tend to be less free and more matter-of-fact, not the least because they often occur with people from the same town and there is the possibility for a real meeting.

> "It's also a bit difficult with it, that if you learn to know someone there, he or she isn't necessarily there again the next day or for some time. It can be difficult to continue from where you were in the discussion ... I've never done it (changed e-mail addresses wih someone). It is, anyway, it is on-line, so that it's really a different thing." (Petri, boy 18)

In cyberspace real life attributes like age, gender and status are not apparent. Cyberspace travellers see this as one of the best aspects of the communication via the Internet, whereas cyberearth youth either move on well-known ground and meet few people from outside their circles, or react as they would do in real life.

> "And then I once wrote to an elderly guy, he was some German guy, really old, a hospital type, who had just grown interested in the Internet ... And another time I wrote to an Australian English teacher, who had a daughter, who was three years younger than me. That type of thing ...."

Question: "How was it then?"

> "Nothing special, really, you don't think about the age when you're writing." (Minna, girl 16, cyberspace)

> "We had been sending some e-mails, it was maybe the fifth one, when I found out – I had thought he was very young, about my age – and then I found out that he was 35 years of age and owned a company, was a director of a company, which imported some chemicals to America, and the turnover was two million. It was a shock to know with whom I had actually been talking!" (Jaakko, boy 16, cyberearth)

Routine and feeling

Considering the earthly attitude and technical interest of cyberearth travellers, it comes as no surprise that for them the Internet does not bring great feelings. Like Jaakko says: "There's hardly any feeling. I manage it with routine."

Or like Petri says: "When you have so much knowledge, you can look at it with an air of superiority. It doesn't really have so much to offer."

On the other hand, for cyberspace people, the use of the Internet brings a lot of positive feelings. They are concentrated when they surf, immersed in the world they are in.

> "I could see nothing but that (the screen). I was totally concentrated on it. It is really a discussion (talking about IRC), I'm talking to someone there. If someone else comes beside me then about something else, I am like 'Shut up, you, I have something to do!' And it is its own world, really exciting, if you meet new people ... It is that you really have a great opportunity to meet people from all over the world." (Tiina, girl 19)

> "Sometimes that happens. If I find a good page, it can happen that I am really addicted to it for a long time. Just because I'm interested in all kinds of weird things, I once managed to find a page where you can see stories and news on all the New York mafia families ... It's like that, I really get excited about things like that." (Minna, girl 16)

> "I'm interested in these toys, and then I happened to be on the Internet and I thought: 'Hmm, could there be some information on them?' and there was an immense amount of www pages. And in a way, after that day I've been totally addicted to it (ironically)." (Leena, girl 17)

Addiction

The young people of this study all use the term "addiction" in one form or another, and they think of their use in terms of it. Addiction is a theme often presented in the media, but it is also one for young people themselves. Modernity puts the young people of today under the pressure of continuously having to balance freedom against homelessness. Fornäs states (1995) that the conflict between striving for intense, close and symbiotic devotion and a distancing reflexivity seem to have become a main cultural theme in late modernity. As addiction is at the heart of this problem area, its place at the centre of young people's discourse is not surprising. All young people in my study also refer to their own use in terms of addiction, even when not directly asked about addiction.

– "Do you have other hobbies?"
– "Yes. I'm not an addict, anyway."

–   "No, you are there really rather little, only a couple of hours per week, I don't think it's much." (from the conversation with Petri, boy 18)

"I don't understand, how you can become so. I've never been myself, I mean, even though I was there quite a lot, but I never was such an addict, you know, that I had to get there." (Jaakko, boy 16)

"I haven't used it such a lot, I haven't got any addiction, as I think that it's a fairly clumsy system ...." (Petri, boy 18)

It is perhaps not surprising that the Internet does not cause addiction to its cyberearth users with their technical interest and the feeling that it doesn't work quite as it should. Maybe their "addiction" would instead direct itself to computing.

But is there really a good case for the thinking in terms of addiction? And if not, how could it be explained, if we don't allow ourselves to be satisfied with the overall importance of the theme in current conditions of late modernity? Maybe it has to do with the fact that the "addiction discourse" in a silent way underlines the difference between cyber reality and reality? For it is discussed in ways which leave the definition of the term open and wavering; it is not clear what the attributes of addiction are. This can be seen from the following two quotations which are taken from a discussion with the same boy:

"He said, that if you once talk with someone, you'll have to chat with him or her all the time, or you want to do that. Well, I don't want to be addicted like that; that I would have to ..." (Tommi, boy 16)

"Human relations, I think it's the most important thing in life. I could not live without friends. I really, really couldn't. I mean, it would be terrible if I suddenly lost all my friends, or my mother or brother." (Tommi, boy 16)

Giddens also discusses ontological security and its relationhip to practical consciousness. Practical consciousness produces ontological security by bracketing out questions about ourselves, others and the object world, which have to be taken for granted in order to keep on with everyday activity. Giddens states that the answers which these modes of orientation give are emotional rather than simply cognitive (Giddens, 1991). Maybe the addiction discourse could be seen as a cultural opposition to the cultural setting of the Internet, a setting which erodes faith in the coherence of everyday life? Anyway, in my study the two people who are the most horrified about addicition are at the same time those two who seem to be the most social in their normal lives; they talk a lot about their friends and families with love and devotion. Would the acceptance of the cyberspace sociality as legitimate mean undermining the importance of the normal life socialising, the root and basis of their identities?

165

Tiina was an addict, and is now renegotiating her relationship to the use of the Internet. She talks about her use mostly in passive terms even though she still uses the Internet quite a lot; and her account is somewhat contradictory. One of the contradictions is directly connected to this very negative attitude; as, interestingly, her experiences on the Internet are altogether not that negative. Tiina tells about her negative attitude:

– "It is somehow such a foreign world, that you immediately feel that it's so far away. I also get the feeling that I should kick my brother out of the door, outside, 'go and have a walk at least!' or 'do something real!'"

– "Why then do you think that it's so 'not real'?"

– "Because they are machines! (laughs a bit) They are machines."

The addiction is still strongly associated with the idea of a "computer nerd". Nissen (1993) asks why it is that this idea of computer "addition" gets so much attention and publicity; why not for example the horse "addiction" of girls. Because computers are machines, and our relationship to machines is contradictory; filled with as much fear as hope?

Tiina visited her IRC groups again after having been away for quite a while. She tells about her first revisit:

– "Many people came to ask me, if I'm the same old person, and where I've been and things."

– "Well, what did you tell them?"

– "Well, I said, I changed the computer for life (laughs a bit) or something like that, because it's a common joke there 'Sell the computer, buy life (laughs a bit).'"

The ideal of freedom, one of the characteristics of our times has been described by Ziehe in the exclamation: "Do something with your life!" Experience is no longer dominated by bad consciousness of wanting too much, but by the fear of achieving too little (Ziehe, 1992). Personal freedom means possibility for experience and openness of the future; but this freedom demands to be used, too. Addiction could be seen as an escape from this obligation; it is the opposite of controlling oneself and one's life. Tiina tells how one becomes an addict:

– "You get excited about IRC and stay there. You chat with people. But soon the stories are told, because the other ones don't have new stories any more. Anyway, they're people who sit the whole day by the computer ... And then they start complaining, ... and then it's all complaining, and then everyone else's stories end, too, and people are not really interested in a new person any more. So, that's how you become an addict."

– "Because there's nothing to say any more?"

- "Yes. Then you start thinking, you start thinking everything, there by the machine: how terrible your life is, that you just sit there and IRC, and everything is going by. But you just can't stop it."
- "Is the discussion like that then?"
- "Well, not directly, few people admit directly that they are addicted - it is really addictive. But yeah, it's a common subject that IRC is a bad thing."
- "Really?"
- "Yes."
- "Why is that?"
- "Because it is just so addictive. You just continue with it. And then everything goes by."

A British researcher, Leslie Haddon, is able to show that computer associated activities are culturally interpreted as male (see Nissen, 1993). This might cause a further burden of proof for female users of the Internet. Tiina also gives the label of computer nerd as one of the reasons for not using the Internet, and two girls have marked the theme with a laugh; one use of laugh in conversations is as a strategy against losing face (Alasuutari, 1993). However, in my study, the girls also use the Internet much more than boys, so the term addiction may also therefore be more sensitive.

"I don't want to have a label of computer nerd. It's that. Then I have a bad conscience if I'm there too much, because everyone talks about it, that the people who IRC have nothing else." (Tiina, girl 19)

"I've read them (media stories about addiction). Terrible stories; something like 'S/he stays the whole day, twenty-nine hours a day with the computer!' I don't know, certainly, they exist, people who are really totally addicted. But I'm not like that myself – or 'I don't think I am (jokingly).'" (Leena, girl 17)

"... my mother has sometimes said, when I've been there for a really long time, that I start to sabotise the whole family, that I am there every day (a small laugh). But I don't know then (an 'official' tone in the voice)." (Minna, girl 16)

Girls and boys

At this point of my study the division line between cyberearth and cyberspace travellers is also the division line between the two sexes: the cyberearth travellers are boys and the cyberspace travellers are girls. Computers have been a rather male-dominated hobby and as the attitude of cyberearth surfers is reminiscent of a similar kind of technical interest, it is hardly surprising that cyberearth travellers in this study so far consist of boys.

However, it is not only the former use of computers which creates this division; all the girls also had computers available at their homes for a long time, and two of them had already had computers as a hobby before their use of the Internet. Interestingly, though, one of the girls actually started her computer career with the the discovery of the Internet. For all of them, however, the Internet was a turning point; it was the Internet which really got them excited.

I do know, however, from my conversations and otherwise, that there are boys with the cyberspace attitude.

> "In the beginning I only learnt to know boys. Then they took me with them to another channel. They asked me: 'Hi, what are you doing here, there are nothing but stupid kids here!' And that's really how it was: a lot of boys from "peruskoulu" (elementary school, comprehensive school), whose stories certainly were on a low level; there they can give out those four-letter words so that Mummy doesn't see."

It is possible that younger users who start their use of computers at the same time as they start to use the Internet are more apt to see it as cyberspace; that the age plays a fundamental role in the formation of user habits. Still, there are plenty of older male cyberspacers, too, so this cannot be the explanation.

> "There was one guy, a really funny guy, with whom I used to chat less seriously. Once he then came to the channel and seemed to be somehow sad, and I asked him through a message (i.e. privately): 'Hi there, are you O.K.?' And he started to tell openly how his father had died."

Several studies have shown that girls and boys have different world views. Helve states in her study on Finnish girls that the critical attitudes of girls are bringing a new political climate to the country. Girls are more critical toward the society, economic growth as well as science and technology. They also generally have a more global attitude than boys (Helve, 1992). These findings fit well together with the girls and boys in my study.

> "If we think of our world; it's really superficial; it goes like "it's really important to earn money, earn money, earn money, go to work in the morning and be a respected member of the society', that: 'Is that all, is all of living just that?'" (Leena, girl 17)

> "Many things are decided because of money. I think it's really stupid; it can be because of a couple of people and their greed that huge areas get destroyed." (Minna, girl 16)

Moreover, it is stated that whereas girls try to build up their identities by establishing close relationships with other people, boys are more inclined toward action and try to build identities which do not depend on other people. Lähteenmaa (1992) concludes that the rebellion and search for excitement of girls is different from that of boys. Their overstepping of limits is generally less visible and filled with sense of responsibility. Still, it is possible to overstep limits even this way; by using cultural imagination. Travelling, an especially beloved hobby of Finnish girls, could be viewed from this angle. Grundström interprets the inter rail travel of young people as a modern test of womanhood, where the limits of one's competence and personality are put to test (Grundström, 1991). Following these lines of thinking, the Internet travellings of the girls in my study could be described as exciting journeys to cultural imagination, or as personality tests in an imaginative culture.

Moreover, it is stated that girls have to engage in more profound identity work than boys, because for girls the world looks less given and less free from conflict and also because they have traditionally been more dependent on culturally given behaviour models, which are now breaking (see Näre and Lähteenmaa, 1992 and Siurala, 1991).

This and the nature of the girls' use of the Internet would create an unstable background for the girls' enthusiastic use of the Internet. The Internet clearly offers girls possibilities to try to overstep the limits of the everyday world. And all this can be done in a way well suited to girls: through active engagement in relationships which on the Internet can be more plentiful and heteregenous than in real life, and without causing trouble to either other people or to themselves.

There is a further reason why the Internet seems to create a suitable place for identity work for girls: all girls feel that it is fairly equal because of its anonymity. The boys in my study have a similar feeling; but understandably, the boys do not elaborate on it as positively as the girls do. However, the girls' experiences have not been only positive. Sexual harassment cases at least in some of the IRC groups are common, and the male domination of the Internet can also be frightening.

> "On the Internet I think that men and women are fairly/really equal. So that I think the atmosphere there is such, that it doesn't matter, if you are a girl or a boy." (Minna, girl 16)

> "I think that it maybe has positive effects for the equality of the sexes. Because it is in such a way anonymous, so that you don't see the person's face or looks, when you're talking with him or her. And in a way, you concentrate more on his or her thoughts. But maybe this is just a hope. Sometimes when you are in a news group and it is a girl's name, so no-one pays any attention to you, or so." (Leena, girl 17)

> "In a way it is very frightening, because it's a very male-dominated world, anyway. Because in some boxes, if you are a girl, everyone will notice that 'Oh, yeah, her name is Leena, so ...'"

Gender

The Internet makes it easier to talk about sensitive matters, for example sex and gender relationships. So, these are often on the agenda there. The relative anonymity of the Internet may also make it easier to try to get contact with the opposite sex. Girls, who are not many compared to the number of boys are very popular in IRC groups and boxes (= similar to IRC but not connected to the Internet).

> "I think that because there are so few girls in there, when you just write about anything to someone and have a few more intelligent opinions, they immediately think 'Oh, she's very smart, she's really wonderful!', like that, you know." (Leena, girl 17)

> "... Sometimes I thought that there was such a wordless competition about girls' attention. Because there were so few girls. Then you were a really good guy if you got attention from girls. That's the reason why so many boys necessarily wanted to be my friends, even if we didn't really find each other that sympathetic, but because I was a girl." (Tiina, girl, 19)

Traditional gender relations have been deeply problematised by modernisation. The Internet with its anonymity offers a place for identity work about gender and gender relations. No wonder, that virtual gender swapping is a normal phenomenon in IRC. (See also Turkle, 1995) Tiina tells how her boyfriend acted as a girl in IRC:

> "He had such a nic (nickname), that one could think that he would be a girl. An American asked him 'are you a girl?' or 'you surely are a girl?' He said 'Yeah, yeah, surely.' And it was actually very nice to look at, when he was thinking what to comment, like 'No, a girl wouldn't say it like this ...', but he really thought about it, about what a girl would say. And it was interesting, really."

General flaming and rules for good behaviour on the Internet have been given a lot of attention in the media and elsewhere. The relatively anonymous situation on the Internet certainly offers possibilities for this type of behaviour. The young people in my study have met flaming on the Internet, but it does not really seem to bother them very much. On the other hand, sexual harassment, which also occurs, is a touchier subject, as it feels much nastier and is generally more difficult to deal with, too.

> "Approximately at least once a day, someone comes to suggest something, you know ... As I once said to someone, putting it at its crudest: it is so that during the daytime kids are asking you about the size of your bra and in the evening, disgusting rude old men are asking you, what clothes you're wearing."

Is it that for some of us the virtual empowerment is a solipsistic affair, an empowerment which entails refusal to recognise the substantive and independent reality of others, as Robins concludes? In virtual reality the continuity between the potential space that supports infantile illusions of magical creative power, and that which is associated with mature aesthetic creativity becomes particularly apparent. Robins argues that techno environments of cyberspace are particularly receptive to the projection and acting out of unconscious fantasies (Robins, 1995). At the same time, the Internet, however, also offers a possibility to deal with these in a way which does not exist in "real life":

> "In the long run, one learnt to be disgusting oneself. My boyfriend was really shocked about what I did, when a guy came to ask about a 'little session with him'. What you do is you follow the discussion for a while, saying yes to everything, and then suddenly say something so that he stops bothering you ... You have to do it that way, that they understand ... When he understands that you are not with it, and thinks 'Help, now she is laughing at me there!', then he doesn't have the nerve to go on with it any more."

What are the consequences of this "moment of disillusionment" (see Winnicott, 1988: 107) for life in the real world? As the Internet is emptier than "real life" from the symbolic communication which Foucault sees strongly bound to power, sexual harassment becomes open and obvious. Foucault stresses that power not only prevents people from doing things, it also forces them to creative action (Fornäs, 1995). Maybe the Internet can offer a further kick into the creative direction in power games; it may be an easier option there than in normal life. And could that have an empowering effect?

Tiina tells how she used this trick together with another girl:

-   "Once in IRC we (with another girl also in IRC that night) decided to give them a lesson. We changed our nics (= IRC names) to something else, something sweet, something like Doctor Love. And then we established a new channel also with an idiotic name, and started to ask these guys (the guys who had been bothering them for a long time) to come there. And again, we played this game, which I told you about. So as to give them a little lesson."

-   "Well, did they get one?"

-   "Well, they did then, when they realised, that it had been some girls they knew, who had really made them go nuts, and who had had a really good laugh on them."

Also otherwise, Tiina feels that she is more determinative in her relationships with boys in IRC than in "real life":

> "It's perhaps that in normal life, I don't so easily tell guys off about things ... In IRC I can easily say really toughly, whereas in normal life it is a bit like well ... maybe more courageous in that way."

Power is, of course, present in the Internet interaction in many ways. In a study by Sproull and Kiesler, for example, which was made in 1983 in a U.S. company, people studied found e-mail to be a particularly practical tool when they had to send a message to a person above them in the organisational hierarchy. The study also gave evidence to the assumption that e-mail communication offers a possibility to a more uninhabited use of words, flaming (see Savolainen, 1996).

The use patterns of the Internet

What services of the Internet do these six young people then use? Are there any tendencies to be found? Do the cyberspace and cyberearth types differ from each other also in terms of actual use of services? The answer is: "Yes, they do."

Time spent on the Internet is the biggest divider: The cyberspace youth spend more time in virtual reality (from approximately ten up to twenty hours per week) than the cyberearth youth (from approximately five to ten hours per week). The largest common denominator is the use of www pages; all of the young people in my study sometimes use this service. How much they use if for information, how much for entertainment purposes, differs from one to the other; it is common, though, also for those who emphasise the use for getting predetermined information, to "get lost" on some other pages every once in a while.

The cyberearth youth use the services perhaps more evenly, as no one service has totally captivated them. Most often, the services they use are determined by real life: if they need a new programme, they go to ftp; if they have a computer problem, they may ask for help in an IRC group; when their friends are abroad, they use e-mail to stay in contact. They do, however, try out new services as these come on to the market, and time spent on the Internet rises accordingly. This is, however, a transitory phase only, for as they have learnt to manage the service, the enthusiasm fades away, and they return to more or less similar pattern of use, perhaps added to by the new service.

The enthusiasm of cyberspace surfers begins with a "great discovery". Interestingly, all the girls emphasise the role of luck in telling about the beginning of their use – just how large a part pure luck really has played is difficult to prove. Time spent then rises for some time as they learn to use the system better and know more and more people, until it attains its climax. At the same time, the use, gradually, also moves towards closer relationships. In terms of services this means a shift from news – or IRC groups towards using e-mail, as the closest and most interesting relationships move there. The use of news or IRC continues as well, but clearly loses its value in the long run compared to e-mail, as that is where the best friends are; a well-known and common rule in real life places and situations, especially for girls.

In most cases the father's computer/s and computer enthusiasm has played a part in the young person's interest and access to the Internet. For two of the boys who have home computers, this had an effect on the beginning of the use of computers; the Internet hobby was already their own inititative. Instead, two of the girls tell, how their fathers actively encouraged them to learn and start using the Internet.

Information, sociality and entertainment

> "It's like – how would I describe it? – it's like nice entertainment. For example, if I'm not interested in anything here (talks about the youth club), if I have a lazy feeling, couldn't play ping-pong or anything, then the Internet is such that you can just sit there half an hour, and travel there, and anyway, you get some useful information."

Not all the use can easily be described as a search for information, but even less can it be described as sociality. This part of use comes close to mass media use, perhaps the paging of yellow papers. Everyone in my study uses the Internet more or less in this way. But is this method of use, as it now would seem to be, based on the social background of the young person? Will I find out more about the use of the Internet for its entertainment value, encounter more differences which are based on the young person's social background, inequality which shows in the young person's possibilities for identity formation? Leisure is rich with fantasy work and identity development, but it can also leave us feeling trapped.

Cohen and Taylor see everyday life as a mixture of "chained activities" which render life predictable, and "escape attempts" which aim to utilise these activities as a precondition for freedom. They argue that everyday life consists of "multiple life worlds", and that the escape attempts in modern society reflect this variety of forms. Common to all these escape attempts is the individual's assertion that "this is where he/she really lives", where he/she suspends self-consciousness because the activity in itself provides an adequate opportunity for self-expression (Cohen and Taylor, 1992). But not all escape attempts offer similar possibilities to empowerment; they may in fact turn out to be organised deceptions or manipulations.

If we are moving from the centrality of civil rights toward the right to take part in information and communication structures, like Lash (1994) suggests, these questions are all the more important. The more the civil society and publicity itself are subordinate to information and communication structures, the more being outside of them is like being without civil rights, like being outside civil society both in the political as in the cultural meaning. Therefore the more important it becomes to be able and willing to use those structures in an active way.

Anita Eliasson

References

Alasuutari P (1993). *Radio suomalaisten arkielämässä*, Helsinki: Oy Yleisradio Ab, Tutkimusraportti 3/1993

Bauman Z (1990). *Thinking sociologically*, Worcester

Beck U, Giddens A, Lash S (1995) *Nykyajan jäljillä: Refleksiivinen modernisaatio*, Tampere: Vastapaino. English original: *Reflexive Modernization: Politics, Tradition and Aesthetics in the Modern Social Order*, Polity Press, 1994

Cohen S and Taylor L (1992). *Escape Attempts*, London: Routledge

Fornäs J (1995). *Cultural Theory & Late Modernity*, London: Sage

Giddens A (1991). *Modernity and Self-Identity: Self and Society in the Late Modern Age*, Cambridge: Polity Press

Glaser B and Strauss A (1967). *The discovery of grounded theory*, Chicago: Aldine

Grundström E (1991). Interrrailaus on modernia. In Lähteenmaa J and Siurala L (eds.). *Nuoret ja muutos*, Helsinki: Central Statistical Office of Finland, Studies 177

Helve H (1992). Tyttöjen kriittinen maailmankuva. In Näre S & Lähteenmaa J (eds.). *Letit liehumaan: Tyttökulttuuri murroksessa*, Helsinki: Suomalaisen Kirjallisuuden Seura

Maykut P and Morehouse R (1994). *Beginning Qualitative Research: A Philosophic and Practical Guide*, London: The Falmer Press

Nissen J (1993). *Pojkarna vid datorn: Unga entusiaster i datateknikens värld*, Stockholm: Symposium Graduale

Näre S & Lähteenmaa J (1992). Moderni suomalainen tyttöys: altruistista individualismia. In Näre S & Lähteenmaa J (eds.). *Letit liehumaan: Tyttökulttuuri murroksessa*, Helsinki: Suomalaisen Kirjallisuuden Seura

Robins K (1995). Cyberspace and the World We Live In. In Featherstone M and Burrows R (eds.) *Cyberspace, Cyberbodies, Cyberpunk: Cultures of Technological Embodiment*, London: Sage

Rubin H and Rubin S (1995). *Qualitative Interviewing: The Art Of Hearing Data*,. Thousand Oaks, C A: Sage

Savolainen R (1996). Tietoverkkojen käyttö empiirisen tutkimuksen kohteena: Metodisia lähtökohtia ja tutkimustuloksia. *Informaatiotutkimus* 15 (1)

Siurala L (1994). *Nuoriso-ongelmat modernisaatioperspektiivissä*. Helsinki: Helsinging kaupungin tietokeskuksen tutkimuksia 1994:3

Strauss A (1987). *Qualitative Analysis for Social Scientists*. Cambridge, NY: Cambridge University Press

Strauss, A. and Corbin J (1990). *Basics of Qualitative Research: Grounded Theory Procedures and Techniques*, Newbury Park, CA: Sage

Suurpää L (1996). Yksilöllistä sosiaalisuutta vai sosiaalista yksilöllisyyttä: Nuorten yhteiskunnallisten identiteettien poluilla. In Suurpää L and Aaltojärvi P (eds.). *Näin nuoret: Näkökulmia nuoruuden kulttuureihin*, Helsinki: Suomalaisen Kirjallisuuden Seura, Tietolipas 143

Turkle S (1995). *Life on the screen: Identity in the Age of the Internet*, New York: Simon & Schuster

Willis P (1993). *Common culture*, Milton Keynes: Open University Press

Winnicott W D (1988). *Human Nature*. London: Free Association Books

Ziehe T (1989). *Kulturanalyser: ungdom, utbildning, modernitet*, Stockholm/Stehag: Symposium Bokförlag & Tryckeri AB

Ziehe T (1992). Nuoriso kulttuurisessa modernisaatiossa. In Aittola T & Sirola E. (eds.). *"Miksi piiriin": Thomas Ziehe koulusta, nuorisosta ja itsestään-selvyyksien murenemisesta*, Jyväskylä: Jyväskylän yliopiston kasvatustieteen laitoksen julkaisuja 1

New media and the process of learning social skills

Introduction

In this paper I will try to highlight that the changing youth culture we now are facing requires a changing learning approach. For this alternative approach we need more effective ways to involve young people to define their needs and to design responses required. Therefore we – youth workers, adults and decision-makers have to take Internet seriously into consideration in our work with young people and in their process of learning social skills. Skills required to link young people into society.

To keep the paper brief I have decided not to include too many references to information given to me by young people. On request it will be provided. Some information will also soon become outdated. I would like to take this opportunity to thank the young people who have shared in an openhearted manner their life stories and visions with me. Without their input this paper would not have been possible.

For the past seventeen years I have worked with young people who have been involved in the misuse of drugs, criminal and social problems. I have also been responsible for a number of projects dealing with youth problems, such as projects for car thieves, glue sniffers, etc. Furthermore I have also designed and arranged projects in the field of youth culture, such as festivals and concerts. The description in this paper of the social context young people live in is based on these and other experiences as well as observations acquired over the past four years during visits to over three hundred different youth projects in more than twenty countries, together with being close to the youth scene itself in these countries. In addition to this, by talking to young people, youth workers, computer freaks and using Internet myself, I have come to the following conclusions regarding new media and the process of learning social skills.

New media

When people talk about new media, they often mean new information technology and Internet. Many people also know that you are able to ask almost any question on Internet and then "surf on the Net" to receive an answer. Answers or guidance as to where to find information are provided by the "global village", Internet users who believe that despite the reality of living in different societies and with large geographic distances in-between them, you should help each other as good neighbours as in a little village. A village spirit where you can lend somebody something and borrow something in return. Furthermore the belief is held that information should be free and available for everybody.

For most people in Europe, including young people, Internet is still new, in the sense of having access to it. Outside Europe in some developing countries, even radio and television are still deemed to be new technologies. The access to Internet alters from country to country in Europe. There appear to be major differences between former eastern European and western European countries and between the countries in the south and north of Europe. These statements are difficult to prove since accurate figures of prevalence of Internet users in each country are hard to get, due to difficulties with measurability. At the risk of being misleading, I have chosen the number of active domains (IP addresses) in each country to give an idea of access to Internet, not taking into consideration com addresses.

Futhermore there are also differences within the countries, due to the socio-economic level in the region which make access to netserver easy or difficult. If we look at Europe as at November 1996, I think, there are still very few young people with access to Internet and even fewer actually using it on a daily base. All facts indicate however that this reality will change extremely rapidly. I believe that Internet is going to "conquer the world" and become as common as radio is today. That fact should force us to take Internet seriously in to consideration in our work with young people and in their process of learning social skills.

I would also like to include old information channels such as television and films, but used in another way, in the concept of new media. Take television for example, where there are now channels and programmes which are only targeting young people, such as the music channel MTV. These television channels and programmes open up the national and international youth scene which would otherwise not be available for many young people. Here they have access to contemporary music, latest youth trends, new events and different lifestyles. Talk-shows like Ricky Lake, which focus on a youth audience, deal with issues that are to a large extent important for young people. Programmes that are very influenced by US values and commercial forces. Every day the Ricky Lake show deals with a new issue like "I am pregnant, but my mother wants me to have an abortion" or "When I told my parents I was gay, I got kicked out ..." Young people obtain access, in this way, to information and knowledge which was not available for their parents' generation.

Global information

Young people are now exposed to new information and knowledge, due to rapid extension of global media coverage, by satellite broadcasting, and expansion of media channels. The rapid expansion of/growth in information technology, sources of information and types of information available to young people have had significant influence on their world-views. This means that we are increasingly facing a "borderless society" or a "global village" on Internet. Information and knowledge are available to young people which they did not or could not always receive from their parents, school or society. Lack of information not only caused by ethical, moral, religious or political values but also by lack of accessibility. The fact that young people are now exposed to a wide variety of information and knowledge through Internet could be judged as bad or good depending on what point of view you have.

In some neighbouring countries the governments obstruct communication between them, which means, for example, that when young people from the neighbouring countries meet in Europe, there would normally be no possibility once back home to communicate with each other, either by telephone, letter or e-mail. Now, instead of using "old media", like telephone and letters they can send their e-mail to a friend in another country who conveys the message immediately. Another example of borderless information, which had great influence is Mr Drazen Pantic and his colleagues at Radio B52, one of Belgrade's independent media outlets. They could, with a simple telephone connection to the Internet, continue to broadcast even when the Serbian Government began to jam their radio signals. Their news bulletins were encoded into RealAudio format and sent to the radio's home page, located on XS4ALL's computer in Amsterdam. That made the B92 radio programmes available via Internet to anybody in the world, including Serbia. All according to a story filed on 28 November by CNN.

Of course, this borderless information network is not considered as good by some governments, politicians or other decision-makers who want to have control of people. Voices are also raised to get control over Internet but the construction of Internet with many small nets linked to each other makes that impossible. Instead of using the phrase "exposed to" you can view "as access to". Access to information for young people can form a foundation for better decisions and actions. This access to new and better knowledge is a reason, I think, why many teenagers now "break out from society" to a larger extent than before, based on the longing for freedom and real democracy.

The widespread use of videos makes it feasible for rural young people, who do not have easy access to cinemas, and for that matter also minors, who are subject to age restrictions to view new films. Videos also reinforce learning since you are able to see the video over and over again. In that way you can learn words, gestures and actions by heart. Anyone with some knowledge of young people knows how they are able to imitate scenes from different videos. I have come across young people, in non-English-speaking countries, who never went to school but who speak fluent English. They have learned it from videos, television and the street. An English dominated by US culture and values, facilitated by commercial forces. While working with young people in developing countries, it is natural to use videos in awareness and educational programmes. Videos are becoming one of the most effective means in reaching street kids in Brazil, Zimbabwe or Thailand. Therefore it is remarkable how little videos are used, not only by social workers but by the whole educational system in Europe, in their approach towards young people.

The above arguments are also valid for Internet. Not only in rural areas, such as the widespread use of Internet for distance tuition in Australia, but everywhere. As a young person you can also be "rurally" isolated belonging to a minority, even though you live in a big city. Let me take an example from the gay world. There are a lot of young gay people who live isolated, invisible lives, bereft of contact with other gay teenagers or with anyone for that matter, with whom they can talk. For an increasing number of gay and lesbian youngsters, on-line communication on Internet is the magic carpet that lifts them beyond their stifling geographic and psychological boundaries to a land of conversation, information and potential life-saving interaction.

So the medium of Internet itself is very empowering to disenfranchised young people. Furthermore, it is very influential because it is so anonymous in its structure. It responds in the same way to youth regardless of race, colour, religion or social status. On the other hand, Internet also facilitates for "destructive" groups like fascists, racists, paedophiles, etc. I will refrain further discussion with a note that this brings us to a more philosophical question; Are perpetrators created by receiving certain information or are they already perpetrators receiving required information. Anyway I think it is astonishing how youth workers have underestimated the use of Internet in working with young people.

Internet, as all other media, is used in a social context. Ms Evie Haraki, Youth Officer, says for example, that Greek young people do not use Internet alone. This differs from our usual perception of the lonely computer nerd. Young Greeks would always do it together with some peers. This is also, she continues, one explanation why Greek young people do not have a need for youth organisations since they are already "organised" as a part of their lifestyle. Everything is done together with friends and in that context learning takes place. Similar learning will in other countries also take place through youth organisations. Out of that knowledge peer education programmes have emerged. In spite of this, a lot of youth projects which I have come across, still undertake individual case work.

Today there are more youth magazines and they are getting more inexpensive, more widely spread and cover a vast variety of topics in order to cover special interests like hip hop, skateboard, mountain climbing, computers, bodybuilding, tattoos, etc. Music stations are increasingly being established by young people for young people, even with some international concepts like the radio station NRJ. Records, CDs, films, videos, Internet home pages, fashions and accessories are produced in a steady stream. Together they are promoting, creating and reinforcing a global youth culture which makes us recognise similar sorts of black clothes with three white stripes or the same sort of music, whether we are in Budapest, Toronto, La Paz or Hanoi. Yet, I believe, youth culture is not homogeneous. It is more like a rainbow, where the different parts confirm different groups of youths around the world. Even then young people are collaborating in the new global youth culture via their own national culture.

Global youth culture

But why do young people feel the urge to get involved in this global culture? I think there is some basic theme, across Europe and moreover in the whole world, but with different emphasis, somewhat similar to rays before they hit the prism. I would like to focus on the alienation young people feel. Teenage years will always produce a period of alienation, of being excluded, somewhat contrary to the world of adults. Recently I have come across a deeper and more genuine alienation and mistrust of that which authority and society stand for. The alienation has one of its roots in the long-term and accelerating youth unemployment, manifested in the fact that young people cannot get into society since they cannot acquire a job. It can no longer be argued that an increasing number of young people are also actually never allowed to join the labour market.

The responsibility of raising the youngsters has been, and still is, only laid on the family – in spite of the changed economic grounds of today, which force both parents to work or make single parents unable to provide for themselves and their children. Instead this should provide grounds for shared responsibility of the raising of children. Society should not take over the responsibilities from the parents, but stand by them and actively and professionally obtain the duty of raising children rather than taking charge when the damage is already done, in terms of negative developments. It is politically naive not to admit the new realities that human beings live in society today.

To cope with the problems of increasing unemployment, homelessness, poverty and growing economic disparities, civil unrest, violence and drug abuse, young people have to learn new life strategies. All these changes that have occurred in people's family situations have put many young people in the position of having to fend for themselves. A position where the required help is often provided by peers rather than society.

On the other hand, some young people enjoy the fact that today there is a greater gap between the generations which makes it much easier for young people to live their own lives. I think this is due to the fact that parents in Scandinavia and in many parts of the western world have lost their role as the real raisers, because of the last decades fast changes in society. It is also stated that the gap has neither been filled by others in the world of adults, nor by pedagogical institutions, but by friends of the same age.

Irrespective of the cause, you can sum up the process like this; young people belonged first to society, then they felt to be outside society and now it seems like young people are creating their own society or what I call "breaking out from society". If we do not act now the ultimate consequence will be that we will wake up one morning to find that a parallel society has emerged out of this situation. A changing social process requires a new learning process and I think youth workers have to take the lead.

Hans Knutagard

The crusaders – a group of young computer nerds

Youth associations in Norway and the challenges of the new information technologies

Summary

I want to address what impact the information technologies in the shape of the Internet, may have on the future relations both between the different parts of the youth associations and between the associations and the different governmental and international bodies. I want to do so with reference to a Norwegian example of associative life on the Internet. The idea is to discuss what possible transformations of youth associations the new information technologies may cause, based on findings of a research project on the relations between youth associations and public institutions on municipal, regional and national levels in Norway from 1980 to 1993.

Introduction

The Norwegian Council of Youth Associations – *Landsrådet for norske ung-doms-organisasjoner* (LNU), includes most national youth associations. The Council can now be accessed on the Internet. Their home page includes links to those of the member associations that provide the same kind of service. At present only twenty-two out of sixty-two youth associations do. This number will most certainly increase as the youth associations seem eager to adapt to the new possibilities of the information technologies. But this information catch-up may imply a challenge beyond that of mere technological improvement for the youth associations.

The account of how the introduction of steel axes into a group of Australian aboriginals disintegrated the whole of their culture, is a classic (Sharp, 1952). Yet the parallels between Lauriston Sharp's account and the challenges ahead for the youth associations as they approach the Internet may seem far fetched. Still, in both cases we are dealing with social groups forced to adapt to new technologies. The story of the Australian aboriginals Yir Yoront may therefore have a lesson to teach the youth associations at the doorstep of cyberspace.

The missionaries who introduced new technology into the stone age economy of the Yir Yoront at the beginning of this century brought on a collapse of their whole culture. The steel axes replaced the old ones made out of stone. The missionaries handed them out to anyone of the Yir Yoront who came to the mission. The missionaries paid no attention to the Yir Yoront system of social distinctions prescribing who should have possession of stone axes and who should not. Both men and women, young and old, who approached the mission would return with their own steel axe. At first sight a clear cut example of technological progress. The new axes did the job in less time and lasted much longer than the old stone axe.

Still, time was not a scarcity among the Yir Yoront, nor was endurance a matter of priority. Worse, the non-discriminatory way of distributing the steel axe made much havoc on the fine social fabric of the Yir Yoront society where control of access to the stone axe was decisive on the social hierarchy that regulated their daily life. In addition, the stone head of the old axe could not be excavated in their territory, it could only be acquired through trade with surrounding groups. With the advent of the steel axe this whole system of trade broke down with repercussions on the social fabric of people far away.

In the case of the youth associations the adaptation to cyberspace may also involve the abandon of former ways of communication within the organisation as Internet may do the job much quicker. But the youth associations may just find out that speed is not the essential thing about communication, the case may very well be similar to that of Yir Yoront to whom time was not a scarce commodity and no improvement could come out of the fact that the steel axe did the job in less time. The introduction of the Internet may be much more than just technological improvements in the world of communications, as the steel axe it may threaten to erode the way youth have associated up until now. More important perhaps, the Internet may, as the steel axe did in the case of the Yir Yoront, confront the youth associations with a whole new cultural make-up. In the case of the Yir Yoront the steel axe confronted them with the cultural make-up of European industrial society, a confrontation that made it impossible for them to make a new cultural reintegration where the steel axe could be assimilated into their world. Instead they found themselves having to assimilate into the industrial culture of the steel axe. What will happen with the youth associations? What will the new information technologies do to their way of working?

To understand their ordeal I believe we have to take into account a particular feature of their organisational make-up. Because as far as non-governmental organisations (NGOs) go, the youth associations are ambiguous creatures. This is because the associations function as an arena of every new generation carving out an identity as youth different from the adult society that surrounds them, and at the same time these associations are tools that adult society uses to invade the youth arenas to make them civic participants. The boy scout doing mountain hiking or the young environmentalist on a stand campaigning against pollution are both involved in activities with their peers, activities that deny admittance to adults - except perhaps in the role as leaders or advisers. But, at the same time, their mountain hiking or fight against pollution through organisations forces them to learn and adopt the rules of adult society. In so many words, boy scouts and young environmentalists are expressions of youth different from adults and youth becoming adults at the same time. I suspect any youth association that is unable to maintain this ambiguity and become only a youth arena or only a tool for adult society, must in the end disappear.

If the Internet can be compared to the steel axes of the Yir Yoront, I believe it is because the new information technologies may disrupt this ambiguity.

The information technologies

We are at present experiencing a mayor shift in the world of information technologies. Just as we are getting familiarised with word processors and spreadsheets, the user interface for the Internet is dramatically improved, permitting the isolated operator of a word processor to access the information highways simply by a click of the mouse button. This new ease of use is coupled with a commercial drive by major actors in the world of telecommunications seeking new revenues. In the world of commerce some even visualise that the reign of the personal computer (the PC) will soon be conquered by the net computer (the NC) which by avoiding the expensive storage and software needs of the PC (which it will substitute by accessing facilities on the net) may produce a computer more accessible to the general public. At any rate, it is not far fetched to predict that the Internet will have an enormous impact on all kinds of social activities.

There is a growing literature on cyberspace and cyberculture. Traditional media such as newspapers, radio and television are versions of broadcasting where information is transmitted from a small group of producers to a large group of receivers. Internet is a new kind of media based on narrowcasting where information is being sent back and forth between participants who are both producers and receivers of the information transmitted. The interaction on the Internet is therefore often interpreted in terms of virtual communities between actors who have almost unlimited means of social imagination at their disposal as they enact identities freed of spatial limitations. Perhaps most important to refurbish this view of the Internet has been Marshall McLuhan's metaphor of "the global village" (McLuhan in Symes, 1995). In accordance with his view we may see the new technologies as further extensions of our nervous system which abolish both space and time so that we are able to experience the whole world as a global village as though as if we were face to face. McLuhan is a media theoretician of the TV era who held an optimistic view of the broadcasting media as making the global village possible. But, clearly, the TV set only made us observers to global events such as operation desert storm where US marines entered Iraq. In contrast, advocates of the Internet want us to believe the net may actually make us participants in global events as it promises to reduce the sharp distinctions between producers and receivers in the information transmission. It is not a view exempt of political ambitions. It is based on a belief that it has potential to break down centralised power, and help form a community that lives on a more integrated basis, with more shared responsibilities.

The Internet clearly has potential for reducing the distinctions between producers and receivers of information characteristic of the traditional media. Any implementation of the Internet facilities that ignores this may do so at the risk of being relegated to the margins of the net activities. But there is naïveté apparent in the political ambitions expressed. The Internet cannot make us participants in world events such as the desert storm any more than the TV did. The Internet remains a channel for information - to gloss its virtual nature may have political implications that contradict the political ambitions of making the net function as a check on centralised power. Information circulating on the Internet may (or may not) heighten our awareness of the political implications of actions such as desert storm, but as any hacker will know, it is action, not information as such, that counts.

I suspect this to be important when the youth associations approach cyberspace; to avoid confusing information with action. The youth associations must be able to maintain the ambiguity that characterises them; being both a youth arena and a tool for adult society. One way of doing that is to become vessels for youth activities on the Internet. But adopting the Internet may increase the distance between the executives at the head of the organisations and the local youth at the bottom. That may upset their organisational ambiguity and transform them into sterile "youth services" at the hand of adult society.

The Norwegian youth associations

The literature on youth associations is either studying youth culture or organisational design. Whereas the first study styles, expressions and symbols youth use in identity making, the second study organisational adaptation. Still, I hope most researchers will agree that youth associations have an ambiguous nature. On one hand they are similar to other voluntary associations dedicated to civic causes, on the other hand they are vessels – or expressions – of youth culture.[1]

Most of the Norwegian youth associations have a long history, but new associations are created all the time. One of the more recent ones is Youth Against Drugs – Ungdom Mot Narkotika (UMN). UMN was established in 1985. UMN has steadily increased its membership since then. No doubt this is related to the ability of the organisation to adapt to important trends among youth. For instance, UMN ran a radio that managed to host the influential hip-hop artists just when that music figured as the vanguard of urban youth culture and they arranged drug-free house-parties when that kind of gathering became popular. This demonstrates their capability to be a vessel

---

1 Or what Sven Mørch calls juvenile revolts against adult society (Mørch, 1992).

for current youth culture. But, UMN is also a typical voluntary association capable of lobbying political decision-makers for specific demands.

The youth associations as voluntary associations have played an important role in the development of the welfare state in Norway. Through local participation in different associations citizens have been able to access national decision-makers in ways they could not hope to have achieved on their own. From the decision-makers point of view, the information they got from organisational contacts was considered more representative – and there for much more credible – than the information passed on from the odd voter.[1] This way the voluntary associations that in the past had been popular movements addressing problems and activities that somehow was neither taken care of by the state nor the marked, now became effective lobbying mechanisms that would manage to draw attention to new fields of activities that the growing welfare state should attend to. An important consequence of this was the reproduction of the traditional hierarchical structure of the voluntary associations, a structure where each voluntary association had an administrative centre at a national level that was heading local branches spread across the country through regional centres.

The Norwegian welfare state is no longer growing in size. In order to meet the popular demand for welfare services some policy-makers have coined the concept "the welfare society" according to which the voluntary associations will have increased importance as providers of social welfare that cannot be met by public services. In accordance with this some researchers argue that we are at present witnessing a social transformation where former voluntary associations based on member activities will re-emerge as operators providing social services on commission from governmental agencies, relegating their members to a marginal role. In short, what used to be voluntary associations will in the future reappear as commercial enterprises. A number of Norwegian NGOs, such as the Norwegian Red Cross (Norske Røde Kors) or Oslo Indremisjon (a christian mission) already function as contractors for governmental agencies providing public services for the population on a commercial basis.

This ongoing transformation is expected to coincide with a changed attitude among the members towards the voluntary associations as they are being less concerned with issues dealing with the national project of political and social improvement. In the future citizens are expected to participate in associative life primarily motivated by their particular leisure interests. As a result

---

1 Knowledge of the mechanisms of the corporate state was of invaluable importance to the Sami activists who in the 1960s, 1970s and 1980s were able to increase the public presence of the Sami culture and language through lobbying the Norwegian authorities through newly shaped Sami organisations (cf. Eidheim 1971). The concessions won through this channel they skilfully used to win influence among a hesitant Sami population in order to enforce the popular support for their organisations which they pretended to have in their dealings with the Norwegian authorities. In the 1990s we are witnessing something similar among immigrants who are increasingly dealing with the authorities through new organisations.

the hierarchical structure of the organisations is expected to be dismembered. What used to be the national centres of the organisations will reappear as commercial agents, while the local branches will perish or be revamped to fit the particular demands for leisure activities in each locality. When contact between the former national centre and the local branches is retained it is expected to be on a strict cost benefit basis. As a consequence the traditional voluntary associations organised nationwide will experience a decrease in popular support – while participation in local organisations depends upon their ability to adapt to local leisure demands.

The Norwegian youth associations are at present experiencing a decrease in their popular support. Official statistics in Norway show that the youth associations in 1980 had almost 750000 members below the age of 25 (cf. NOU 19:1995). In 1995 the number of memberships were reduced by more than a third to less than 500000. The statistics may give a distorted view of the situation. This is partly due to demographic changes where the cohorts between 12 and 25 are markedly smaller in size than they were fifteen years ago. Partly it is because the youth associations have improved their registration routines inhibiting a common fallacy of the past of counting members who failed to renew their membership. Still, the fact remains that the traditional youth associations experience a weakening social position.

As voluntary associations become providers of public services we may expect them to become increasingly dependent upon governmental funds. This development has been documented in a study of the Norwegian voluntary associations (cf. Statskonsult, 1995). Our research documented a different development in the youth associations, where an increase in governmental subventions from 1980 to 1993 was matched by a similar increase in their own earnings (Moshuus 1996a).[1] The share of the income from their own earnings have not diminished. Since their earnings comes from services rendered to their members, the increase of these earnings may serve as an indication that the dramatic decrease in their member support is exaggerated. More important, perhaps, it may give us reason to believe that the youth associations are not being transformed into producers of welfare services for the government. But we may suspect that the increased earnings from member services indicate that the relation between the national centre and the local branches is gradually being transformed from a traditional relation between organisational levels into a relation between buyers and sellers of services. What used to be a mechanism of organisational redistribution of goods produced by joint voluntary efforts, is gradually converted into a cost-benefit relation (Moshuus 1996b).

In view of these gradual changes of the internal relations between top and bottom of the youth associations, we may guess that the associations adapt

---

1 Admittedly, our data is restricted as we only investigated a selection of the youth associations in a limited number of settings.

to the new information technologies most often caused by initiatives from the top of the organisations. Because the computers represent capital investments beyond reach of most local branches. The national centres may use computers to get the administrative jobs done in less time. It is not only a matter of efficiency but also a matter of compliance to governmental demands for measures that may permit them to sanction any abuse of governmental funds. This way, the adoption of the Internet may further the hiatus between top and bottom. Whereas the young executives of the organisations may communicate by e-mail and browse different home pages for information, the local affectionate may not have access to computers. The outcome of the adoption of the Internet may in light of this very well be the final breakdown of the internal cohesion of the youth associations.

On the other hand, as I have argued, the youth associations are more than just voluntary associations, they must also be vessels for current trends in youth culture. Or to follow what Ola Stafseng has argued in relation to youth culture and socialisation, the youth associations, must serve youth as one setting where they may perform role-playing games where formal education may be seconded by informal "self-education" (Stafseng, 1989). So, when the organisation Youth Against Drugs, UMN, succeeded as the host of major youth trends such as the hip-hop, they managed to address the issue of drugs through imaginative ways that made drug prevention part of modern trends in youth culture among larger groups of youth. This is the challenge for the established youth associations when they adopt the Internet. They must adopt the Net in the same way as young people do.

The Internet is already a setting for associative life among young people. The forming of the group "crusaders" may serve as an example with certain similarities to what UMN managed to do when they hosted the hip-hop artists.

The crusaders – a group of young computer nerds in Norway

These are notes from an interview with a male "computer nerd".[1] A computer nerd is the term for the mutually recognised cohabitants of the Internet. My interlocutor was 26 years old and worked as a systems integrator at a computer firm. He described himself as a self-made who works professionally with computer communications.

I told him I had done research on voluntary associations among young people in Norway and that I wanted to know more about the social milieus that existed among young people interested in computers. We agreed that he would tell me the story of the group that has come to be named "crusaders".

---

1 There are many similarities between my interlocutor's story and the milieu of hackers described by Michelle Slatalla and Joshua Quittner in *Masters of Deception: The Gang That Ruled Cyberspace* (Harper-Collins, 1995). An excerpt can be found in the electronic journal "Wired on the URL": http//www.wired.com.

He dated his story back to the 1970s. The story started in a very internation-al context, in an American milieu of what he called "electronic freaks". These freaks were isolated individuals who were constructing their own rudimenta-ry computers. They first became aware of each other's existence through attendance at university courses at the MIT (Massachusetts Institute of Technology). The stories of how they forced their way in to the building to continue their activities at night are known by most young computer nerds today. In this environment it soon became popular to hack the code of copy-righted programmes and the first hackers were born. Once the code was hacked the programme could be used without any licence from the producer.

It was Sir Clive Sinclair and his creation of computers at an affordable price that really made computers accessible to young people. Sinclair's machine "ZX80" came with a simple chess programme, but the ZX users could soon benefit from a rapidly growing industry of game producers. Some even start-ed producing their own programmes. The programmes were stored on cas-settes and through the ZX magazine the users were able to swap their games for access to those of others.

The Sinclair machine developed into a refined version called ZX Spectrum. It was soon to be rivalled by the Commodore 64. In 1982 the number of peo-ple working with these cheap computers had increased and diversified. On both machines youngsters hacked game codes like their heroes had done at the MIT. Once the code had been hacked, the game could be swapped for games hacked by others. The obvious motivation was to get access to as many games as possible without having to pay anything to the producers. According to my interlocutor these game producers were "large corpora-tions".

Once the code had been hacked the game became an asset, called "warez" with a limited warranty. The warranty is determined by the amount of time the game has been available on the market. In the beginning when the com-puter nerd was dependent on the regular mail system a hacked game retained its value as an asset until at least two months after the game had been introduced on the market. Today with the Internet, the warranty is reduced to six hours. As long as the hacked game is an asset it can be swapped. This way young computer nerds were soon swapping games all across Europe through the mail.

Each hacker was entitled to leave his personal imprint on the hacked product. At first the imprint only consisted of a plain text string presenting the hacker by his pseudonym and the date when the programme was hacked. The most famous game hackers were known as "Bud Spencer", "TRSI", "Mr Gurkan", "1001 Crew" and "the Vikings". They were located across Europe.

The hackers soon started putting more creativity into their particular imprint than on the actual hacking of the game code. These imprints became known as "intros". The intros soon included both graphics and music. At a later stage, the most creative hackers stopped hacking game codes all together, dedicating themselves to making only intros. These products became known as "demos".

The pseudonyms often represented entire groups of youngsters who worked as a team. Some were dedicated to hacking, while others specialised in swapping the end products. The first of these groups was a German group called "the 1001 Crew".

From the mid 1980s the computer nerds started to gather during holidays on occasions called "copy parties". On these occasions that could last a few days the participants could exchange games and compete in hacking games, making intros and demos. Participants would find their way to these copy parties from all over Europe.

Through the 1980s these copy parties diversified into different "scenes". "The hacker scene" included the best and fastest hackers, "the elite scene" those with the largest collections of the newest in hacked games and the "demo scene" that included the best makers of intros.

Among the hackers prestige could be won by demonstration of speed hacking the newest of games first. The best game hackers depend upon having "suppliers", people who work in the computer corporations who can provide them with the new games even before they reach the stores. Among the elite, what matters is the magnitude of their collections of hacked games. To be a true member of the elite you should have a collection of seven thousand games. In order to have a collection of this size the collector must have many "warez" or assets that makes him an interesting partner for swapping.

On the demo scene what counts is display of creativity. The demo scene got under way with the German group TRSI (Trident Red Sector Inc.) when they made the demo "Megademo" in 1988. A production that today is considered a classic. A demo group always includes a programmer (coder), musicians, graphic designers, swapper and a systems operator (organiser).

Along with other Norwegian groups like andromeda, cryptoburners and spaceballs, the group called the crusaders was formed as a demo group in 1988, consisting of twelve young boys from Oslo. Today they are group of twenty members. Two of the members have become part of the group through electronic media like Internet as they live in the UK and Finland. Today there is also a demo group consisting only of girls called the crusaders girls.

The original members of the crusaders all worked at a computer store in Oslo. The crusaders have produced demos and music CDs that have been distributed on a regular commercial basis, but outside the normal stores. At least one of the CDs sold more than 1500 copies.

Since 1992 the crusaders, have been arranging an annual "demo party" during Easter week called "the gathering". Together with "the assembly" each autumn in Finland and "the party" each Christmas in Denmark, the gathering is considered the major demo party in Europe. This year 2500 young computer nerds were present at the Gathering. At the Gathering a Norwegian association of computer nerds was formed that at present includes 1800 members.

My interlocutor emphasised that the name "the crusaders" was chosen without any religious intentions. He explained that all names in the milieu is chosen for the sound only. Any name in use is respected by all others. If anyone tries to present themselves by a name already in use, the whole computer milieu will react and make it impossible for the violator to succeed in his intentions. Each group member also has his own alias. My interlocutor's alias is "Shady". Other members of the crusaders are Dr Awesome, Fleshbrain and El Cubo, to mention but a few.

The milieu lives by an informal honour code that prescribes conduct on the Internet and elsewhere where the computer nerds meet. My interlocutor compared the code with that of the knight order in the middle ages. Outright breaches of the code may cause the group members to be ostracised from the group.

One of the major wrong doings is to be caught taking commercial benefits out of your position on either of the scenes that make up the computer parties. The demo scene, the hacker scene and the elite scene are mutually dependent on each other through the basic swapping arrangement that permits the computer games and demos to pass between the participants. If anyone takes out a commercial benefit he is bound to benefit from the efforts of others and put the whole concept of swapping into jeopardy.

Other major breaches of the code consist of using the work of others in your own productions with out giving due credit. A group member may also put his position at risk if his collaboration is judged as sloppy by the others. Non-respectful conduct on the Internet may also harm your position within the group. All these breaches of the honour code are considered as examples of "lame conduct" by the computer nerds.

On the other hand you build your own reputation among the society of computer nerds by collecting favourable opinion among the established group members as you deal with them on the Internet demonstrating familiarity with their technical jargon and through your updated knowledge of the events that take place in the milieu.

Take for instance the elite scene. Besides the different copy parties when the computer nerds may swap hacked games face to face, they are normally confined to the Internet where they must have access to the private archives of other collectors in order to swap. These archives are illegal as they include games with the copy protection hacked. So their owners change the Internet address at intervals to avoid the police. In order to build a reputation as a nerd on the elite scene you need to demonstrate that you are considered a credible swapper by the number of archives you have access to. As your reputation grows you may step upwards and finally get access to the archives most wanted by the police.

In Norway the most famous archives used to be those belonging to the aliases "the Red Baron" and "Purple Haze". These archives belonged to hackers who played hide and seek with the police and the Norwegian telephone company as they manipulated the telephone system changing phone lines continually. Their archives were supposed to include only the games of the best quality and anyone who had access to them enjoyed the highest reputation among the young computer nerds. Both of these hackers and archive owners have now retired.

The youth associations and the steel axes of the Internet

The group of Australian Aboriginals, the Yir Yoront, perished as a culture group because they where unable to reinterpret the new technology, the steel axes, so that the technology would fit into their way of living. Instead they found themselves forced to adapt to the ways of living of which the steel axe was part.

The Internet is sometimes called an unregulated "new frontier" because it produces a new social space where little law enforcement exists. The group crusaders is one example of what exists in that space. As should be clear from the above the group formed among participants who want to portray themselves as "rebels" or "hackers" outside the law. Their heroes, Internet aliases like "the Red Baron" and "Purple Haze", had gained their heroism from their ability to fool what they call "the large capitalist corporations" behind the computer programmes. They were offering their comrades the programmes for free. But as my interlocutor's tale also shows, the hackers conduct on the Net was not without social control. Their conduct had to comply with moral standards he compared with that of the knight order in the middle ages if they wanted to maintain their position among peers.

But the Internet is also a new frontier similar to that which the Yir Yoront encountered as the steel axes invaded their territory. As the steel axes the Internet may well provoke the final break up between top and bottom of the youth associations. The local youth may either find the executives' endorsement of the Internet for communication as terminating the remaining local contact with the national headquarters as the technology feels alien to the local devotee. Or, when the local young people adopt the new technology, they may find membership of the youth associations superfluous as the Net fulfils their interests.

And, yet, this is where the group of young computer nerds who formed crusaders has relevance for the youth associations adapting to the Internet. The story of the group crusaders and the gathering they organise one week every year with an attendance of some 2 500 youngsters bears resemblance to one of the findings of the research we did on the Norwegian youth associations. In that research we recorded much difference between the social role played by the youth associations in different local communities with equal levels of municipal subventions. In most local communities the associations seem to find their members deflecting away from their traditional engagement in favour of exploiting alternative leisure activities either found as part of improved municipal services or as part of a competitive commercial offer. Still, in one local community the youth associations manage to maintain high levels of engagement among their members in spite of dwindling municipal subventions. Apparently this may be explained by their exceptional access to other kinds of earnings. In Seljord, a rural village located in the heart of Norway, the local youth associations control and supervise a huge annual fair which is a stable provider of a yearly profit which can be redistributed to the organisational activities. Yet, the profit is dependent on the capacity of the youth associations to provide the necessary number of voluntary workers. An additional explanation of their continuing hold on their membership must be sought in their capacity to serve as an arena where participation in the local community may be enacted. Otherwise we would be unable to explain their ability to provide sufficient numbers of voluntary hands. A closer scrutiny of the informal community in Seljord will probably reveal that the social fabric consists of activities and encounters run on a daily basis through the different voluntary associations that operate in the village. The associations have even managed to build a large cultural centre which much bigger villages envy. They did so with very limited public investment, and it is run with hardly any public subventions. The parallels to the group of computer nerds should be obvious. When the group crusaders succeeded running the annual gathering with incredible crowds of youth attending from across the country it is because they too manage to function as a social arena for an informal community.

The importance of being a social arena brings us around to the last important lesson that the group crusaders carries for the youth associations adopting to cyberspace. The activities that brought the computer nerds together forming the crusaders, was a sequence of skills they taught themselves. Starting out playing computer games they developed through collecting games, hacking them, adding their own imprints and finally dropping the games all together devoting their skills to the imprints that became fully-fledged computer programmes of their own creation. In the end they had become computer professionals, each of them developing different specialities. Being part of this loosely knit association they went through a complex socialisation where all of them now are integrating into adult society based on the skills they acquired. In other words they have managed to cultivate that ambiguity that makes youth associations "tick". The crusaders has been that invention – in cyberspace – of expressions familiar to youth associations in other contexts of being youth different from adults and being young people becoming adults at the same time. This should carry warnings to the efficient young executive at the top of the organisation to avoid introducing the Internet from the top.

Another important conclusion in our research was that the economical centres of the organisations were being moved from the local levels, where traditionally most activities where conducted, to the national level where the administrative centres were operating. This was the unintended consequence of discrepancy in public policy on municipal and national levels. While governmental youth policy has provided the youth associations with steady annual subventions for almost two decades providing the organisations with the necessary framework to plan and develop their activities, on the municipal level the associations have experienced a steady deterioration of their public subventions. This has weakened the local levels in the youth associations across the country and pushed the organisational impetus towards the national centres of the associations. Adopting the Internet from the top in this situation may not be such a good idea, it may turn out to counterproductive to the intentions of self socialisation that the crusaders had succeeded so well with.

If the youth associations shall succeed adapting to the Internet, the adaptation must come from local initiatives. The Internet strategy of the youth associations must mimic the self socialisation of the youth who formed the crusaders in a revolt against an unsophisticated technological world of adults in order to end up as fully-fledged adult members of a less technophobic world. If the youth associations do not, they might experience that the Internet will become their own unmaking as the Yir Yoront who perished – as a culture group – in the encounter with the steel axes.

Geir H Moshuus

References

Escobar A (1994) Welcome to Cyberia. Notes on the Anthropology of Cyberculture *Current Anthropology* Vol. 35 no. 3 June

Escobar A (1995) Anthropology and the Future *Futures* Vol. 27 no. 4

Grue L (1985) *Bedre enn sitt rykte*, En undersøkelse av ungdoms fritidsbruk, STUI Oslo

Klausen K K & Selle P (red.) (1995) *Frivillig organisering i norden Tano*, Oslo

Kuhnle S & Selle P (eds.) (1992) Government and Voluntary Organisations, *A Relational Perspective*, Avebury, Aldershot

Lorentzen H (1994) *Frivillighetens integrasjon* Universitetsforlaget, Oslo

Moshuus Geir H (1996a) *"Små beløp – Stor innsats" Om økonomien i barne- og ungdomsorganisasjonene lokalt, regionalt og sentralt fra 1980 til 1993*, Ungforsk rapport no. 4, Oslo

Moshuus Geir H (1996b) Utfordringer for barne- og ungdomsorganisasjonene i Tormod Øia (red.) *Ung i 90 åra*, Cappelen, Oslo

Mørch S (1992) Ungdom og masse *Psyke og Logos* no. 2 vol. 13

NOU (1988:17) *Frivillige Organisasjoner*

NOU (1995:19) *Statlige tilskuddsordninger til barne- og ungdomsorganisasjoner*

Selle, Per og Øymyr, B (1995) *Frivillig organisering og demokrati*, Samlaget, Oslo

Sharp, L (1968) Steel Axes for Stone Age Australians i E LeClair og H.K. Schneider (red.) *Economic Anthropology*, Readings in Theory and Analysis. Holt, Rinehart and Winston. New York 1968

Shields R (ed.) (1996) *Cultures of Internet*, Sage, London

Stafseng O (1991) *Youth Culture and Language Socialisation*

Statskonsult (1995) *Statlige overføringer til frivillige* organisasjoner Rapport nr. 3 Statskonsult, Oslo

Symes B: *Marshall McLuhan*

URL: http://www.aber.ac.ungdomskulturer/~ednwww/benmcl.html

Amit-Talai V & Wulff H (eds.) 1995 *Youth Cultures. A Cross-Cultural Perspective*, Routledge, London

Øia, T (1994) *Norske ungdomskulturer*, Oplandske Bokforlag, Oslo

Pedagogy of the information society

Rural youth in the United Kingdom: information, advice, and the role of technology

Summary

This paper is a summary of a verbal presentation made at the above symposium, which explored the information and advice needs of rural youth. It is structured in two parts. First, some general information is presented about the experiences of rural youth in the UK, a group of youth frequently neglected by researchers and policy-makers. It will be demonstrated that many rural youth experience considerable difficulty in accessing information, advice, and services. Second, some recent initiatives are discussed, which use novel methods to get information and advice to rural youth. The issue of the use of new technology in the provision of information and advice for rural youth is discussed. Finally, a number of organisations working with rural youth in the UK are listed.

Rural youth: issues and needs

Young people living in rural areas in the UK, and in Europe more generally, rarely receive attention from researchers, policy-makers, or politicians. This undoutedly has something to do with the image of the rural situation as easy-going, comfortable, pleasant, and unproblematic.

In recent years, however, many youth workers and researchers have demonstrated that this image is, for many young people, very far from reality. Although there can be many positive aspects to rural life – including knowing a small group of people well, peace and quiet, and access to the countryside – there are clearly also disadvantages, particularly for young people. A number of extracts from recent publications demonstrate this well:

> "The notion of an idyllic rural childhood has helped to obscure the fact that the little research that exists suggests that families in rural areas may experience considerable difficulties ... including isolation, material deprivations, lack of support and few opportunities for children to socialise with their peers." (Statham and Cameron, 1993, p. 1)

> "The idyllic image of the English countryside has been exposed as a myth." (Observer, 20 March 1994)

> "Young people in rural areas can suffer particularly from isolation. Poor transport adds to feeling of isolation and housing problems can magnify family tensions." (Turner, 1992, p. 54)

"In reality, the countryside is a place of poverty, isolation, poor housing, bad services and social conflict." (Observer, 20 March 1994)

"Perhaps the greatest issue is a feeling of powerlessness, of not being noticed, of not knowing what to do to improve their situation. Sometimes young people are all too visible in their communities. Stereotypes once given, are hard to change." (Leach, 1996, p. 4)

"Many myths surround the notion of life in a rural environment. Perhaps the most common is that it is idyllic, peaceful, happy and easy. For many young people living in rural areas life is too peaceful." (Youth Clubs UK Newsletter, 1994)

"Living in a rural area can be very secure for some young people as a safe and familiar community. For others village life is boring, lonely and does not stretch their social skills, and without transport they are dependent on the willingness of parents to take them out to other events." (Turner, 1992, p. 54)

During the last few years it has therefore become clear that many young people in rural areas lack the information, resources and facilities that are essential for healthy development. As such, living in a rural area is central to the topic of "Youth in the information society" – for many rural youth a key problem is the difficulty of accessing information and advice. This lack of information has clear implications for young people's future prospects, health and well-being. It is this issue which is considered in this paper.

The problems facing young people who grow up in rural areas are often multiple in nature. They include: high rates of youth unemployment; limited options for education and training; a scarcity of affordable housing; and limited public transport (see for example Fabes and Banks, 1991; Wallace et al, 1993). Homelessness and drug use amongst rural young people are on the increase. A recent report (Lifestyles in Rural England, Rural Development Commission, 1994) demonstrated a number of important facts, including:

– four out of ten rural families are now living in poverty;

– one household in eight has no car;

– one in twelve families has no telephone; of these 40 per cent are more than a quarter of a mile from the nearest phone box.

As a result of social isolation, feelings of marginalisation, and limited career, leisure and information opportunities, young people's health and psycho-social development may well be adversely affected. Adolescence is a time when peer support and the availability of information and advice is particularly crucial; consequently rural young people are particularly hard hit. This is demonstrated by a number of facts published by the National Youth Bureau (now the National Youth Agency) in 1992. The problems for rural youth that they identified included:

– Difficulties of access: in particular to health care information, advice, and facilties. Numbers and choice of general practitioners is often limited (with no choice at all in many areas), and specialist services are rare. In rural Shropshire for example, travelling over twenty-five miles to the nearest hospital is the norm.

– Isolation: including a limited peer group, loneliness (in particular a lack of peer support and of specialist youth services), lack of privacy in small communities, and difficulties for young people of detaching themselves from parental involvement in their activities. (Indicative of this isolation, a survey of 14-16 year-olds in North Yorkshire found that 22 per cent of this group lived five miles or more away from their best friend, and 38 per cent only saw their best friend once a week; see North Yorkshire County Council, 1989). Facilities for socialising and meeting people of similar age are often also severely limited, with many communities having no village hall or youth club.

– Difficulties of developing individual identities: many young people living in rural areas reported feelings of marginalisation, loneliness, low expectations, and low self-esteem. There was also found to be little tolerance of unusual dress and lifestyles in rural areas, and few opportunities for gay or lesbian young people to "come out".

Fabes and Banks (1991), in Working with young people in rural areas demonstrate that youth work in rural areas has only begun to emerge as a distinct area of practice in the last ten years. This is as people begin to realise that "... genuine hardship and poverty exist in rural as well as urban areas" (p. 3). This paper confirms the finding of previous research that there are a number of problems for rural youth, including:

– a limited peer group, with few people of the same age;

– loneliness, as well of a lack of peer support and services;

– lack of privacy;

– parental involvement in all of their children's activities (especially because of dependence on parents for transport);

– poor access to health care/education/training/careers and benefit advice;

– high reported incidence of incest;

– less tolerance of lesbian and gay lifestyles;

– feelings of marginalisation and low expectations.

Similarly, Kendrick and Rioch (1995) confirm that most research focuses on urban youth. Yet, they say:

> "Activities and opportunities for young people are restricted in rural areas. There are fewer leisure and recreational provisions which tend to be concentrated in urban areas..." (Kendrick and Rioch, 1995, p. 46)

201

Transport issues were key, these writers suggest. Isolation is particularly noticeable if the young person has no access to a car:

> "Private car ownership was considered to be a pre-condition of rural employment and access to social activities. In this respect young people in their late teenage years who had neither a driving licence nor access to a car were reported to be severely disadvantaged." (Shucksmith et al, 1994)

These suggestions are confirmed by Meadows and Birch (1995), who undertook research concerning the needs of young people in north Norfolk. Their research was conducted with 117 young people in rural areas, and they found in particular that:

– problems with transport in rural areas led to a vicious cycle of no transport, and difficulties of getting a job; this often led to homelessness.

– of the young people interviewed 70 per cent said that they would benefit from a one-stop advice agency that was especially geared towards young people in rural areas.

Meadows and Birch (1995) concluded that

> "The research project confirms that both individuals and groups of young people interviewed by the team experienced a sense of isolation, coupled with a lack of affordable accommodation and perceived lack of employment prospects, limited career choices and opportunities, lack of social and cultural activities and proper access to advice and guidance." (Meadows and Birch, 1995, p. 3)

Use of illegal drugs has become a particular issue in relation to rural youth. Winchester and Hampshire Community Drugs Advisory Service undertook a survey of two thousand 14-15 year-olds in rural areas. They found that one fifth of their sample had tried an illegal drug. Reasons given by the young people for using illegal drugs included boredom, lack of leisure facilities, and poor transport to get to other leisure activities. Similarly, young people coming to DASH (the Drug and Alcohol Service in Hereford), from rural areas "... are usually very isolated and by the time they get to us they are experiencing major problems..." A recent article in Community Care reported that "... the growing problem of substance misuse in rural areas has been largely overlooked."

There are also clear issues for young people in rural areas of getting access to information, advice and services about other topics such as sexuality and lifestyles. In a report published by the National Youth Agency (NYA, 1994) some key difficulties for young people in rural areas were identified:

– friendship patterns are limited – few opportunities to interact with same age peers;

– many rural communities are oppressive – little tolerance of unorthodox dress or behaviour;

– many rural youth experience isolation, claustrophobia and a poorly established self-identity.

Indeed, this finding is reflected in projects which have explored what rural young people say they want in terms of service provision. For example Steel et al (1995) in their report Meeting the needs of young people in the Leiston area, asked young people what they most wanted in terms of services provided for them. The most common responses included wanting information about:

– drugs;
– sexuality and health;
– careers, employment and training;
– personal and family relationships;
– housing;
– money and benefits.

Reflecting this, many youth workers express concern over the difficulties of working with gay and lesbian youth in rural areas. Young people in rural areas are very visible; those exploring their sexuality are quickly labelled and noticed. In general, there is less support for rural youth – helplines and support services are town centred; there are also fewer role models available. Cox (1994) concludes that:

> "Teenagers without public transport may find it difficult to seek confidential advice about for example contraception, pregnancy and drugs..." (Cox, 1994)

It is clear from this brief review of the literature, that young people living in rural parts of the UK are often severely disadvantaged in terms of access to information, advice, and the resources needed to make decisions about their lives and futures. The following section explores some of the ways in which youth workers and voluntary groups are responding to these needs.

Recent developments aimed at improving access to information for rural youth

There are many projects in the UK now which are devoted to improving rural youth's access to information and advice. Most of these have had to adopt novel methods in order to reach this group of young people. Many of these projects are also now starting to use information technology, such as e-mail, telephone helplines, and videolinks. (Note that although some of the projects mentioned in this section are no longer in operation, they are included here in order to demonstrate the type of projects that are and have been available).

Many of the projects aiming to reach rural youth are "mobile" projects. Fabes and Popham (1994) describe a number of mobile youth projects that are now in operation. These include:

- Rea Hamlet Hopper in Shrewsbury – a converted removal van, which picks up young people and tours around.
- Lancashire Association of Boys Clubs – a twelve-seater landrover with sports trailer – takes sports and leisure resources into rural areas for young people to try.
- The Tackle Express in Norfolk – a caravan which tours rural areas providing advice and information.

Many mobile projects operate in an area of 150-450 square miles. They include buses and minibuses which tour round rural areas and pick young people up, or stop in an area where young people can then call into the project. What all the projects have in common is that:

> "... they all took what they had to offer out to where young people could take advantage of it." (Fabes and Popham, 1994, p. 62)

Most rural mobiles include a coffee bar, to give a sense of a meeting place:

> "Providing somewhere for young people to come, sit, talk, listen to music and to 'be' in some degree of comfort is a major linking theme in the world of rural mobiles." (Fabes and Popham, 1994, p. 63)

Funding is, of course, a constant issue for almost all of these projects. Most projects are usually funded by a partner, such as the European Social Fund or the Rural Development Commission. Most projects also rely on one paid worker and some volunteers. Volunteers can, of course, be very difficult to find, especially in sparsely populated areas.

The key to effective rural mobile work is to find ways of reducing the negative aspects of living in a rural environment – including isolation, visibility, difficulties of leaving home, access and advice (Fabes and Popham, 1994). Issues being addressed by mobile projects include:

- Access to information and advice – usually leaflets are available, and sometimes a database is available. Information provided includes welfare rights, issues concerning leaving home and homelessness, and general information which in towns is provided by Youth Information Shops, Citizens Advice Bureau, etc.
- Personal development – projects aimed at personal development aim to enable young people to use the information they get – e.g. courses on personal safety, health care, the impact of crime.
- Participation – most projects actively involve young people in management and planning.
- Curriculum – the programme of a project must be developed through consultation and negotiation.

Again, it is clear from this that the needs of rural young people are not different to those of most young people who live in non-rural areas. However, the difficulty for rural young people is actually accessing this service.

What follows below is an account of nine projects, mainly (but not exclusively) mobile projects. Each aims to provide information and advice to young people in rural areas in a novel way. They are not, of course, a representative sample, but do give some ideas about the variety of projects currently under way in the UK:

"Just Up Your Street":

This service is a mobile youth centre run by Dorset Youth Service. The project was set up because of the difficulty of maintaining regular individual youth clubs in the area, a result of the sparse populations of young people, and difficulties with transport. In response to this a mobile youth centre was set up, which consisted of a thirty-foot vehicle which has:

– electric lights;

– sink and water;

– information, games and activities;

– soft seating and outside equipment.

This vehicle takes youth workers into rural communities, with the aim of providing a similar service to that which young people in towns and cities expect.

The North Cotswold Mobile Project:

This project was set up to make young people in rural communities feel less isolated. It is funded by a variety of organisations, including Children in Need, Gloucester Social Services, and National Playbus. It covers a large geographical area, and includes visits to sixty-four parishes in North Cotswold. It provides:

– information and advice (e.g. counselling, health advice and information);

– resources and equipment (e.g. sports equipment, games);

– training and support (e.g. education and training advice).

South Downs Mobile Youth Project:

This project was set up in 1994 to provide information and advice to young people living in a rural area on the south coast. It is staffed by experienced youth workers, social services staff, and most recently by a nurse. In its first year it dealt with the enquiries of over one thousand young people.

National Association of Youth Theatres:

This organisation now runs in rural areas as a way of providing information and support to young people in rural areas. Its aim in rural areas is to "... alleviate the problems of isolation and lack of support through setting up support groups of local youth workers from existing agencies to ensure the continuation of youth theatre".

Lancashire County Council Youth Service:

This youth services offers a rural mobile service. This provides information and advice to rural youth about topics including:

– education;

– employment and training;

– family and relationships;

– specialist counselling services;

– justice and equality issues;

– health;

– housing;

– sport, leisure and travel;

– money and finances.

Most importantly, the service offers free standing phone lines, so that young people can access the full range of services to them, and also access national information databases.

"Over the Hills and Far Away":

This is part of the rural contact project in Hertfordshire. The service provides information and advice to young people in a large rural community. They quote from one young woman who uses this service:

> "People think that when you're 18 you should know where to go and what to do. But you get fobbed off when you're a young person, and out here there's no one to talk to – that makes you feel even more on your own. Some people go for weeks with hardly seeing anyone."

It is clear from their evaluations that this project is providing an extremely valuable service.

"In the air tonight – BBC Radio Lincolnshire Livewire":

This is a youth club on the air – a radio programme put together by young people to involve, educate and entertain rural young people in the area.

Lancashire County Council:

This Council has various projects which aim to meet the needs of young people in rural areas there. The projects are using a variety of technologies to open up young people's opportunities in relation to education, training, and employment, including:

– the Internet;

– Telecentres;

– Mobile Information Technology centres;

– CD rom access;

– Teleconferencing facilities.

Those responsible for this service also undertook a survey of six hundred young people in the area, who said that the topics they had most difficulty getting information about were the following:

– religions;

– European Union;

– working in Europe;

– shopping rights;

– tenants rights;

– politics;

– housing and homelessness;

– leaving home.

Sussex Rural Community Council:

This organisation has a scheme called Password, which is based around four villages in Sussex. It is a sort of information and advice shop, based in the village hall or youth hut. The service was set up because of a study which showed that 90 per cent of young people had not used an information and advice service, but 85 per cent said they would like to do so.

Conclusions:

This paper has aimed to illustrate some of the difficulties for young people in rural areas of accessing information and advice on topics crucial to healthy development. The information and advice young people need is very diverse, and includes information about health, sexuality, education, training, and employment, housing and homelessness, and leisure. The paper has also described the use of mobile projects which are now being used in many parts of the UK in an attempt to meet the needs of young people living in isolated rural communities.

It is important to conclude this paper with a note about the use and value of technology to young people in rural areas. It is clear that technology does, and can, make a very positive impact on the lives of rural youth. Young people can now access work and training opportunities via telecentres, health and advice information via the Internet, and participate in campaigning via fax, the Internet, e-mail and teleconferencing. These are all enormously beneficial to the young people concerned, although of course the success of these services is greatly affected by the extent of the service provided, its funding, and the training and skill of those running the schemes.

Research is needed into the impact of technology upon the lives of young people in rural areas. It is possible, perhaps, that for certain young people technology increases their feelings of isolation, and lack of contact with sympathetic or same age young people. Thus having access to a computerised data base for basic health care advice may be of little use to the young person in a rural community who feels that they have no one to talk to. This is not to devalue the potential importance of technology in the lives of rural youth. Technology should be viewed as one way of opening up opportunities for rural youth, and of providing them with information and advice. However, the starting point must be the young people themselves, and the information, advice and services that they say they need to lead safe, fulfilling, and enjoyable lives.

Dr Debi Roker

References

Cloke P (1994) *Lifestyles in Rural England*, Rural Development Council, London

Cox J (1994) Rural general practice, *British Journal of General Practice*, September, 388

Couchman C (1994) *An Everyday Story...? An initial fact finding study on issues affecting children, young people and their families in rural England and Wales*, The Children's Society, London

Fabes R and Banks (1991) Working with young people in rural areas. *Youth and Policy*, 33, 1-9

Fabes R and Popham D (1994/5) Mobile facilities with young people in rural areas, *Youth and Policy*, 47, 59-67

Fabes R and Popham D (1994) Mobile Youth Work, *Rural Viewpoint*, summer, p. 12

Kendrick A. and Rioch C (1995) Knowing the back roads: Rural social work and troubled young people, *Youth and Policy*, 51, 46-57

Leach S (1996) *Over The Hills and Far Away: A model of detached rural youth work from the Rural Contact Project*, Community Council of Hereford and Worcester, Malvern

Macdonald et al (1995) *Routes to rural opportunities: A research study*, Oxford Brookes University, Oxford

Meadows L and Birch H (1995) *Assessing the needs of young people in the north Norfolk district area*, North Norfolk County Council

National Youth Agency (1994) *Nothing Ever Happens Around Here: Developing Youth Work in Rural Areas*, NYA, Leicester

National Youth Bureau (1990) *Deprivation in rural areas: Young people's perspectives*, NYA, Leicester

NCVO (1990) *Mental Health in Rural Areas*, NCVO: London

NCVO (1994) *Substance Misuse in Rural Areas*. NCVO: London

North Yorkshire County Council (1989) *Growing up in a rural area: A response to the needs of young people in North Yorkshire*, NYCC: Northallerton

The PASSWORD project (1996), Sussex Rural Community Council, Lewes, Sussex.

Statham J and Cameron C (1994) Young children in rural areas: Implementing the Children Act, *Children and Society*, 8, 17-30

Steel G (1995) *Meeting the Needs of Young People in the Leiston, Saxmundham and Aldeburgh Areas: An evaluative study*, Suffolk County Council

Turner L (1992) *Issues in rural mental health*, Sussex Rural Community Council, Lewes, Sussex

Wallace et al (1993) *The employment and training of young people in rural south west England*, Youth Network Occasional Pape, City University, London

"What Works?": For Young People and Communities in Rural Lancashire (1996) Lancashire Youth and Community Service, Preston

Youth Action (1994) 'In the air tonight', *Youth Action*, 51, p. 10

Youth and Policy (1991), Special Edition 'Focus on Rural Youth', No. 33, May 1991

Useful Organisations (all UK)

Community Transport Association: Highbank, Halton Street, Hyde, Cheshire, SK14 2NY

Teleworking UK: Clydesdale Development Company, Clydesdale Business Centre, 129 Hyndford Road, Lanark, ML11 9AU

Good Practices in Mental Health, 380-384 Harrow Road, London, W9 2HU

The Rural Housing Trust: Victoria Chambers, 16-18 Strutton Ground, London, SW1P 2HP

ACRE (Action for Communities in Rural England): Somerford Road, Cirencester, Glos, GL7 1TW

National Youth Agency: 17-23 Albion Street, Leicester, LE1 6GD

National Council for Voluntary Organisations, Rural Team: NCVO, Regents Wharf, 8 All Saints Wharf, London, N1 9RL

Rural Development Commission: 11 Cowley Street, London, SW1P 3NA

Rural Media Company: St Peter's Church House, St Peter's Square, Hereford, HR1 2PG

Youth Clubs UK: 11 St Brides Steet, London, EC4A 4AS

"The information society" – a society that includes the poorest young people?

First of all, a few words about the Fourth World Youth Movement:

– It brings young people who live or have lived in extreme poverty in various parts of the world together, so that they can broaden their horizons and talk about their lives and hopes, and it supports them in their efforts to overcome destitution.

– It also brings together young people who have never known poverty, but are resolutely joining its hardest-hit victims in overcoming it.

We can testify that this kind of encounter and exchange between young people from different social backgrounds is something which they themselves want and which is possible.

My name is Jacques Ogier. I am a cheese-maker by training and a permanent volunteer with the Fourth World Movement. Peggy and I are not researchers (though some volunteers are) or administrators, and we are not exactly what is usually called "practitioners". We are activists. This "status", if it is one, puts us in close touch with young people, and that has shown us that extreme poverty is universal. What Alan and David from Ireland say is equally true for Zoltan from Hungary; what Arame from Senegal says also applies to Nixon Pacheco from the United States; what Didier from France says can be said by young people the world over.

That brings me to my first point: at the opening of the symposium, we heard how important it is for researchers, practitioners and people from the ministries to work together. I would add that the first people we should be involving in our work are young people themselves, and particularly the poorest among them.

Another point: installing computers with free Internet access in public places will probably not be enough to get the very poor to use them. For that to be possible, we have to create the right cultural conditions and help them to overcome certain fears. Let us hear what Alan and David have to say:

> "We know Mandy who is 21. Mandy has a 3 year-old daughter Rebecca. She is a single parent and is trying to survive on the government's lone parent allowance which is not enough for her and Rebecca to survive on. She sometimes had to go without so that her daughter could have had what she needed. Mandy says that she loves her daughter and would not change her for the world, but it is especially hard when you are a single parent. Mandy would like to be inde-

pendent but she and Rebecca are forced to live with her parents and her five brothers and one sister. That is ten of them in a three-bedroomed house. Her family just about survives from week to week.

Mandy left school at 14 with no qualifications so getting a job is very difficult. The only jobs available are washing-up or working in a chip shop so the pay is not very good.

Mandy finds it hard to socialise because she has no money so entertainment for Rebecca and herself is difficult. They spend the weekend playing games and walking if the weather is suitable. There is a leisure centre in Athlone which Rebecca loves but Mandy does not take her there because it is too hard to explain why she cannot have chips drinks and ice cream like all the other children.

To try and earn more money now and to ensure a better future for them both, Mandy attends a community training workshop where she learns skills like catering, hairdressing and computing. She is acquiring qualifications which will help her get a better paid job so that maybe some day she will be able to give Rebecca the same opportunities that the other children have.

Mandy also works a a volunteer with Athlone Community Youth Project which is a project set up to help young children living in areas of high unemployment and school drop-out. So Mandy is also working towards improving the lives of other young children in her locality."

(Extract from the testimony of Alan and David, Irish delegates at the 23rd Fourth World Youth Movement European Assembly on 14 October 1996.)

Rebecca found a community to support her, but who will support all the other Rebeccas round the world in their search for knowledge?

The main source of information which the poorest families have (at any rate in western Europe) is television. The computer equipment companies have got the point and are selling game consoles which can be connected to television sets, providing network access via built-in modems. Even for the Internet, are we going accept second-class access for the penniless and socially excluded, allowing them, at best, only to consume information and culture?

One may well wonder whether giving the poorest young people access to the Internet is a good thing or not. But the Internet exists, and they see very clearly that something important is starting up here. Didier, a Fourth World Activist and conscientious objector, who is doing his alternative service in the Fourth World Youth Movement, had this to say at the end of a day spent trying out the Internet with young people in the street:

"It's hard to get young people to look at the Internet because it's totally new to them. They just know the games, but they don't know anything about information on the Internet. For young people from poor backgrounds, it's a closed world. They see it from another angle. They see it as something they're cut off from. It's a closed world, because it's something for the haves, not the have-nots, and they feel they're not part of that family. People develop with the things they learn, but they don't try to share them. Some young people in poor neighbourhoods can't keep up with the way things are changing today. We've got to trust them with the Internet, so they feel they're not worthless. We've got to tell them that it's there for the ones who don't have the money, so they can come up with new ideas of their own. The world has changed without them. We've got to tell them we're here, that they can communicate with today's world. They're afraid. 'Why did they invent that thing' they ask. We've got to tell them, 'We're going to look at the world of the Internet with you', and show them as much as we can. We've got to help them with the questions they put on the Internet - that way, they'll get their answers."

What Didier is saying here is that the most underprivileged young people will not get access to the network unless the ones who use it all the time make room for them, not just so they can get information, but so they can use it to express their anger and their hopes and get a hearing.

For several years, the Fourth World Movement has been experimenting with an internal network which provides a kind of introduction to the Internet. The part set aside for young people is called Yodem, from **Yo**uth mo**dem**. We find that young people get on better with the network if they have already met and talked to people "on the other side". In this way, the network becomes a preparation for, or extension of, actual face-to-face meetings. Virtual meetings are just not enough for the most underprivileged young people, and this is where the network of networks takes on its full significance.

Lastly, before I give the floor to Peggy, who will develop what I have just been saying, I would like to say that the things we are trying out in the Fourth World Movement are extremely modest, in terms of the number of people and places we get to: we operate with the resources we have, and those are very limited. But the work we do is worthwhile, because it reaches the very poor, and that gives it universal relevance.

We would find little or no disagreement with the statement that the "information society" that is now evolving must not exclude anyone. It is easily agreed as well that this poses a challenge for us in regard to those who do not have ready access to the evolving technologies that give access to massive quantities of information, the most obvious example being those who cannot afford it.

But, as Jacques has mentioned we could not meet this challenge by giving each household a computer, even if that were imaginable. Nor could we meet this challenge by putting a free computer and electronic communications centre in each public library, training included. We would not be meeting this challenge because we would not be reaching the poorest.

We would not be reaching a certain woman in Brooklyn who would not have a go on the computer that was part of the street library front of her building because she did not want to risk breaking it. We would not be reaching the young people who never go to a public library because they are ashamed of not being able to read or write. We would not be reaching the young people whose hard lives have made learning in a normal school environment very difficult. We would not be reaching the young people whose families for generations have been excluded from the rest of society leading them to not feel the confidence or the self-worth to be a part of the modern world, or a new society and who have been excluded for so long that the "norms" and changes in society in general do not necessarily apply to them.

The poorest do not have the strength or the knowledge to create their own place within the technological world and on the internet, not without the help of those who already have their place in this part of today's world.

I will explain in three parts how the Fourth World Youth Movement is trying to meet this challenge:

– The importance of being in the modern world and our experience using the internet with this in mind;
– Projects that are aimed to make sure the poorest young people succeed;
– Working with modern technologies with an aim much broader than accessing the labour market.

Being part of the world

From what I have heard over the past two days, we do not necessarily agree on whether to call the society that we are evolving into a society of information or a society of learning or otherwise. Perhaps we simply cannot say exactly what the evolution will entail. But we do seem to agree that a change is taking place and that new technologies and the access to information that these technologies provide play a significant role in this change. To change society so that the society that we are evolving into, whatever we call it, could be a society without exclusion and poverty those people who are living the worst reality of these problems must be a part of the making of this change. We could not imagine making changes for the equality between the sexes as a group made up solely of men. By the same logic, we cannot be trying to fight social exclusion without the participation, the advice and the experience of the those who are the most excluded. So, to be changing a society where new technology is more and more important, it is vital that the poorest have their place within the technology of today and tomorrow. Without their participation, their exclusion will not only continue but will become more severe in an "information society" that they have no part in and have not helped to create.

Nixon a youth from the USA is one of the many young people that can help us understand the importance of this idea. This is part of what he wrote for October 17th, The World Day to Overcome Extreme Poverty, this year:

> "With the street library, kids from the neighbourhood, including myself when I was little, gather around to hear stories, read books and learn about the computer. It was the first time there was a computer in the neighbourhood. It is important to learn these things for modern times, because in order to break the poverty chain we young people have to make ourselves useful to build the future for us and for a better society."

As Jacques has said, the poorest people are not completely disassociated from the information in today's society. As Fourth World Movement volunteers, we have constantly seen that the poorest people watch a lot of television and through this media have access to information (however we may criticise its quality). But the information society that is evolving has many other media that the poorest people do not have access to: Internet being at the very least the most talked about. To include the poorest people in this development poses a challenge but also gives a great opportunity because of the "interactivity" of new media. This can give the most excluded people a chance to participate as others citizens do, which is something television does not do.

As citizens of the world, the poorest young people have a fundamental right to have access to these modern technologies to be able to work in skilled jobs but also in order to access information, to communicate with others, and to contribute to the dialogues taking place through electronic communications. In this way, they can have the same tools as others to participate as citizens and be the best of themselves. But also, by participating, discussing, giving their opinions, sharing their dreams and their experience, they will be a part of the making of a new "information society". A society that is created with the participation of the poorest will be more whole and just because a society that includes the most excluded will be will be a society for everyone.

Again, our work with the Internet has just begun but here are some examples from projects that we have done with young people and the Internet which can show how the poorest young can people be a part of the creation of an "information society":

Using Internet Relay Chat to call other young people to the fight against extreme poverty.

Many things are being discussed on the Internet. Are the poorest included in these discussions? Are we discussing how to include them? Are we discussing on the Internet how we can end poverty?

This is an example of how, on a chatline, two young English women helped a young man in the States believe more strongly that young people can do something to fight poverty.

Taking part in conversations already existing on the Internet, so that poor young people have a voice in a variety of issues.

There are many dialogues already taking place on the Internet about human rights, social justice and many other political and social issues. To have a complete discussion, the opinions and experience of the poorest should be included.

This is an example of how two young women in the Fourth World Youth Movement, one from England, one from Slovakia, contributed to the discussion about children's rights on UNICEF's "Voices of Youth Page", and therefore were able to express the issues most important to them.

Introducing modern technologies.

Before doing anything on the Internet young people must be capable of using it. Learning the skills is important but even before that, young people, especially very poor young people, must believe that these technologies are not out of their reach and are something they are capable of using.

By looking for information about their interests on the Web, young people have been able to understand how the Web works and have finished our "Internet workshops" with the desire to find access to Internet in their own areas, and with the knowledge that Internet is a part of the modern world that is for them.

Projects for success

If we want to ensure that the poorest young people succeed, we have to create projects with their success in mind, and the challenges this poses. I will give examples of projects with information technology but we could give other examples in other domains.

Access to materials, training, and the ease that most young people from other backgrounds have with information technology starting now from a young age rarely exist for disadvantaged young people.

But with young people who have a background in poverty and exclusion and therefore are less capable than others of succeeding at school, in training projects, etc. we have seen a consistent and remarkable interest and ability in information technology, as a means of learning, training, communication and creativity as well as out of a profound curiosity of the technology of the modern world.

With these young people we try to provide the best conditions possible for learning: an environment where they feel comfortable, without a lot of pressure to succeed but showing determined, patient, and deep belief that they can. Our workshops are rarely simply to teach skills but rather to get the young people involved in a practical or creative project which they will find interesting and useful. Through this interest, and by doing work in groups, they can learn skills by building something for a larger purpose. And with the finished project they have proof of success.

Examples of projects for success:

Computers as a tool in a bigger project.

At the Fourth World Youth Movement Workcamp Training Session in February 1996 we began a map to illustrate and plan the manual work that was being done throughout the week.

Working together, and feeling like one is part of something and belongs somewhere can help one feel comfortable and capable to learn something new. It is not just the organisers of the workshop that give instruction, the young people, who come from all different background, help each other.

This aspect of being a part of something and not being alone is vital to the Fourth World Youth Movement. We are fighting poverty as a Movement not as individuals, and as a movement made up of young people from different socio-economic backgrounds and different countries. Therefore communication between the young people in the Movement is very important. And to make sure that everyone has chance to communicate we use different media: a monthly bilingual journal, visits, international events, personal correspondence and our own electronic communications network, all of which intertwine and support each other.

Arame, a youth we know in Senegal, underlines this:

> "In the Fourth World Youth Journal I see people working with computers. It is a good system. We will have to work a lot with young people, especially on communication so that young people can speak with other young people and so that they know how to communicate with others who are on the outside."

(Extract of the testimony, Contribution to the 23rd Fourth World Movement European Assembly, October 1996, by Arame N'Diaye, Parcelles Assainies, Dakar, Senegal.)

Yodem: The youth movement's electronic network – to keep in touch, share ideas, and build something together.

The Youth Movement uses the network to share news, send personal messages, messages on a certain theme, and messages that contribute to a campaign.

One example of a personal message:

Eric, 22 May 1994

HELLO EVERYONE. MY NAME IS ERIC. THIS IS THE FIRST TIME I'VE BEEN IN CHAMPEAUX. I'VE BEEN ATTENDING THIS YOUTH COURSE FOR THREE DAYS NOW, LEARNING HOW TO BE AN ACTIVIST. MY REAL REASON FOR COMING WAS TO MEET OTHER YOUNG PEOPLE WITH PROBLEMS LIKE ME. I WANTED TO ASK SOME QUESTIONS. AND I WANTED TO FIND OUT MORE ABOUT THE MOVEMENT AND LEARN SOME THINGS I DIDN'T KNOW. ONE THING I'VE LEARNED IS THAT WE DON'T NEED HELP FROM THE TOWN TO GET ACTIVITIES GOING WITH YOUNG PEOPLE OR CHILDREN IN MY NEIGHBOURHOOD. WE WERE ABLE TO SAY WHAT WE THOUGHT AND FIND OUT HOW THINGS ARE FOR OTHER YOUNG PEOPLE IN THEIR CITIES. ERIC FROM SAINT-POL-SUR-MER (NEAR DUNKIRK).

More than access to jobs – "rethinking about human activity"

Information technology can be seen as a tool not just in paid jobs, but also for other kinds of "human activity", activities which are becoming more and more important to recognise and explore as employment is becoming increasingly difficult to find: activities of creation, of self-education and growth, and of teaching, communicating with and supporting others, for example.

The importance of computers for creativity and self-expression.

An example of how a "disadvantaged" youth can find an expressive outlet with computer technology: Fourth World Movement Workcamp Training Session April 1996.

One participant was a young man from an estate in the Paris area who had a hard time getting involved in most of the activities: the manual work, the discussions, group-living, etc. who with his friends caused trouble for the others during the workcamp, and who has not had much success at school. He learned how to use the drawing programme, with one of our workers, by finding a photo of his basketball idol on a CD Rom and copying it and changing it to his liking within the drawing programme. Later, on his own, with two hours of concentrated and determined work, despite several technical problems, he made a beautiful drawing. He would not stop until it was exactly right. This young man found an outlet for expression, for creativity, by using computers.

We must continuously ask ourselves how we can be including the poorest young people in the quickly evolving information society. What projects can we create? How can we be running these projects so that the poorest can be included? Which parts of the Internet and other growing media must the poorest have a voice in? How can the poorest young people not just access the information and learn the skills but be active participants in this important evolution? How can we work together to make this happen? The examples in this paper should give us a starting point for answering these questions.

I would like to end by telling you about one young man that we have in mind when we are talking about the "very poorest young people". He is named Zoltan and lives about one hundred km from Budapest in a village of two thousand people. In this village there is a rate of over 90 per cent unemployment and no money, investment, projects or hope in sight for this to change. Zoltan has a profession, as a tractor repairman, but there are no tractors in the area, broken or otherwise, to repair. There is one telephone in the village, in the mayor's office. There is one library in the village, in the community centre which has no financial backing and which might not have either heat or electricity this winter. Zoltan is a part of the Fourth World Youth Movement and therefore knows other young people throughout Europe who are in similar situations of difficulty. I saw him just before coming to this conference and he told me that it is important for him to know that these other young people are thinking of him, and his family and his friends, that this gives them strength. When we are talking about a new society of information, technology, communication, where does Zoltan fit in our discussions? What responsibilities do we have towards him in our work and our interests with European young people? I hope that you will keep him in mind.

Peggy Simmons, Jacques Ogier

Youth and Internet in Turkey: some facts

There has been a lively debate about where an Internet connection appeared for the first time in Turkey: some say it was TR-Net which established the first connection, although it is known that the Egean University's and other accounts existed a couple of years before the founding of TR-Net.

Indeed, TR-Net, a project group founded by TUBITAK and Middle Reatern Technical University in 1991, was preceded by the exclusively academic net TUVAKA at the Egean University. METU and TUBITAK's main aim was to set a connection accessible to anybody who requested it. TR-Net's equipment and staff were jointly financed by METU and TUBITAK. Today, income is used to maintain and upgrade the system.

The first step in establishing the connection was the link between METU and Washington (NSFNET) which was opened on 12 April 1993. Major universities followed suit and established their own connections.

The problem of getting access to the Internet in Turkey is not purely technical or financial, but a legal one. Since the key to the Internet is data lines, primarily telephone lines, and the Turkish state-owned Telecom holds the monopoly over these lines, one can say that Internet in Turkey is under governmental control. Thus, the rental of telephone lines by third parties is illegal in Turkey. Given the fact that data exchange on the Internet is primarily through the telephone lines, Internet can also be said to be illegal.

It can be argued that the legislation was adopted before the Internet technology was developed and that the respective laws are void. However, the law is active and basically serves the interest of the government of monopolising the means of communication in the country.

Many Internet providers have appeared in the recent years but their activity has no legal foundation. Legal problems led Microsoft to refuse to establish a network in Turkey. Only a few pioneers like IBM took the risk to set up networks that can be dismantled at any time by the government.

The ways for the citizens to establish an Internet connection in this country are the same as everywhere else: the main connection sites being schools; students and paying clients obtain access through the universities; others connect via modem through private providers or universities. Obtaining access from universities was difficult at first and students had to be ingenious to find a way out, sometimes even sharing an account with friends. Engineering and graduate students were given access first but recently nearly all universities already "hooked" started giving accounts to all students.

For those without access to these facilities, there are new establishments such as Internet cafés who provide computers and access for fee and in a social atmosphere.

IBM Net was the first specialised provider of Internet accounts in Turkey. Due to legal uncertainties, the connection was established via the Netherlands. An additional problem is the state of telephone lines: in some places they are not digital which makes the connection fragile, noisy and slow.

Gradually, Turkish companies started looking for ways of improving the infrastructure. The computer company ESCORT found a backbone link with a doubled capacity for data transmission. Moreover, services of local providers often offer richer and more diverse contents and graphically more attractive sites. They also give more emphasis on sites created in the country.

Despite all the technical and financial difficulties, Turkish youth quickly accepted the Internet. Long before professional outlets were opened, students were establishing their own Bulletin Boards and exchanging e-mail. The first BBS served exclusively for swapping software and had a phenomenal success. They were, and still are, based in student bedrooms, providing a space for chatting, trading and forming of interest groups. Today there are over fifty BBS in Istanbul and their sysops (system operators) seem to know each other and form a tight net themselves. The reason for this may be the limited number of BBS and the restricted specialised press which makes it necessary to learn and solve problems through personal contacts. Some BBS require a membership fee, others can only be entered through someone you know.

Turkish students abroad started using the Internet much earlier than their fellows who were in the country. They created a support line whereby news from and to Turkey were exchanged in the mother tongue. This link has raised the awareness of expatriate students of their country and the world of friendly chat soon turned into serious debate on various issues.

The small virtual community of Turkey unites, as everywhere else, people who, being of different ages and social milieus, would have never come to know each other had the Net not existed. Web sites were set up for Turkish Soccer teams, for friends and helped connecting people from all over the country. In the summer of 1996 a virtual wall was made as a result of a virtual meeting where the Internet users protested against the slowness of the system. If the numbers of users continues to grow at the present rate Turkey will soon have a very active army of young virtual travellers. They all believe the government should understand the importance of the Internet phenomenon and improve the quality of the infrastructure that connects Turkey to the rest of the world.

Meral Alguida

Sales agents for publications of the Council of Europe
Agents de vente des publications du Conseil de l'Europe

AUSTRALIA/AUSTRALIE
Hunter publications, 58A, Gipps Street
AUS-3066 COLLINGWOOD, Victoria
Fax: (61) 33 9 419 7154

AUSTRIA/AUTRICHE
Gerold und Co., Graben 31
A-1011 WIEN 1
Fax: (43) 1512 47 31 29

BELGIUM/BELGIQUE
La Librairie européenne SA
50, avenue A. Jonnart
B-1200 BRUXELLES 20
Fax: (32) 27 35 08 60

Jean de Lannoy
202, avenue du Roi
B-1060 BRUXELLES
Fax: (32) 25 38 08 41

CANADA
Renouf Publishing Company Limited
5369 Chemin Canotek Road
CDN-OTTAWA, Ontario, K1J 9J3
Fax: (1) 613 745 76 60

DENMARK/DANEMARK
Munksgaard
PO Box 2148
DK-1016 KØBENHAVN K
Fax: (45) 33 12 93 87

FINLAND/FINLANDE
Akateeminen Kirjakauppa
Keskuskatu 1, PO Box 218
SF-00381 HELSINKI
Fax: (358) 9 121 44 50

GERMANY/ALLEMAGNE
UNO Verlag
Poppelsdorfer Allee 55
D-53115 BONN
Fax: (49) 228 21 74 92

GREECE/GRÈCE
Librairie Kauffmann
Mavrokordatou 9, GR-ATHINAI 106 78
Fax: (30) 13 23 03 20

HUNGARY/HONGRIE
Euro Info Service
Magyarország
Margitsziget (Európa Ház),
H-1138 BUDAPEST
Fax: (36) 1 111 62 16
E-mail: eurinfo@mail.matav.hu

IRELAND/IRLANDE
Government Stationery Office
4-5 Harcourt Road, IRL-DUBLIN 2
Fax: (353) 14 75 27 60

ISRAEL/ISRAËL
ROY International
17 Shimon Hatrssi St.
PO Box 13056
IL-61130 TEL AVIV
Fax: (972) 3 546 1423
E-mail: royil@netvision.net.il

ITALY/ITALIE
Libreria Commissionaria Sansoni
Via Duca di Calabria, 1/1
Casella Postale 552, I-50125 FIRENZE
Fax: (39) 55 64 12 57

MALTA/MALTE
L. Sapienza & Sons Ltd
26 Republic Street
PO Box 36
VALLETTA CMR 01
Fax: (356) 233 621

NETHERLANDS/PAYS-BAS
InOr-publikaties, PO Box 202
NL-7480 AE HAAKSBERGEN
Fax: (31) 53 572 92 96

NORWAY/NORVÈGE
Akademika, A/S Universitetsbokhandel
PO Box 84, Blindern
N-0314 OSLO
Fax: (47) 22 85 30 53

POLAND/POLOGNE
Głowna Księgarnia Naukowa im. B. Prusa
Krakowskie Przedmiescie 7
PL-00-068 WARSZAWA
Fax: (48) 22 26 64 49

PORTUGAL
Livraria Portugal
Rua do Carmo, 70
P-1200 LISBOA
Fax: (351) 13 47 02 64

SPAIN/ESPAGNE
Mundi-Prensa Libros SA
Castelló 37, E-28001 MADRID
Fax: (34) 15 75 39 98

Llibreria de la Generalitat
Rambla dels Estudis, 118
E-08002 BARCELONA
Fax: (34) 343 12 18 54

SWITZERLAND/SUISSE
Buchhandlung Heinimann & Co.
Kirchgasse 17, CH-8001 ZÜRICH
Fax: (41) 12 51 14 81

BERSY
Route du Manège 60, CP 4040
CH-1950 SION 4
Fax: (41) 27 203 73 32

UNITED KINGDOM/ROYAUME-UNI
TSO (formerly HMSO)
51 Nine Elms Lane
GB-LONDON SW8 5DR
Fax: (44) 171 873 82 00

UNITED STATES and CANADA/
ÉTATS-UNIS et CANADA
Manhattan Publishing Company
468 Albany Post Road
PO Box 850
CROTON-ON-HUDSON, NY 10520, USA
Fax: (1) 914 271 58 56

STRASBOURG
Librairie Kléber
Palais de l'Europe
F-67075 STRASBOURG Cedex
Fax: +33 (0)3 88 52 91 21

Council of Europe Publishing/Editions du Conseil de l'Europe
Council of Europe/Conseil de l'Europe
F-67075 Strasbourg Cedex
Tel. +33 (0)3 88 41 25 81 – Fax +33 (0)3 88 41 39 10 – E-mail: ce.publishing@seddoc.coe.fr